Woman to Woman
An Oral History of
Rape Crisis in Scotland
1976–1991

Edited by Eileen Maitland

Published by Rape Crisis Scotland 2009
Tara House, 46 Bath Street, Glasgow G2 1HG

Copyright © Rape Crisis Scotland 2009

ISBN 978-0-9561486-0-5

Cover illustrations by kind permission of Angela Hayden –
http://angelahayden.net/
Front cover: Circle of Women
Back cover: BW Woman#4

Printed by Hampden Advertising Ltd

Dedication

This book is dedicated to all women who have been involved in the fight against violence against women.

In particular, it is dedicated to Frances Oboyle, Kate Cavanagh and Ingrid McClements, whose contributions to this movement were immeasurable.

Contents

Acknowledgements

Our heartfelt thanks go out to every woman who took the time to take part in this oral history project, and to every woman who played a part in the development of the Rape Crisis movement in Scotland. We hope that their voices will help:

> *"To inspire younger women, younger generations to keep on, not so much a struggle, but ...a sort of an opening of the mind, a strengthening of the connection ... between women and a better understanding of the world around us and that a lot of good things ...can and will go on happening. But not to sort of sleep on our laurels the way sometime women think these days that they've got it all because it's not true. It could ...be taken away so easily."* [Florence Germain]

We would also like to thank Professor Dorothy Griffiths and the Feminist Review Trust for funding this publication, and for their patience and support, Angela Hayden for very generously allowing us to use her beautiful images on the cover, Sean Feeny at Hampden Advertising for support and advice on preparation for printing, and Anne Muir for extensive use of recording equipment for carrying out the interviews, and advice on good practice in oral history and file preservation.

Introduction : The way out is to tell

Healing is a continuous process.

Rape affects all aspect of one's life and being and one has to work continuously to become whole and intact.

Pieces of myself are coming slowly together. I am different, but I accept that.

The way out is to tell:

Speak of the acts perpetrated upon us, speak the atrocities, speak the injustices, speak the personal violations of the soul.

Someone will listen, someone will believe our stories, someone will join us.

Charlotte Pierce-Baker – author of Surviving the Silence
http://www.survivingtothriving.org/quotes

On 27th November 2006, over 100 women gathered at the City Halls in Glasgow for a celebration. This moment was the culmination of 30 years of commitment, care and concern, clamouring and campaigning that characterised the Rape Crisis movement in Scotland, from its first determined steps in the mid 70's, to the fully-fledged feminist support organisation and force for change it is today. Many of the women who attended the party that night were among those whose efforts at the very beginning had made it all possible. This document puts together the testimonies of many of the women involved, and tells the story of why and how the Rape Crisis movement emerged in Scotland, and what it meant to them to be part of this unique piece of Scottish herstory.

The 2006 anniversary brought sharply into focus all that had been achieved in the course of the preceding three decades, and the emphasis it placed on the scale of that achievement seemed to highlight the importance of documenting the process, and the memories of those women who shaped it. As a result, Rape Crisis Scotland decided to undertake an oral history project, and recorded a total of 33 interviews with women in Glasgow, Edinburgh, Aberdeen, Dundee, Inverness and further afield. In offering up their testimonies, these women bore witness to the determination and commitment which gave birth to the Scottish Rape Crisis movement: a birth no less painful or fraught with anxieties than any other – and often just as rewarding.

Note

This document is by no means an exhaustive account of the experiences of women who were involved in Rape Crisis in Scotland during its first 15 years. There are many women whose names and contributions remain unrecorded but who nevertheless played just as significant a role as the women whose testimony is documented here. Their words pay tribute to the determination, resilience, ingenuity, courage and compassion of all the women whose monumental efforts forged the Scottish Rape Crisis movement which continues the fight against sexual violence today.

Early days:
Motivation, planning, and involvement –
by design and by chance

The individual centres emerged in very different ways – some were the result of months of planning, while others sprang up virtually overnight, and developed on much more of an ad hoc basis. All of the centres developed to some extent on a praxis model – their shape and service model being formed in response to the needs of their service users, though inevitably circumscribed by the extremely limited resources that were available to them. The first services began in the major cities of Scotland and served mainly women in urban areas in the early days. However, this is not to say women in rural areas were neglected: although the advent of centres such as those now established in Argyll and Bute, the Western Isles and Perth and Kinross seemed like a distant dream in the mid-70's, the few services that did become established during this period often went to great lengths to support women at considerable distances from their urban bases. Indeed, centres such as Glasgow, particularly during the period it was funded by Strathclyde Regional Council and was known as Strathclyde Rape Crisis Centre covered vast geographical areas and travelled widely to provide support to women outwith the cities.

Statistics published in The Glasgow Herald at the end of 1980 showed that there was growing concern over a conviction rate that stood at around 23% of the number reported – in 1979, when 145 cases were reported (90 of these were in Strathclyde), 50 were proceeded against, and 34 of these resulted in a conviction. It seems horribly ironic that this rate of conviction now seems like a distant ideal – figures for 2006/7 showed that while the figure for reported rapes rocketed in the intervening years to 922, the number of corresponding convictions was a mere 27, giving Scotland at the time of publication almost three decades later one of the lowest conviction rates anywhere – 2.9%.

Motivation: the prevailing culture

Many of the women who became involved in Rape Crisis had been involved in left-wing politics, but were disillusioned with the way that issues of gender were sidelined or ignored. The failure of other political systems to take account of the realities experienced by women, pushed many towards the wholly feminist agenda underpinning the Rape Crisis movement:

> "We had the broad left, we had the Socialist Workers Party, we had the International Marxist Group… We had all shades of red. As long as it was red, it was there and, but within that, not really an awful lot of discussion of where women fitted in. The issue was class, and we didn't even really talk about poverty. We talked about class and Capitalism. And there wasn't any recognition of where gender or race or disability…where any of those issues sat within that understanding of what society was about." [Lily Greenan]

> "I was very politically active, but I'd been involved in party politics, and you know, they were so sort of male dominated and confrontational and men scoring points off each other, you know, that I felt that a lot of the wood wasn't being seen for the trees…I mean, the women's movement and women's issues were raised, but…really, it was a bit of a struggle and there wasn't the focus that I wanted…I wanted to focus more on the needs of women…rather than try and fight it from a party political perspective …I thought I want to be somewhere where people, more or less, were all aiming in the same direction, you know?" [Rona Clarke]

"I think like many women…I'd been very interested in feminist politics during the seventies but hadn't been very active…I had kinda been more at the edges of it and I was in my twenties… it just was a kind of coming together of, you know, wanting to join a women's group, knowing that I felt very strongly about sexual violence in particular against women and children, and wanting to join women who wanted to do something. I mean, it was as simple as that, really." [Siobhan Canavan]

"I suppose it came about because I had become interested in the Women's Movement generally and had been involved in things like the pro-abortion campaign and just generally meeting up with other women and talking about issues that, you know, we hadn't talked with other women about in the past" [Moira Kane]

"I got involved because I was really quite political as a young woman. So anything with supposedly left wing politics and injustice and humanity, humanitarian issues really interested me. And the first thing I did when I left home was to work in an organisation called Simon Community which supported homeless people. And it was very, the project I was in, in the community was very much geared towards men, which was really good and it was supporting them to kind of have like sober and healthy lives. But it wasn't enough. And I heard about Rape Crisis and volunteered." [Heather Forrest]

"I'd already been quite involved in some of the other aspects of what the women's movement in Edinburgh had been doing, so I'd been involved in…the regional women's liberation group that formed in Edinburgh…probably around sort of '70, '71, and also been involved in a group which was called, rather grandly, the Women's Legal and Financial Independence Group, that had met, done a bit of work around…various sort of issues around employment and also family law issues…I'd had some, less direct involvement with…Women's Aid, which really started to operate, in Edinburgh, from about '73, '74… So it was a sort of natural progression, I think, probably, from that and the issue had become…quite big" [Sheila Gilmore]

"Definitely considered myself a feminist at the time. All my friends were feminist…I was in a book group and that was a feminist book group and we only read women writers …it was definitely political in those days and I think that's probably what motivated me." [Brenda Flaherty]

"When I was at University in England, I was on Nightline and then when I lived in London for a few years I was a Samaritan helper, and then when I came up here I phoned the Samaritans and they didn't want me, so I suppose I was looking for something else to do and the Women and Health group was very good. Where you met lots of people and they were feminists as well so when that ended, naturally progressed towards Rape Crisis." [Maureen Porter]

"Nightline was already in existence…that was a student body thing…it was from my doing that as a volunteer, I think, that started opening my eyes up to the issues around rape…but… it was not a specialist line for people who had experienced that…Samaritans gave us training…so that was…very useful." [Kathy Litteljohn]

"I don't know what happened…out in society there, but it did change and people now will come – they're wanting to add it to a CV or they're wanting counselling experience – that's become very popular – but not then." [Norma Benzie]

Sometimes, involvement in Rape Crisis work developed out of unusual or unlikely circumstances:

"Actually I had a boyfriend that suggested it…I was quite young – I would be just turned 18 I think, and this was actually my first boyfriend. I remember meeting him at a dance, and thinking I won't dance with him a second time, I'll just get rid of him…I thought one of the things that would get rid of him was if I told him I was a feminist and he said "Oh do you read Spare Rib?" and I had never actually seen a copy of Spare Rib but I'd heard of it and I quite fancied reading it. So I started going out with him and felt emboldened to get a copy of Spare Rib and I think he actually saw a notice up about Rape Crisis in Glasgow looking for volunteers – this would be 1979, so I phoned up and after a while I think he thought I was getting a bit too involved – that's how I got involved with Glasgow." [Morna Findlay]

And personal experiences of the ever-present threat of sexual violence were another major motivating factor:

"Being groped was so commonplace that you just didn't even register it. You just kinda went "Oh fuck" you know "bastard" you know, you kinda swore a bit but you didn't let it get to you because you couldn't, 'cause it was so commonplace. Sexualised comments…being commented on by complete strangers was the norm. So you just got on with it. You might be irritated by it, you might be annoyed by it, but you didn't react to it. I think I'd begun to react – I'd begun to get quite pissed off about it." [Lily Greenan]

But the reasons for the interest and commitment that so many women gave to Rape Crisis centres were as complex and diverse as they were themselves:

"Some women came in because they were rape survivors…[ ] was somebody who was absolutely there for the support of women…she was a rape survivor herself, and she was an absolute backbone…terrific woman. And others would come in…because they were looking for like-minded women. Sometimes because they…thought they might be lesbian, but didn't know what to do about it, and that worked very well sometimes, and sometimes it didn't for them…Others came in, because intellectually, perhaps, they really wanted to do something, or politically, they wanted to do something, and others came in 'cause they wanted to change the world." [Aileen Christianson]

Helen Mackinnon had just returned from 6 months travelling in India, Nepal and Sri Lanka in 1979 when she joined the Rape Crisis centre in Edinburgh:

"I had always been interested in women's issues and health issues. But when I was away travelling, it sort of gave me time to have a good think and …it certainly – through looking at what was going on in India and Nepal and Sri Lanka at that time…issues around poverty, women's position as part of that and even like the reading that I was doing when I was away, it really fired me up to think that I needed to do something more immediate around issues, women's issues when I got back…once I did get back, I thought that Rape Crisis was a nice mixture because it was offering practical help as well as political lobbying. And so that's what I did.

And it was funny because…when everybody else was sort of joining feminist groups in my early 20s, because by that time I think I was about 29 or 30. In my early 20s I was training to be a nurse, I was at university and then I was doing nursing and then I was like a ward sister and I was heavily involved in the health service. And I was more like, not an onlooker, but I felt more peripheral to the sort of major feminist movement that was going on at that time so I kind of felt…almost like a late starter." [Helen Mackinnon]

She recalls her memories of the first of many visits to Broughton Street:

"The first introduction was…at a meeting, it was a Saturday, and there was people from all over Scotland there to talk about Rape Crisis…there was women knitting and it was also a very cold room…And I remember that's when I first met Jan, Jan MacLeod. She was there and she must have just been a young, young woman…it was just her I remember and Aileen." [Helen Mackinnon]

Helen spent around 9 months with Edinburgh Rape Crisis before she moved through to Glasgow to take up a new post:

"It was quite intensive though because at that time I didn't have a job... So it meant that I was on the rota... I did manage to invest quite a lot of time in it, which was really, really good...I wasn't sort of doing a day job and then rushing. And it felt really like one of the most important things in my life to do it...it...really sort of, hit the spot in terms of it being meaningful and making me feel good. And what I learnt in these first six months ...was to be continued once I went to Glasgow. " [Helen Mackinnon]

Dorothy Degenhardt's experiences took her on a similar path to Helen's:

"I took a year out of work which would be '78–'79. And I travelled in India and Pakistan and Kashmir and Bangladesh and...became more aware of the position of women in those countries and then I realised when I got back that actually it was similar for some women in Britain. And then I became much more involved, or interested in women's issues and feminist stuff...I came back and worked in a hostel in Edinburgh for people coming out of psychiatric hospital and prison, and then again, there was a new women's hostel being set up in Edinburgh for women offenders, an alternative to prison or women coming out of Cornton Vale and I was in at the beginning of that. So that will be '82–'85, ...the majority of women that worked there were feminists. And we tried to run it, which was very challenging, as a feminist collective...Being interested in women's issues and then the follow on from that was getting involved in Rape Crisis." [Dorothy Degenhardt]

The First Centres

Glasgow [Jane Dorby, 1976-c1984, Jan Macleod, 1977-1985, Anita Grassey, Naomi Gibson, Lorraine Warmbath, Liz Hunter, Morna Findlay, 1979-82, Helen Mackinnon, 1981-85, Rona Clarke, c1980/1/2?, Isabelle Kerr, 1980-82, 1985-90 & 2006-, Frances Monaghan (Action Against Incest), 1982-89, Rhona Watson (Action Against Incest), Kathy Litteljohn, 1975-6, Ann Hamilton, Caroline Armit, 1977-1985, Heather Low, Heather Forrest, 1983-89, Marcia D'Oliveira, Patricia Bell, Sheila Inglis, Alison Hack, Susan Gibb, Irene Audain, Dorothy Kemp, Dorothy Brownlie, Kate Laverty, Maria Laverty, Sheila Brodie, 1987-97, Lesley Ross, Linda Reid, Lyn Harvey, Morag McSween, Angela McCusker, Julie Harkin, Irene, Pauline.]

Glasgow Rape Crisis, which was the first centre in Scotland, emerged from a Women's Group at Glasgow University:

> "Well my understanding is that it grew out of the Glasgow Women's Group that they had a women's group or a women's liberation group in Glasgow…and round about 1975…it split into different interest groups. And one of them was about rape and it turned into the Rape Crisis Centre and one of them was about domestic violence and it turned into Glasgow Women's Aid. And then they had other ones that were to do with employment rights and abortion rights." [Jan Macleod]

Jane Dorby, who had already been involved with the women's movement in London by the times this happened in 1976, recalls:

> "I came up to Glasgow and I was studying and working, and I met a person called Naomi Gibson. And Naomi had said they were interested in starting a Rape Crisis centre, but I initially got involved in the women's group at Glasgow University… and we used to meet on a fortnightly basis, and we would discuss… feminist theories, and there was a very strong split in the group for abortion campaigns and Rape Crisis, and I chose to establish, along with Naomi and a few others, the Rape Crisis Centre. So we managed to get a small premises in Holland Street. And we got the phone lines up and running and we kept that kind of very maintenance establishment thing." [Jane Dorby]

> "The Scottish Council for Civil Liberties had a little office on the ground floor of a close in Holland Street. And we just had a phone in there, it wasn't even our own room we just were allowed to go in to one of their office rooms, we used to do evening rota, Monday, Wednesday and Friday and sometimes Sunday. And literally all that they had was the phone and an answer phone and a notebook. So we were there for a while, but I mean the good thing about it obviously was it was rent free. And then they moved down to Hope Street, which was with the Volunteer Centre and they gave us more or less the same arrangement, we had access to a desk and a meeting room." [Jan Macleod]

> "Someone knew someone in Civil Liberties, very, very nice people at the time, and they had a spare room. It was Civil Liberties who rented it, and they gave us a back room free…the only thing we'd to pay for was the phone line. So we shared it with civil liberties – it was actually very good, there was a good network there, because they had lawyers and things as well, and people we could get in contact with." [Jane Dorby]

A small piece in the Glasgow Herald under the headline "Funds needed", from February 1978 highlighted the difficulties with accommodation that were faced by the Glasgow centre:

> "After frustrating months of having no fixed address the Glasgow Rape Crisis Group now occupies premises (albeit small and temporary) in the city centre and can now make some start in helping rape victims seek justice and begin mending their lives. Meanwhile, the search for more suitable premises

will continue and, of course, funds will be urgently needed to ensure that the group's therapeutic and practical counselling becomes a long term project.

If you think you can help, or if you need help, please contact the group c/o The Citizen's Advice Bureau, 212 Bath Street, Glasgow G2 (041-331 2345/6/7)" [The Glasgow Herald, 15th February 1978]

"It was this tiny little cubby-hole office and I remember I fitted a mortice lock to it…and then after that we moved to the Volunteer Bureau…in Wellington Street…for a while we really were virtually in a cupboard…we'd go in about half past 6 or whatever…and unlocked a big cupboard …the phone line and the answering machine was in the cupboard …that and our books – logs, diary and whatever…set up on a table…" [Caroline Armit]

Kathy Litteljohn recalled her own involvement at the very earliest stages of Glasgow Rape Crisis:

"I worked in Nightline, at Strathclyde University…I was a student doing languages and psychology at Strathclyde between '73 and '76…it was in about the end of my university course at Strathclyde in about 1975…It was very much at the start with Jane and Jan…it was before we'd even been able to get funding… We started going to Holland St because SCCL gave us a little dingy room to meet in…I was…in the Nightline and between our experience of calls there and…information in the press about some really high profile cases that were going on with really huge issues around the way the legal system was treating women, the way the…police were treating women – it was just really glaringly… such a huge issue…I can't remember how I linked up with some of the women…I knew Ann Hamilton because we had a mutual friend who was my flatmate, and I think it must have been that plus the Nightline contact that then women were getting together to talk about it…but it was so, so at the early stages…

There was Lorraine Warmbath…and she was very…focussed and very knowledgable, Jan Macleod, Jane, and… Caroline Armit…those are the key people I remember…Things were…very informal, because we were having to meet at Lorraine's flat, or latterly at SCCL, Jane's flat…

"Lorraine…gave us…lovely…strong and clear impact about the issues – about oppression and feminism and…how the system militated against individual women…" [Kathy Litteljohn]

Kathy's involvement lasted a year, until she was accepted to do a continuing education course at Edinburgh University. Even in the context of her new (social work) course, she found herself having to confront a deep-seated reluctance to engage with the subject of rape:

"I …had to put up a dissertation topic for personal study…I wanted to do issues around rape and how… the caring services dealt with it, how the legal services dealt with it. I was told no, don't be so stupid… there's nothing really around that you can use for research, there's not a lot of material, and, it was a guy of course…and that just fired me up…to prove him wrong…" [Kathy Litteljohn]

Caroline Armit was working as a medical secretary in a hospital at the time:

"If it hadn't been that, it would've been Women's Aid…I think originally as I remember now I'd only really just offered just to go along and do the typing…but very quickly realised …it was just on its really very beginning stages…I didn't really know anybody." [Caroline Armit]

In Glasgow, in spite of the fact that they were operating largely in the dark, the group lost no time in setting up the Rape Crisis line, planning and teaching themselves as they went along. Their own commitment, enthusiasm, determination and stamina were the only resources they had:

"It wasn't really a problem. We had energy by the bucket loads… we just moved in, and as soon as we moved in, we said we'll need a table, yeah, let's get the phone in and let's try and fund raise and we just did it, you know? It just happened – it was very organic, actually. It was very easy." [Jane Dorby]

"It was so early days…there wasn't a knowledge base…a research group base to work on…there wasn't databases…there wasn't computers… there wasn't emails, there wasn't like websites…there was nothing then…we were just kind of…feeling our way…

We were having to…affirm and educate one another…cause everyone was at different stages and some people were more political and some people were more legal, some people were more…feminist, some people were less feminist…some people were more confident dealing with the authorities…although… it was an amorphous group really, there was incredible strength of feeling and commitment…it was just invigorated every time something else came out in the press…there was an awful lot of judges saying stupid things…that was the climate at the time…" [Kathy Litteljohn]

"I think we all knew we were just gonna do our best – I think the feminist thing really had kicked in then…" [Caroline Armit]

The women prepared themselves and educated one another through discussion, consultation, using whatever means they could:

"Sunday meetings were held in people's houses…just thinking about it and considering what on earth is this about – just making sense of it in so much as we could make sense of what we knew to be true… hence being a feminist!" [Caroline Armit]

"We would sit together and…I don't think anybody was terribly into kind of roleplay sessions and formalised stuff and all that kind of thing but we did try to prepare as best we could…Helen Mackinnon for instance…when she joined us…and there was somebody else before that…Kathy Litteljohn – had a bit of training…but you really were sort of working it out as you went along…but sensitively trying to think about what would be best – there was no other models about particularly and …there'd be meetings down in London and things…would be helpful…there was communications as to how they were working." [Caroline Armit]

Advertising and fundraising

Glasgow Rape Crisis publicised its activities "on the hoof" and in more formal ways:

"We got small stickers, and we went around public toilets, put them there. Naomi was at university, Anita was at university and they did Glasgow University and Strathclyde, and we held a disco, I think, if I remember, at Glasgow University for the first time…For fundraising, and it was also publicity, and we did a lot of phoning around and things like that. Yeah, very basic, but mostly, I remember doing fly posting around the west end and the city centre, and wir bucket and spade and wir car." [Jane Dorby]

"We had to do a lot of letter-writing at the beginning to try and contact different people…that was done collectively…" [Kathy Litteljohn]

"It always felt hand to mouth…you were out fundraising – flag days – in order to get the rent money… they had to be booked ahead of time…get your allotted day and everything…We did sort of exhibition things in Buchanan Street pedestrian precinct I remember…with boards …that somebody got from Glasgow Uni…"Rape is an Aberration"…we did that quite a few Saturday mornings – at the time I felt was probably quite brave…but it was just out there trying to be conscious-raising…what I do remember is being back in the office…with the Gestetner running off more leaflets because we'd done really well and handed out piles of leaflets so it was a lot about letting people know that there was such a thing as a Rape Crisis centre…" [Caroline Armit]

"It was in the Yellow Pages. It was called Glasgow when I joined. When we first got funding, which must have been about 1980 or something like that, we got a small amount of Section 10, it became Strathclyde…I think when I started, they used to advertise occasionally at the back of the Evening Times. And they also had little stickers that people put round women's toilets and things like that." [Jan Macleod]

"We did quite a lot of press releases – we hoped that we would get onto the radio or television quite often or get articles in the paper. We were actually relatively good at that." [Morna Findlay]

"But I do remember at one point, and it must have been the early 80s, we were fundraising money and we had this incredibly ambitious sort of rota of advertising in local newspapers so you have like the whatever, the Ayrshire Advertiser…every month you had an advert in a local paper, where possible we would try and get free publicity through …phoning them up and asking to do a small article." [Jan Macleod]

"We advertised in different ways. We'd have posters which we would take round and put in doctors' surgeries. We'd send them to schools as well. Not an awful lot of schools would accept them because of… the underage thing and they'd just think it would not be appropriate, but obviously it was because that's where lots of young girls were. And if they were given empowering skills they might have been able to say no. Or tell someone. And certainly to help them kind of think about, you know this is not normal. Maybe I should phone and do something. We also had little stickers and things which we'd put around phone boxes and things…And little leaflets that we'd take around. We did do various talks to quite often women's groups. And we'd do a lot of that campaigning as well…we were out in different places like Kirkintilloch, Lenzie, Renfrew, Eastwood." [Heather Forrest]

Getting information out and accessible to women who might need it was often dependent on the attitude of people like GPs:

"It was…quite difficult to get the information out. And that's I think [what] motivated people to get more money to produce better packs and write better leaflets and things like that and try and organise for it to go out to surgeries…but it was difficult…it depends on the doctors and what they thought and how they dealt with individual women…and whether in maybe some surgeries there was a woman doctor who might be quite supportive…then maybe you could have the information there, or they might write for information." [Sheila Brodie]

Although some of the messages that the Rape Crisis workers were trying to get out met with scepticism, there were often women with whom it clearly resonated:

"Some thought we were being quite extreme. And didn't believe us…But quite often, there'd be one or two women at the end who'd kind of like sneak up to you as you were …putting your leaflets away and they'd be going give me a leaflet and I know what you mean when you said that, it was, it really touched a nerve and so I think people didn't want to believe it." [Heather Forrest]

"…You would get a mixture, but by and large…you were really just aiming to be speaking to one or two women and groups of women or Mum & daughter…folk were maybe out shopping…that type of thing and that …bit of it felt absolutely fine because you were having a conversation for four or five minutes and then people were really interested because …everyone knows about and fears rape – and domestic violence as well – it's very very tied up with that so you knew that … people really want to find out more and discuss it a bit …" [Caroline Armit]

Finding the resources to support the services they worked so hard to develop for women was a constant challenge. In the early days, things were very often hand to mouth, and fundraising was often on a relatively small scale by means of things like flag days and one-off fundraisers. Funding was sought and acquired from many different sources and activities, often with a great deal of effort and inventiveness:

> "Well, we did things like discos, Glasgow University, we sent letters to the Labour Party through my sister, and they had affiliated funds, so that became a regular income – they would give, like, maybe £200 a year from the different groups across the west coast, and we established that as a fund. Fundraising was not a problem." [Jane Dorby]

> "Sometimes…cheques would arrive out of the blue – one from Saints & Sinners…charity…and the other I remember was somebody wonderful…voluntarily cut hair and sent us her money…we were relying on wee bits of money coming in so I don't really remember any big advertising…" [Caroline Armit]

> "We had discos, which would raise a fair bit of money as well. There was a regular disco on a Friday night anyway, a Lesbian Line disco, and you know, you would just do that, and part of the money would be taken for the Rape Crisis Centre. So these were the two main methods of fund raising, and then, again, it was putting into the…Soroptimists and the Royal Society of Foresters and things. You would just get money from sort of bizarre sources. Again, I do remember Jan was very good on that, because I think Jan had then been on to get a job. She was working. After she graduated, she was involved in social work, and that seemed to be an Aladdin's Cave for finding out about where you got money from." [Rona Clarke]

> "I remember one time we got a donation from a Charitable Trust that sought us out and, this woman phoned up and asked for information and…she said they'd decided to give us £500. And I remember nearly dying cos you know it was like a huge amount of money, I couldn't believe it. Just for nothing you know. I mean even these days you wouldn't be sort of put out of somebody gave you a £500 donation with no strings attached, but then it really was quite a lot of money. And also, we did fundraising …in the Star Club which was over in Carlton Place… we would do fundraising discos there, we used to do raffles, we had a party one time I remember in the big flat that I shared with other people in Clouston Street and charged people three pounds or something to get in…I think there was about 80 people at it. And then what else did we do? Blinking collecting days, shaking the can." [Jan Macleod]

Flag days were recalled with mixed emotions by women:

> "The fundraising days were really interesting – always got a good response and there was a bit of a carnival atmosphere for us. You used to do it in pairs, generally…Sauchiehall Street was our pitch…I used to do it with Caroline Armit for a few years. And some people did Byres Road, and some people did Argyle Street. I think you were actually allocated, you couldn't just go wherever you wanted… and we always had a bit of a party at night, afterwards, counting all the money, etc., that was very gratifying, and the discos were a good laugh, as well." [Rona Clarke]

> "We did do collecting in the street. That was very successful…The public were great because, you know, I mean, we weren't just shaking the cans, we were actually going up and speaking with people… And that was quite good, you know? People were quite keen to listen, and quite happy to wear a sticker. So that was quite interesting. We did, we were allocated a day, you know the way the Charities Commission does it? So we were allocated a day, and I think we did that regularly for a number of years…" [Rona Clarke]

"We used to do these can collections up and down Buchanan Street and Argyle Street, and you'd have to get permission from the council to do them and it's quite a bit of a faff getting all the cans sorted and all the rest of it. But it was a way of raising money… And once or twice we had the women's choir – Eurydice, doing things round the pubs for us…the choir's still around." [Sheila Brodie]

"The dreaded flag days….Which for some bizarre reason were always in December or January." [Isabelle Kerr]

However communicating the purpose of the fundraising could sometimes pose a challenge!

"I remember we did have this flag day and people thought we were what, collecting money for the rates, the Rate Crisis …I was one of the flag collectors on that day …it was good fun and it was bloody cold… but…it felt very energising and bonding…I suppose you would call it team building today…and we did get a lot of money." [Helen Mackinnon]

This also happened in Aberdeen:

"We were out on the streets doing flag days. People used to think that we were called the Aberdeen Rate Crisis Centre and they would say "I'm not giving money for the rates – I pay my rates!" [Siobhan Canavan]

Kay Carmichael, who was the Principal Officer for offenders supported Glasgow Rape Crisis in applying for Section 10 funding from the Social Work Department of Strathclyde Regional Council. This was funding for the provision of services that the department might otherwise have to provide themselves, and paid for a part-time administrative worker. It was the first such funding that the centre received and Glasgow Rape Crisis became Strathclyde Rape Crisis.

"When we got the sort of relatively small amount of money, Section 10 funding…it was one of these mixed blessings…We got it from Strathclyde Regional Council so we then had to call it Strathclyde Rape Crisis and…from having like, you know about £40 a year to cover Glasgow we probably had about £400 a year to cover the whole of Strathclyde which is about 20 times as big. Geographically a lot more than 20 times." [Jan Macleod]

The consequences of this meant that Strathclyde Rape Crisis supported women over a huge geographical area:

"I remember one time Liz phoning me up and saying what bus do you get to Orkney? I was like Liz what are you talking about, she said I've said to this woman that I'll go and see her. I was like Liz, Orkney's an island. She's like oh. She's not a clue about Orkney. So like she never actually went, but I remember supporting a woman in Dunoon for quite a long time, and that was a whole day trek…I had to get the train and the ferry and all the rest of it. Port Glasgow. Ayrshire. Prestwick yeah." [Jan Macleod]

Isabelle Kerr joined Glasgow Rape Crisis in 1980:

"It was a friend of mine who had decided that she wanted to volunteer for something. Now it, looking back she had absolutely no idea whatsoever I think, what Rape Crisis involved, but she had announced that she wanted to be a volunteer…of course she, she didnae want to do it herself. She said oh well you need a pal to go alang wi you so, and I said well I don't know anything about Rape Crisis and she said oh well we can, we can dae stuff like make the tea. You know it'll just be doing something so I said right ok then. So I contacted Rape Crisis and said me and my pal are really interested in becoming volunteers and then she decided she didnae want to do it…but of course she kind of piqued my interest by that time. So…it was Jan Macleod who replied to me and said why don't we meet up and have a chat and I can tell ye all about Rape Crisis and see if you still want to be a volunteer…

It just kinda happened completely by chance…I'm ashamed to say, that I didnae start out on some, you know fabulous political crusade…it just seemed to happen in such a strange way …there are times when I've thought no I canny tell anybody how I got involved with Rape Crisis cos it's just so embarrassing…I just want to sort of let people think that I drank in feminism in my mother's milk you know. That is not the case, cos I have to confess my mother is not anything that would even approach a feminist I'm afraid." [Isabelle Kerr]

Early meetings made a strong impression on the new recruit:

"They all seem to be incredibly knowledgeable and of course they were all studenty types, well it seemed like that to me…therefore I just thought, they just know so much more than me, you know I'm just, I'm destined to make the tea forever more…that was what I thought. And …well you get sucked in, it's a kind of old Hotel California syndrome isn't it, you know you can never leave." [Isabelle Kerr]

By the early 80's, the centre had moved to Wellington Street.

"It was okay in the evenings, the collective evenings, when you were all coming out in a group, but otherwise, it wasn't a very nice location – but the story for voluntary organisations as you know, they always had to be in the cheapest accommodation." [Rona Clarke]

"What I do remember is that Rape Crisis basically were housed in a cupboard. And there was like the phone and the answering machine on and that was all in the cupboard and that was locked up and then when you came in you opened your cupboard…so Rape Crisis centre used to live in a cupboard." [Isabelle Kerr]

"The area was really isolated, and you had to go up…hundreds of stairs to get to it…you were kind of solely responsible for opening the building and locking it up, and if you were on the phone line and you had a call that came in at ten…you can be on the phone to eleven, twelve…it was no a great area to be working in." [Frances Monaghan]

And by 1985, when Isabelle Kerr returned from Aberdeen and rejoined the Glasgow collective, they had moved premises again, to a building also occupied by One Plus:

"It was in Hope Street, by that time… just above that Cookies…It was 39 Hope Street." [Isabelle Kerr]

"At one point…we'd actually used a house that me and Irene lived in because there was no other premises…it was all a very cloak and dagger at that time and on the door, it said Weight Watchers… And it only had two wee rooms…so it was really quite small and we had a wee kind of kitchen area. And that was the only premises we had, so it was quite small and contained… And the phone was in one of those rooms so…we'd have our meeting in there and the phone would be on there at the same time. Sometimes we did bring women there as well, it would just depend… Some people didn't want to be in a room on their own, like some of the volunteers kind of thought if no-one was in during the day, they didn't want to be in that building on their own because it was in the corridor and there was no one else around…" [Heather Forrest]

"They had this old…brown and orange sofa…all the stuffing was coming out of it…there was bits of furniture, basically from women's houses…a kind of coffee table that you pulled up and it was a drinks cabinet underneath (laughs) it just looked really odd, you know?…It was all there was, really…all very kind of hand-knitted…there was a real kind of make do and mend feel about it, there was never any money…" [Linda Reid]

Confidentiality was always paramount:

"We used to say to the women that…these are some rooms that…we get the loan of… we never gave out the address because there were fears of…maybe if it was a women's partner that had raped her finding out where she was…following her and …attacking her there…all these kind of issues…It was a bit cloak and dagger." [Sheila Brodie]

Heather Forrest joined Glasgow Rape Crisis in 1983:

"It took up lots of my life. I wasn't working at the time because I think I didn't try hard enough to get a job because I was doing lots of things for Rape Crisis and I very quickly got involved…at that point we were open Monday, Wednesday, Friday, 7pm till 10pm. And I would usually do one if not two of those evenings." [Heather Forrest]

Similarly, Helen Mackinnon, who had joined the Edinburgh Rape Crisis collective for several months in 1979, subsequently joined Glasgow Rape Crisis when a new job took her through to the west. She joined the Glasgow collective at the beginning of 1981, when the centre was based at Wellington Street:

"I started out in Edinburgh and then I went through to Glasgow and I did three years in Glasgow Rape Crisis in the Women's Support Project…And then I came back to Edinburgh to work… And I think I came back and I was part of the Edinburgh Rape Crisis collective a few years later…for a few months. And then I just moved on to the Management Committee for the Women's Support Project in Glasgow." [Helen Mackinnon]

Helen and Heather Low both worked with the Incest Survivors' Group. The number of women in the collective varied over the years:

"I think, initially, when I was involved, there seemed to be about eight people and then it was bigger than that. I'd say up to about fourteen, fifteen people, and there were always people who didn't come, but who were on the books, as it were…People would drop out, …if they were doing their final exams, etc." [Rona Clarke]

By 1985 the number of women in the Glasgow collective had increased significantly:

"There were loads and loads of women involved at that time. And I had just…came back into the centre. And also at that time, Action Against Incest were operating alongside Rape Crisis – they were kinda sharing premises and that was…when I got to know Frances Monaghan. They were specifically engaged wi Action Against Incest…they had a phone line on as well." [Isabelle Kerr]

"At that time of course…the telephone line was opened Monday, Wednesday, Friday…seven till ten… the collective meeting was on a Wednesday" [Isabelle Kerr]

"We would have our meeting on a Wednesday, from sort of six-ish till about eight-ish or nine, sometimes it would go on quite a long time and then we would all rush out at ten o'clock and go to the Toby Jug which is round there somewhere." [Heather Forrest]

The extent to which the Glasgow collective documented its work was limited:

"There was Minute books from the meetings and that was all. And I think the standard of minute-taking was probably quite good sometimes and quite horrendous and non-existent at other cases."
[Heather Forrest]

Around 1986, Strathclyde Rape Crisis decided to create a video, entitled "**Every Woman's Fear**". Rona Clarke, Helen Mackinnon, Susan Gibb, Heather Forrest, Sheila Inglis and Alison Hack were on the sub-group that organised this, and worked closely with the film-maker Diane Barry:

"In an effort to spread the message, you know, we thought, oh this would be a good idea to try and get involved in video…then instead of us going out, … we can send something out…because we were… frequently asked to do talks which were very difficult to do, because it was always during the day, and a lot of us were working or… it was quite often fairly remote places and we thought, well, if we've got a video, we can send this out." [Rona Clarke]

The group were successful in raising money to fund the making of the video:

"We went away for a planning weekend, we approached Scottish Screen and got a grant of about £500 to make it…this was all over a period of a good few months. We liaised with the Rape Crisis Centre at what they wanted to be in it, etc, etc. So we went ahead and we made it, and we got people filming in my house. We employed an actress…was it Libby MacArthur?… In fact, she's very involved in River City, she's one of the main actresses…you know, to do some of the voiceovers, to make it seem a bit more professional, and the rest of us did sort of walk on parts and things like this… what we were trying to do was… we wanted somebody… who had good speech to talk about… what rape was and whom it happened to and you know, all the myths and facts, basically…So we used Libby to do that, because, well the rest of us were a bit inhibited and…maybe we felt we wouldn't sound as good, and Diane thought it would be good to have Libby as well…somebody who's a trained actress…a trained narrator, rather… it wasn't really dramatised that much, but…we would have…stills of people, you know, wandering about in the daylight…to show that it didn't happen at night necessarily…and just sitting in their house.

But…we didn't want it to be a kind of shlock horror type of thing either… we were talking about… what's best for women and things that women can do to boost their confidence and…we had an extract from people doing self defence and personal safety, which was really interesting. There was a woman who was a lecturer in Glasgow at the time, called Cathy, I think her second name was Miller – she was lecturing at Strathclyde, and she was very involved in women's safety, women's personal safety and… was good at karate, etc, but she'd established some techniques for women to learn to improve their personal safety, which didn't involve…going for five years to karate classes and that sort of thing.

So she was really good and we filmed her and we filmed women doing a few techniques. But, unfortunately, therein lay the downfall of the video because when we finished the video and showed it to the Rape Crisis Centre, the collective at the time, they decided that they were unhappy with the content, because they didn't like the element of the personal safety in it, because they felt that was implying that women should do so… which was not at all the way we felt it was portrayed at all…we were just talking about what, how women can make themselves feel more confident in general… like simple tips, like being aware of your environment, etc, etc, and reacting to your instincts, even if somebody's your brother-in-law, or it's a doctor – if you're not comfortable with them, you're entitled to get out the situation… But anyway, they weren't happy about it, and they contacted Scottish Screen and were threatening to sue us and all kinds of things, you know? So eventually, they refused to distribute it…they didn't want it…So you know, all these copies just lay mouldering, you know?

Nobody'd really said anything…even though we had run it past them, because, at that time, that was all quite new – the idea of personal safety classes…So that was, let me see, that would have been 1986, 87 that was all ongoing. I mean we had a launch for it, but really, the people we wanted to take it, i.e. the Rape Crisis Centre, wouldn't take it. So it was a twenty minute video which we enjoyed making. It was an interesting process." [Rona Clarke]

The centre applied to the Social Work Department for Urban Aid funding to set up the **Women's Support Project**; this was awarded in 1983.

"That just really seemed to embody everything that we wanted, in terms of getting a message out to a much wider group of people, doing training so that, you know, other people could then take the message elsewhere into their areas of professional practice, etc so that, to me, was a big, huger milestone – and then I felt, also, with the Women's Safety Centre, that was very important as well." [Rona Clarke]

"You'd got to tackle it at different political levels as well as the individual level which was why, arising out of … that knowledge and expertise came the Urban Aid mission that created the Women's Support Project to try and cope with some of the educational…consciousness-raising awareness training – all that stuff that needed to happen alongside services to women…" [Caroline Armit]

Rona Clarke recalls her involvement in it:

"I had been a personnel officer at one point and people felt I might know a bit about drawing up personnel policies, etc – so I was involved in that, and that was really interesting, setting up the Women's Support Project. Really, really rewarding … so I was involved in that – the Women's Support Project management committee for a few years…" [Rona Clarke]

Marcia d'Oliveira was the Women's Support Project's first paid worker.

One institution which was useful was that of women's officers, something which existed both within Strathclyde Region and Glasgow City Council, posts which were intended to develop work with women and promote the interests of women and awareness of gender issues across the council:

"Strathclyde Regional Council had women's officers. One was Ann Hamilton, except she was Ann Robertson then." [Sheila Brodie]

Other initiatives and organisations that were developing around the same time focused on women's issues and interests also contributed to a burgeoning sense that these issues were beginning to feature on the agenda:

"There was quite a lot of women's organisations kind of springing up. There had been a Women's Centre… I think it was Miller Street… There was Women's Aid, there was Rape Crisis…there was… the idea of producing a women's directory, there was a Women's Library – there was a lot of…activity. And it somehow enabled a bit better access to funding. If you had somebody in the council who was kind of promoting." [Sheila Brodie]

Another initiative that achieved much success a few years later was the **Women's Safety Centre**, which originated as a pilot project undertaken by the Women's Support Project:

"They were looking at putting together personal safety stuff, personal safety courses – and that was because a group of women had kind of got together and said 'Well, women who are contacting Rape Crisis Centre have identified that they've experienced abuse or violence at some point, on some level. Women who are contacting Women's Aid have obviously identified their experience in abuse and violence, the same with Action Against Incest. What about all the women out there who have experienced abuse and violence, are living, today, with abuse and violence, who are at risk of abuse and violence, but don't call it that, and they don't know how to identify it and they don't know how to name it?' So…the Women's Support Project came up with this idea of doing awareness raising in local communities, but because they got East End funding…it meant that they were restricted to the East End…Inner GEAR [Glasgow Eastern Area Renewal] it was called.

Strathclyde Rape Crisis Workers, mid-1980's

…So they got that, and they were the ones who said, 'Look, women aren't going to turn up to talks about domestic abuse. They're not going to turn up to talks about child sexual abuse', you know, so we need to think about that, so in a pub, again, one night, where all the best ideas come, I think…I remember this conversation being bandied about, about, well what about a personal safety course? How about that, you know? And they're like, mm, aye, women find it easy to talk about their public safety and then once you get in the door, you can talk about all that sort of stuff. What exactly is it that women are experiencing? You know, where is it women are most at risk? It could be used as a tool to inform, to educate, to raise the issue, and give women skills, and that became quite problematic between Rape Crisis Centre and the Women's Support Project and all that sort of stuff because some of the women in Rape Crisis Centre were saying 'oh you can't talk about personal safety because that's putting responsibility onto the women'… And we could see it as well. We could see it, but my argument was, well see while I'm waiting on men taking responsibility for abuse and violence, I want to know how to defend myself, d'you know what I mean?" [Frances Monaghan]

Edinburgh [Aileen Christianson, 1978-1996, Lily Greenan, 1981-1988 & 1992-1999, Leti Volpp, Barb Bates, Jane Cairns, Pat Christie, Kathy Knowles, Anne Leuchars, Janine Roberts, Annie Currie, Sarah Noble, Cynthia Graham(Cindi), Caroline Hickson, Carol Targett, Sarah Scott, Christine Knight, Gail McKinley, Eileen Scott, Sheila Gilmore, 1977-mid 80's, Helen Mackinnon, 1979, & 1985-87, Morna Findlay, 1983-4, Guin Williams, Nadine Harrison, Liz Elkind, Liz Alpert, Margaret McCutcheon, 1983- , Margaret Cunningham (Terry), Sue Hammersley, Sos Hancock (became Sos/Susan Dance), Kathy Kerr, Kathy Anderson, Judy Cottrell, Jane Meagher, Sally Wainwright, Linda Blythe, Amanda Jones, Michelle Jones, Elaine Bain, Bernadette Kelly, Sue Jennings, Christina Aitken, Julie [?], Liz Hammersley, Dawn Wilson, Michele Burman, Gail Robertson, Alison Smith, Simona Hughes, Charmaigne Leslie, Moira Kane, Tina Maison, Evelyn McHugh, Margie [?], Heather Dewar, Heather Marshall, Kenna Chisholm, Carolyn Dougill, Bernadette [?], Manda Green, Carole Dixon, Zam Walker, Jess Anderson, Naomi Wolf, Marie McArthy, Fran Loots, Fione Watson, Lesley White, Kim Stapleton, Kirsty Kerr, Karen Dalton]

The Edinburgh Rape Crisis Centre opened on 1st July 1978 after a period of planning which lasted around 2 years. The Glasgow Herald of the same day contained this account of the new centre:

> "A Rape Crisis centre opens in Edinburgh today to offer a confidential support service to women who have been raped or sexually assaulted. It is being run by a group of 30 women interested in changing attitudes of the courts and the police towards women who have been raped. Although set up to help women, they will not refuse to help any male victims. The Edinburgh crisis centre is the third of its kind in the United Kingdom. The others are in London and Glasgow.
>
> Miss Eileen Scott said the centre believed there were between 400 and 800 rapes and sexual assaults in Edinburgh every year. In 1976 there were 13 prosecutions and, assuming the normal proportion of prosecutions to complaints in Scotland, this would amount to a total of 80 complaints in the city.
>
> However, most rapes were never reported, and studies in London and America suggested the figures as high as nine out of every 10 attacks were not reported. The 30 women, who include some who have been raped and have recovered, will operate the centre by telephone for four hours every evening from Monday to Friday and eight hours, afternoon and evening, on Saturdays.
>
> Miss Scott said that although they had no financial support other than private donations they hoped to get a Government grant." [***Women in bid to help rape victims*** in The Glasgow Herald, 1st July, 1978]

The first ever issue of MsPrint, a Scottish feminist publication which appeared during the second half of 1978, also included a short account of the new service, which ran as follows:

> "In Edinburgh a Rape Crisis Centre opened at the beginning of July. The centre exists for women who have been raped, or sexually assaulted, who want advice or counselling, or who want to talk to someone sympathetic about the experience.
>
> The Centre will be open from 6.00 p.m. to 10.00 p.m. Mondays to Fridays, and from 2.00 p.m. to 10.00 p.m. on Saturdays. The telephone number is 031-556 9437. The Centre can also be contacted in writing through P.O. Box 120, Head Post Office, Edinburgh EH1 3ND." [MsPrint Issue 1, p.9]

The Edinburgh centre's first premises used by the Edinburgh collective were in Forth Street, just below Picardy Place; shortly afterwards, the centre was run from the Women's Centre in a basement in Broughton Street:

"It was not in great condition, but we may have had some money through Women's Aid, ...there was a connection...it was pretty much run on a shoe string at that time, and the later premises were in Broughton Street, which was another basement, but it was a slightly better basement." [Sheila Gilmore]

"It was dark, it was pokey, it had a bare light bulb in the main big room. It had kind of cushions that people sat on – there were some chairs, but there were more cushions. It was a bit scabby, basically." [Lily Greenan]

"It was...a place that you passed, you know, loads of times on foot. All of a sudden it... completely took on a different significance that all this hive of activity was going on in this sub-basement" [Margaret McCutcheon]

"The loo was outside under the pavement. One basement room, I think there may have been water in the corner, I don't even remember, but it was freezing, sitting round in fur coats – we were still allowed to wear fur coats in those days (laughing). Scabby old fur coats we bought at Oxfam." [Aileen Christianson]

"Women before me had gone to great effort to get the place and to get electricity in it or you know get it properly rewired...these things were not to be taken for granted...when I arrived, I think it had just been done up or we were just saving to get it done up. And there was no grants or stuff...

I remember Aileen put a particular effort into the kitchen and the dishtowels. I do actually remember saying well I'll buy trays. And I remember sort of bringing them back and thinking it wasn't to folks' taste, the trays. You know it's funny what you can remember...I think it was a very bright contemporary tray out of Habitat or something. And it seemed maybe a bit too gaudy or whatever...

I do also remember...great big notice boards and they were very interesting in their own right ...sort of radical and alternative information...that was good. And...I do remember we had...the big gas cylinders. They were smelly and they...created quite a damp climate. But they had to be exchanged and it meant that...you had to be there on a Saturday morning at a certain time to get these canisters delivered or you'd to take your car...I don't want to make too much of that. But it was actually quite hard work and it was like two hours of your time just to go and do it...Whereas now... everything's done to support what I'm doing at work. I mean obviously I wash my dishes and I make my tea sometimes, but...you don't just go off and have to sort the heating." [Helen Mackinnon]

"The voluntary sector seemed to be just a mass of posters...it was like the wallpaper. I remember it being very cold and damp in the winter and just full of old sofas and things like that that people had brought in and hotchpotches of desks and tables and because it was a basement it felt quite low as well, you know in terms of ceiling height. So you felt ...slightly cocooned I suppose, in a different world." [Margaret McCutcheon]

A short history of Edinburgh Rape Crisis, entitled "Still a long fight ahead", which was published in "Grit and Diamonds" (a history of the women's movement in Scotland published by Stramullion in 1990) highlights the backgrounds of the women who formed this group:

> *"It was founded by a group of women in the Women's Movement who knew that women who were sexually assaulted often received further bad treatment from professionals, friends, or family that they told. The collective was made up, as many Women's Movement groups then were, of several incomers to Edinburgh, mainly English and American women, as well as Scots women. Their analysis of rape was that it was a violent, not a sexual crime used to control and limit women's lives, a view still held by the collective today. Those original women who had the energy and commitment to start the centre at a time when our view of rape was seen as*

26

extreme and challenging deserve all our thanks. None of them remain in ERCC, but the patterns of working established by that first collective have provided the framework that we still use: Thursday meetings for collective business; phone access to the centre for several hours a week (though our hours have varied); individual meetings with women for support; confidentiality; a resistance to the idea that we are 'counsellors', as opposed to women supporting women; a refusal to use the term 'victim' to describe a woman who has been raped because we feel this traps her into a passive stereotype." [Edinburgh Rape Crisis workers in Grit and Diamonds – Stramullion, 1990]

Sheila Gilmore joined the Edinburgh group shortly after completing her law degree:

"I got involved with the Rape Crisis group that was just trying to set up in 1977, and I think I knew a few of the people who had already started to meet…probably around sort of Spring of '77, and I'd just finished my law degree in, I suppose the May/June of that year, so I had a bit of time in hand, and got involved… they'd already been meeting…only a matter of probably a couple of months…with a view to getting a centre set up…some of them, probably, were people I already knew through other parts of the kind of women's movement in Edinburgh." [Sheila Gilmore]

She recalls the lengthy planning process that preceded the opening of the centre:

"A lot of it was educational, I think, in terms of understanding the issues. Reading some of the literature that was beginning to appear at that time, and things like, I suppose Susan Brownmiller and other books…a lot of it was American, but also trying to get up to speed on some of the…Scottish legal issues, to some extent, and having just finished a law degree, I suppose I was quite interested in that as well…I'd done quite a bit of stuff on family law and a bit on criminal…So I was particularly interested in…that side of it, but it was also…people trying to get themselves ready to do counselling which…I think only, probably some of the group had had any experience of, at the time." [Sheila Gilmore]

Not all of the women who were involved in the planning process became part of the collective:

"Originally, it was only about, probably eight or nine. It was quite a small group, from memory…And that's why I think we were a bit ambitious with what we originally thought we could achieve, in terms of coverage, you know? 'Cause it was asking quite a lot of people to go and sort of sit to person the phones and whatever. But we tried…we saw it as both a counselling service and as a lobbying group… and I suppose to some extent, people sort themselves out into what they particularly like doing…I preferred, was more interested in the kind of lobbying and educational side of it than the actual sort of person to person counselling, which I wasn't that keen to do and I thought it was a bit too much like work, I think." [Sheila Gilmore]

"I actually listed how many women were in the collective, and there were about 15, and there were five who weren't doing phone calls, who were doing public work like me, and there was maybe two who had just come in and weren't yet ready to do phone calls, so that only left nine, eight or nine actually doing the phone calls. And we were never 24 hour – we were never more than maybe four, sometimes five evenings in the week and a Saturday opening, but mostly it was three evenings in the week and that was always a problem, although of course initially we got very few phone calls 'cause women didn't know about us." [Aileen Christianson]

"I think at that sort of low key level…it did work quite well. I mean, it was quite a small group, but people were all quite keen. Once we'd…been a bit more realistic about what could be done, and appreciated that however much we might like to be open every day, that really wasn't…particularly practicable." [Sheila Gilmore]

"Three Thursdays of the month were collective meetings and the fourth Thursday was a drop in for anybody who was interested in joining." [Aileen Christianson]

Aileen Christianson met Barb Bates, an American woman who was part of the original collective, about 2 years prior to this, and describes her own reluctant involvement in the new enterprise:

"I knew about this group that was planning to open a Rape Crisis Centre because Barb and I were in a consciousness raising group together, and I thought bloody hell, that's much too like hard work, oh much too serious, I'm not getting involved with that. And then …they had a sort of display down at the end of Princes Street, and that's when Nadine Harrison joined, I'm pretty sure. And I kept clear…at the time, I had an allotment, and there was one Saturday morning when Barb had said, oh we're doing a fundraising at the end of Princes Street in – whatever the church is called, St John's or something – if you want to come by. And I said, oh maybe…and it was raining – so this friend, who'd been going to go to the allotment with, he said well, why don't we just go down and call in? And so in I went, and Barb was there, and she said, oh it's really difficult because there's so few of us and we really need people on

Lily Greenan & Aileen Christianson

the phone, and I said ach well, I suppose I could do that (laughing). So that's how I joined, in a totally absent minded fit of, it was raining and I couldn't go to the allotment, and I think really, I was quite right to have avoided it, because I knew how heavy going it was gonna be… However, I went along to a training session in December 1978, and that was it…the combination of the actual phone work, and going to see individual women, and helping them, and supporting them and learning from them, and the other side, the legal side, and working towards changing things, which, of course, was very long term, it just turned out to be something that completely fascinated me. So that's how I ended up, I stayed with it for eighteen years." [Aileen Christianson]

The catalyst for Margaret McCutcheon's involvement was a visit from collective workers at Moray House:

"A very small group of women from the Rape Crisis collective came to speak at Moray House Student Union…it was part of the Student Union activities that I was involved in and we…as a women's group in the college invited them to come and speak…that was where I first…learned about the work…they gave this talk which was dead inspiring and…I thought to myself oh, you know I really want to get involved, and spoke to the women at the end of it and said how could you become an unpaid worker? How can you get involved in the collective?" [Margaret McCutcheon]

After several years in Glasgow, Helen Mackinnon returned to Edinburgh to rejoin the collective as it entered what many of those who were part of that collective recall as halcyon days:

"It's a bit like Dr Who and all the spin-offs…I came back to Edinburgh 1985, so it was about three and a half/four years…It was just a really, really productive time…we've since talked about it as a golden age …we all have our golden ages don't we in terms of when things were going really, really well?" [Helen Mackinnon]

Edinburgh Rape Crisis took every opportunity to advertise their services to women:

"There was the opening day, where we had a stall in Princes Street, outside the Register House, and the Evening News covered that. Any time we were asked to do an interview by the Evening News, we always would say yes, because that was a good way of getting the word out to women in Edinburgh. I think there was one time when we actually had an ad on a couple of buses for a few months, but it was incredibly expensive and so we didn't pursue that…So a lot of it was word of mouth, speaking to journalists if they rang us up… and equally, doing television reactions, we would try and do that as well 'cause it would make women see that we existed. Obviously, we were in the phone book and I think after a while, we were in the front of the phone book…but the problem with that kind of thing was, if you're in the phone book, people think you should be there all the time, so occasionally on the answer phone, we would get messages from people being pissed off that we weren't there…And we would do talks as much as possible – we'd do talks to women's groups or sometimes to mixed groups, to anyone that asked us. Anything to simply spread the word." [Aileen Christianson]

"We were actually quite ambitious to start with, and…after the first rush of enthusiasm, was a kind of scaling down…I think we originally thought we were going to be…offering a service most evenings and six days a week kind of thing, and we actually found that was…more than we were able to do with the number of people involved." [Sheila Gilmore]

The question of whether to accept or resist funding from external sources raised many questions within the Edinburgh collective in its early days:

"It was very much the culture of the organisation…that…the voice of the organisation was saying we don't really want to go down the road of taking funding because we'll then compromise our ethos and values." [Margaret McCutcheon]

But the limits on the service imposed by such a view resulted in frustration among some collective members and the realisation that significant progress would depend to a certain extent on obtaining more sustainable funding:

"They were interesting times basically but for me it felt as though if you really wanted to provide something that was more than two half days a week of a phone line where it was hit and miss where somebody, when they needed to talk, what were they gonna get ...an answering machine saying call back...? And you know women didn't have phones, they didn't have mobile phones...you might be out in the cold at a phone box." [Margaret McCutcheon]

By the time Lily Greenan joined in August 1981, there were around 20 members of the Edinburgh collective, and some of the original members who had founded the collective in 1978 were already beginning to move on. Lily returned to Edinburgh Rape Crisis full-time in 1992 as the centre's first paid worker.

The decision within the collective to apply for funding to take on a paid worker was only taken after an extensive period of consultation with its members through a working party dedicated to looking at this issue. Questions raised by this group in a report produced as part of the consultation process highlight the complexities of the issues with which it was confronted:

> *"1. Commitment of volunteers. What kind of commitment are volunteers prepared to make to the group including paid workers?*
> *2. What status will the paid worker have in the group?*
> *3. How would communication within the group proceed – how would individuals find out what is going on?*
> *4. Is the idea of an availability rota a good one and what other links could be forged between paid workers and volunteers?*
> *5. How would we organise the finances of the group in terms of paying the workers, bills, etc. Would we have a volunteer dealing with salaries, N.I., etc or would we employ a "superior" worker for this?*
> *6. What conditions of employment would we suggest? What about dismissal procedure, union membership etc?*
> *7. In view of all these questions (and hopefully answers) do we think it would be a good idea and a feasible one to employ paid workers in the collective?"*
> *[From Report of working party on paid workers (Edinburgh Rape Crisis)]*

Agreement having been reached that the group should apply for funding for a paid worker led to protracted discussions with Lothian Regional Council and led eventually to the funding for a worker being granted. The Social Work Committee of Lothian Regional Council had already begun paying half of the centre's running costs in the summer of 1987, and ERCC also received some support from Edinburgh District Council's Women's Committee which did alleviate the group's financial situation to a limited extent.

Although the different centres shared a common purpose, some focused on particular areas, and developed certain strengths and expertise within those. As Aileen Christianson observed:

> "Edinburgh became a centre which was obsessed with the whole legal situation."

The Edinburgh collective became heavily involved in lobbying for legal change:

> "There was a fair bit of debate about legal changes at that time...Around evidence, around issues of corroboration...and the whole question of...anonymity..." [Sheila Gilmore]

Sheila Gilmore wrote an extensive article on the subject of rape, the many myths surrounding it, and the legal situation in Scotland, for the first issue of the Scottish feminist publication "MsPrint" in 1978. Entitled *"Is rape a problem worth being concerned about in Scotland?",* the piece offered detailed recent statistics and looked at the limited impact that any prospective legal change would bring, if it was not accompanied by a change in attitudes to women. It also summarised the typical conduct of a rape trial, issues of corroboration and rape within marriage, as well as outlining concerns around current police practice.

A report produced by the Edinburgh Rape Crisis Centre in 1982 summarised the many many efforts they had made to that date to effect legal change. These efforts had culminated in an unsuccessful attempt earlier that year to pursue a Private Members Bill to restrict the questioning of women in rape trials on their sexual history:

> "Our proposals were that evidence of the woman's general character, previous sexual experience, and attitudes should not be allowed in rape trials. At present this is allowed in Scotland. In England, since 1976, such evidence is not normally allowed, but a judge can allow it at his/her discretion. We proposed that such evidence should never be allowed, and there should be no question of the judge having discretion to allow it. The defence use this evidence to suggest that women of certain character/behaviour cannot have been raped and must have "consented". The attention of the jury is distracted from what actually happened, and from evidence of threats or actual violence. And thus popular prejudices about rape (that women "ask" for it etc.) are used to secure an acquittal. This is why rape has a very low conviction rate – approximately 56% of cases coming to court result in a conviction, compared to approx. 78% of murder cases and approx. 85% of theft (1977-78 Scottish Criminal Statistics).

> This change would not help in all cases. It would not effect the defence's capacity to suggest that women "asked for it" by drawing on the surrounding circumstances – eg. where the rape took place; hitchhiking; being in a pub before the rape; being protected by contraception at the time of the rape; even if a woman is brutally beaten up as well as raped all these can <u>and are</u> used by the defence to maintain that it was "sex" which "went wrong", <u>not</u> rape. Until public attitudes change, of course, it will go on being possible for the defence to use these kinds of tactics – often successfully – against all the overwhelmingly forensic and other corroborative evidence available to back up the woman's evidence. But we have always felt that at least some irrelevant circumstances <u>could</u> be excluded by this first legal change.

> Our second area of change was to forbid questions about previous sexual intercourse with the accused (at present admissible) as irrelevant to <u>present</u> consent. This would also lend force to the fact that rape within marriage <u>is</u> a crime in Scotland. In 1982 for the first time there have been 2 prosecutions of husbands for raping their wives. In one case the man got off even though the rape took place outside <u>in the snow</u>. The jury clearly took the view that his wife (separated from him for a month) must have consented. In the second, the man pled guilty but his wife was reconciled with him afterwards. Our suggested change would make it more possible for these charges to be brought and perhaps for them to stick. It is small comfort to Scotswomen raped by their husbands that it is theoretically possible to complain of rape by their husbands (something that it is <u>impossible</u> to do under English rape laws) if it remains even more difficult to get a conviction than in nonmarital rape.

> Edinburgh and Strathclyde Rape Crisis Centres sent off to various Scots MPs (who had expressed an opinion in the debates or were local MPs) a short summary of these proposals in Feb. 1982. Some of them referred our letter to Malcolm Rifkind, then Minister for the Scottish Office responsible, and he referred it to a civil servant in the Scottish Office. We were politely told that it would be inappropriate to tinker with the rules of evidence piecemeal before the Scottish Law Commission had presented their recommendations on <u>all</u> Law of Evidence. The Scottish Law Commission in their Memorandum No. 46 had recommended that evidence that a complainer was of "bad moral character or that she associated with prostitutes" should be excluded, but they did not accept that evidence of previous sexual intercourse with the accused should not be admissible. We had already submitted our comments to them in 1981 on these questions. The other excuse for delay was a promised Scottish Home and Health Department research

project on police procedures in rape complaints and on legal procedures in rape trials. – Presumably they hoped that this report might magically absolve the police and the legal system of any responsibility in the extra difficulties women witnesses in rape reports and trials have to face. It still hasn't appeared but it is unlikely to fulfil that function when it does.

Willie Hamilton was the only MP to state unequivocally that he would do whatever he could, though several others were cautiously interested. We duly went ahead and had a small bill drafted into the proper form, the Sexual Offences (Evidence) (Scotland) Bill. Then, shortly before the new parliamentary session, we sent this to our selected MPs, in the hope that it could be presented as a Private Members' Bill, that being the only chance for changes of this sort to get on the statute book. When John Corrie came first in the Private Members' ballot, and none of our MPs featured at all, we duly wrote to him too, despite the unlikelihood of him touching it. Consequently, on none of our MPs being placed in the ballot, and John Corrie choosing an ostentatiously noncontroversial bill, we are left where we were before – stalemated: still waiting for the Scottish Law Commission's recommendations, the Scottish Office research document, and the possessors of a small bill with no chance of entry onto the statute book. Since the whole exercise was always in the nature of a test of MPs' willingness as well as capacity to change anything we cannot be said to be either surprised or disappointed.

Rape Crisis Centres through their support of raped women are obviously constantly aware of the fact that legal changes may make no difference at all in the protection offered to women witnesses in rape trials etc. The Scots among us are also aware that the chances of putting through changes which only affect Scotland in a Parliament that meets in and is dominated by England are slim indeed. So the exercise inevitably produces rather a negative conclusion. To take MPs at their word of January and February and pursue the matter to its logical parliamentary conclusion – a draft bill – proves only what we suspected anyway: that a lot of Parliamentary as well as media hot air was spouted in January and February. And that if we depended on legal changes to improve our protection as women at risk of male violence we'd wait a long long time. The media was desperate for instant action on the subject at the time. And instant action is the one remedy that is definitely not on offer to women living in Scotland." [**Extract from Edinburgh Rape Crisis Centre report for Scottish Joint Action Group Broadsheet no.1**]

Spare Rib published an article by Aileen Christianson in which she outlined in detail the differences between the English and Scottish legal systems on rape and sexual violence – an area around which there was often a great deal of confusion. She concluded:

"At the moment we are only tinkering within the confines of two male defined legal systems. Whilst pushing for proper and fair application of the law as it exists, we should also continue campaigning for more radical change than has hitherto happened in either system. Changes on 'English' law do not apply to Scots law. At present any legal change in Scotland is delayed by lack of parliamentary time in London for Scottish affairs. Women in Scotland must, therefore, also fight for a Scottish Assembly to change our laws for ourselves. Meanwhile knowledge of the law in both systems can only help our common battle to change society's attitudes to rape." [Spare Rib, issue unknown, pp. 54-55]

Michele Burman, who later carried out a great deal of research into sexual offences legislation in Scotland, had worked as a volunteer in a Rape Crisis centre in South Africa while she was a student at the University of Cape Town:

"I became a volunteer worker at Rape Crisis in Cape Town…I can't remember now if this would've been 1978 or 1979…I was studying psychology and sociology…

I'd always had…a heightened sense of gender inequality, gender discrimination…I mean, growing up in South Africa as I did, it was also intersected with concerns about racial inequality… there were some advertisements around the university, about Rape Crisis centres… I'd never heard of Rape Crisis centres at that stage and I didn't quite know what they were, and…I went along to a meeting with other women students, a couple of my friends at the same time and we really got interested and thought that this was something that we could make a contribution to – I'd had two friends who'd been sexually assaulted, actually quite proximate in time to that and so I think all of these things cohered…and I went along and actually worked for…not for very long, about two years I think…doing support work and…outreach work, and education work, this was a long time ago…

We had a number of campaigns, and a number of talks at schools going around to schools and giving out information, leaflets we …gave some, lots and lots of meetings across the university that I was at, and the other couple of universities in and around Cape Town area." [Michele Burman]

Later on, Michele developed links with Edinburgh Rape Crisis when she came to Scotland:

"Some years later I came to Edinburgh as a student…a criminology student…and, I went to Rape Crisis which was in Broughton Street at the time…I did go to several meetings there because I was thinking about whether I could or I should work, and, I can't remember the reason why – but that was where I met Lily Greenan for the first time…I think that probably would've been in 1984 or 1985. Cos I remet Lily in 1987…so there was Lily, and there was …Aileen Christianson…I remember down in the basement in Broughton Street…" [Michele Burman]

This connection deepened significantly a couple of years later, when several workers at the centre became involved in the research into the impact of sexual history legislation that Michele and her academic colleagues were undertaking (see page 120).

With two stints at Edinburgh Rape Crisis and several years in Glasgow, Helen Mackinnon experienced two quite distinct groups, with quite different characteristics informing their approaches to a common goal:

"The Glasgow group was very different from the Edinburgh group and I mean they both had strengths… the differences were that I think Glasgow …felt for me, and this is maybe not right, but it felt more pragmatic… I mean you were allowed to use words like counselling…you could say look we've got a counselling group or we need to get counselling training…so it was a little bit more rough and ready…and there was potentially less ideology…I mean the feminist analysis was the same which was great…it just was different approaches…I think what happened with Edinburgh was…in the early 70s at the beginning of…the women's movement…and…women meeting together and health groups and so on, there was a lot of highly middle class professional women and…I don't want to say that's as an insult because it's not at all, but you had GPs and lawyers, very intellectual women who were meeting as part of what they were doing. And they were not even remotely exclusive, it wasn't like that. But I think that was where that started, whereas the Glasgow Rape Crisis started out of slightly different roots and it started possibly out of…almost like Red Clydeside and women's roots in socialism in Glasgow… And you know the whole sort of working class strength… it changes with every woman that comes and goes, but I think at that time, that was probably the continuum that we were on. "[Helen Mackinnon]

Morna Findlay had also been involved with the Glasgow centre, and also Aberdeen Rape Crisis, before joining the Edinburgh collective in 1983:

"When I came down here, to Edinburgh, being Morna no-friends, I thought, I'll join Edinburgh Rape Crisis…I remember Aileen Christianson was there…you know, people come and go – she was always there…I think Lily arrived just around then." [Morna Findlay]

"She was such a force…People like that are just amazing, I mean…Aileen always just seemed to have such energy" [Moira Kane]

Moira Kane too, joined the Edinburgh collective after leaving Aberdeen:

"I can't remember how long I did the actual…phone line thing because by this time I was a social worker and it felt like, you know I was working with children and families – you're doing a lot of that kind of work, so I think I gave up that, and then I was on the committee for a while but (laughs) I'm not a good committee person…but I did stay on for a while." [Moira Kane]

In their account of ERCC's inception and early development, Lily Greenan, Leti Volpp and Aileen Christianson recalled:

"We have continued as we began, a collection of women volunteers, fluctuating between eight and twenty in number. The inevitable changing of the collective members brings its own problems. By good luck between 1982 and 1988 a few women stayed with the collective consistently which helped with continuity. Because of being in a city there has always been a reasonable number of women offering themselves as volunteers. From the early days of joining in ones and twos and learning as we went, we've changed to twice-yearly intakes with experience-sharing sessions prior to joining. But as with any long-term collective we find a recycling of issues and problems, a constant need to re-invent the wheel." [Grit and Diamonds, Stramullion, 1990]

Aberdeen [Siobhan Canavan, 1981-c1987, Elizabeth Shiach, 1981-87, Liz Hall, Claire Darling, Margaret Byrne, Margaret Cosgrove, Moira Kane, 1980-83, Morna Findlay, 1982-3, Bernadette Kelly, Chrissie Bruce, Isabelle Kerr, 1982-5, Maureen Porter, 1981-88, Isla Laing, 1983-1990, Fran Henderson, Maggie Havergill, Brenda Flaherty, 1983-, Sue Hunt, 1983-89, Leslie Brown, 1991-96, Connie Hadden, Jenny, Elma, Paula Smith]

In Aberdeen, the establishment of the Rape Crisis centre was the culmination of months of detailed planning by a group of women who had already been very active in campaigning against the Corrie Bill on Abortion. The group had originated as a consciousness-raising group typical of many that emerged as part of "second wave" feminism in the 1970's. Maureen Porter had been in Aberdeen since 1977, and involved in a Women and Health Group, which included many active women in Aberdeen:

> "Siobhan was one of the active people and that was when I met her. I think our first meeting was in a pub. In Aberdeen centre, but after that we sort of met in people's houses. And I think that was about 1980." [Maureen Porter]

In 1980, Siobhan Canavan had recently arrived in Aberdeen from Liverpool to work at the university when she met Elizabeth Shiach on a National Abortion Campaign march and was invited along to a meeting:

> "The Women's Group had got to a stage where it wanted to kind of turn itself into more of an action group… it was almost like the last meeting of the Women's Group before it kind of… moved into something else…there were about four or five other women there, and very soon after we met…one of the local councillors in Aberdeen whose name was Catherine Nikodem…And she was a very strong woman who was on the Council and in fact went on later to help establish the Women's Committee in Aberdeen on the City Council, and we met in her house and she said 'Right, let's see what it would take to get a grant from the Council and so on to get a Rape Crisis Centre started.'" [Siobhan Canavan]

> "I don't think there was a specific event…there was an earlier Rape Crisis group in Aberdeen which had been set up as a result of an attack, attacks on women, students, and it was set up by a number of students, it never got to the stage of becoming active, but I don't think our group was, the impetus, was from that – I think it was very much from discussion, political discussion and analysis and …maybe a wish to respond in a practical way, and do something to effect change – both individually for women, and also change, locally, people's attitudes towards violence against women." [Elizabeth Shiach]

An English-based women-only publication entitled Feminists Against Sexual Terrorism (F.A.S.T.) included a mention in its April 1979 issue of the intention of some women in Aberdeen to set up a Rape Crisis centre:

> "We received a letter from Aberdeen sisters who are intending to set up a Rape Crisis centre…." Our problem is that we have a small but dedicated group and very little money, so sending people to conferences was completely beyond us. We organised a Reclaim The Night here in February which was very successful, and we managed to raise some money at the same time. Still, the distance between Aberdeen and points south, and B.R. fares being what they are, our chances of attending further conferences, in England at least, are rather remote. But we would like to communicate with other groups." If anyone wants to get in touch with Aberdeen women they can send a letter to us and we will forward it, OK?" [F.A.S.T – Feminists Against Sexual Terrorism Newsletter No. 2, April 1979]

Like Isabelle Kerr, Morna Findlay worked initially as a volunteer in Glasgow, and then subsequently moved to Aberdeen:

"I joined Rape Crisis in Aberdeen in '82 when I moved up to Aberdeen…Isabelle was a member at that time… in Aberdeen…I must have left Glasgow probably, because I was a final year student at the time, and I think Isabelle joined Glasgow, because though she was involved in Glasgow Rape Crisis…our paths didn't cross…so I didn't meet her until Aberdeen." [Morna Findlay]

"I remember being a bit surprised when I arrived in Aberdeen, because some people were married… the demographic was a wee bit different from the Glasgow group which, when I was a member…there were quite a lot of students…and people that were…you know, I thought they were older, I was only 18, so we're talking about, like mid-20's. And in Aberdeen people were a bit more mature, but still of the same outlook." [Morna Findlay]

"I got the impression that the Aberdeen group was a bit-more close-knit…that it was smaller…in Glasgow at that time there were people who kind of drifted in and drifted out…really I didn't get any kind of training [at Glasgow] when I arrived at all and the first time I took a phone call…was purely by accident…We talked about training and we tried to arrange training sessions…I remember us being not very pushy in terms of people attending training sessions and sort of saying things like "Well, how, you know if you can manage a few hours one week that'll be fine, if you can't manage the next week that'll be fine and we were quite lax and in some ways I think some of us felt we were giving the impression that you could be a member of Rape Crisis without actually doing very much…just drifting in and out." [Morna Findlay]

"I'm sure we had a lot of discussions about…when you were speaking to somebody…what kind of attitude you would take…one of the main ones I would remember was always as you would expect… to absolutely believe what the woman was telling you…reaffirm…that you were there for her to tell you whatever…that you wouldn't be judging it in any way." [Moira Kane]

The group in Aberdeen initially comprised 8 women, who met in each others' houses every Monday for many months of planning before the service began operating in June 1982:

"We just thrashed it out between us…we had huge debates about violence against women and what would we say, if men said they wanted to be involved and what would happen if, you know? There were lots of stuff like that, and then we had to look for premises. We got a small grant, I think, from the City Council. It wasn't that much, and we had to set about looking for premises and…you know, all the things that a voluntary organisation has to do – to set up a PO Box and work out what our bottom line was on certain things. And then we tried to train ourselves. There was no training, I mean, there was just nothing [laughs], absolutely nothing. We trained ourselves, mostly from… the internal resources that we had, you know? People who were either social workers, teachers, psychologists of one kind or another or women who had worked with women." [Siobhan Canavan]

"We were ensuring that we all had the same view of the issues and that took quite a lot of talking through, but I think what I remember was just people's enthusiasm and commitment to get a centre opened up in Aberdeen…" [Isla Laing]

The opening of the new centre in Aberdeen was noted in the Glasgow Herald of May 27th, 1982, in an item entitled "Help for rape victims":

"A Rape Crisis centre is opening in Aberdeen next week to offer women help in coping with the emotional and practical problems surrounding an assault. From June 3, victims will be able to telephone Aberdeen 575560 for confidential support and advice. The centre will provide a sympathetic listener and, if wanted, information on medical procedures or how to report the matter to the police. Volunteers are willing to accompany victims during medical examination and legal procedures. Similar centres are already operating in Edinburgh and Glasgow. The Aberdeen line will be open from 6 p.m. to 8 p.m. on Mondays and 7.p.m. to 9.p.m. on Thursdays." [The Glasgow Herald, May 27th, 1982]

The Aberdeen group had support from Edinburgh Rape Crisis, who had been established for several years at that point:

> "We invited some women up from Edinburgh Rape Crisis. Two women – Aileen Christianson was one, and…I have a feeling that Lily was the other one… So we met with them in my house, plus two women came through from Inverness. They were also at…a similar stage to us and talking about setting up a Rape Crisis group, so they came through and…we had a lot of talk about just generally how Edinburgh ran – they'd been running for some years by then.
>
> How they ran, the issues, the funding, the structure, their training, to really help us get a handle on what we were trying to do. What could we expect, as well, what it was like? Answering the phone, what sort of calls would we expect, and just experiences – how, you know, what publicity they did… what their experience was of working in the Rape Crisis Centre, as well. I would imagine we talked about funding as well… " [Elizabeth Shiach]
>
> "Aileen Christianson came up to talk to a group of us and we got a room in the university in Old Aberdeen … there were quite a number of people there and she came up and told us about how they'd gone about it down in Edinburgh…and from there we had lots of business meetings and meetings to discuss how we would go about it." [Moira Kane]

Amazingly, the group were able to access some funds from the previous Rape Crisis group which had had similar intentions, but had never quite got off the ground :

> "We certainly got the bank details, the bank account off the original Rape Crisis group and after about nine months, managed to get hold of that money that was in that account … they'd opened a bank account, they'd had Reclaim the Night march… they'd never become active, but they had raised some money… I think it was like, a couple of hundred pounds which was a lot of money… but you had to get signatories and things, to try and get, release the money to us, so we constituted ourselves as a Rape Crisis group, presumably using someone else's constitution as a…basis for what we drew up." [Elizabeth Shiach]

Ironically, the very wealth which made Aberdeen a more prosperous city (in financial terms at least), than its more deprived counterparts in the south, made fundraising even more of a challenge for the Rape Crisis collective there, as the "urban-aid" type funding which benefited centres like the one in Glasgow, was not something that was open to them as it did not exist in Aberdeen, with its oil and gas revenues.

> "We opened on a shoestring budget and that was something that never really altered…we secured some funding from Aberdeen City Council…" [Isla Laing]

A great deal of preparation, lasting around a year, went into planning the Rape Crisis Centre in Aberdeen:

> "We did things like visited the hospital. To find out what happened if a woman went to the hospital. We visited the STD clinic to find out about that, we spoke to the police, we spoke to the fiscal service – so we went off and found out…whoever had done the visiting wrote a little bit up…so that we had a handbook of information." [Elizabeth Shiach]

"We went to the police, we had training with the police. They showed us the cells and they showed us where they treated women and where they examined them and where they talked to them and so on." [Maureen Porter]

The collective drew up a constitution:

"I remember having quite a number of meetings about that…how that would work." [Moira Kane]

The Aberdeen collective was a very tight-knit group of women, whose bonds extended well beyond their shared commitment to support survivors of sexual violence:

"I would say that what was very good about the early days of the Rape Crisis group was it was a very strong group 'cause we knew each other well. We'd been meeting…for the year before so we knew each other well, we …were a social group as well…and that held us together… I remember a weekend up in Strathdon, where we all went away to this hostel, well very, very basic hostel, I think it's been slightly upgraded since then – Jenny's Bothy…I can remember Morna was there, Isabelle, Siobhan, Bernadette, Isabelle's …kids were there. Probably Liz was, I'm not sure, but we all…had a great weekend…went walks with lots and lots of laughs. So I think that was an important part of the group – it was very cohesive." [Elizabeth Shiach]

"As a group we were incredibly skilled, cos everybody was doing a job somewhere or had worked in voluntary capacities. There was masses of skill in the group, so it was really just using what people knew anyway…" [Liz Hall]

They also held a public meeting to talk about what they were doing, and other women were recruited at that point. The women in the group had a great mix of skills and experience that proved invaluable in setting up the new centre. As a psychologist, Liz Hall was heavily involved in the planning stages in helping the group to develop listening skills:

"I was doing it by the seat of my pants, really. But I think we all were. We all were doing everything by the seat of our pants, really, cos nobody really knew how to set up a Rape Crisis Centre." [Liz Hall]

"I did several days, well, it seemed like days, on listening skills and how to talk to people on the phone. We had phones set up in adjacent rooms so that people could talk…I think that's when we used the university. We did role-plays, we did lots…and as the time got nearer and nearer for the place to open, people were panicking. 'What do I do if…' and 'how do I say' and 'what…?' So I think I was much more involved with that part of it." [Liz Hall]

"It was a counselling approach. Not advising people what to do but just listening to them, which was probably the first time that some of us had heard that sort of approach." [Maureen Porter]

Liz Hall's professional status coupled with involvement in the Rape Crisis collective did raise potential problems:

"Siobhan and I would often meet and discuss different women, some of whom were my clients, and that was actually quite difficult, cos the boundaries are really difficult, but… the clients knew that was happening…Some of them would be my clients at work, or patients as they were called." [Liz Hall]

"I think one of the most difficult things for me was when I was working as a psychologist, but having volunteers from Rape Crisis…helping a woman who I was seeing, and they were saying 'We can't let this happen' and I was saying 'But I can't do anything about that' and I think that got very messy, it got very messy…then I didn't know whether I was working as a volunteer or as a therapist…we were all doing a bit of both, really." [Liz Hall]

Aberdeen Rape Crisis workers

Isla Laing recalls her own involvement :

"I got involved before the Rape Crisis centre in Aberdeen actually opened, but prior to my involvement there had been a group of women meeting and looking at the possibility of setting up the Rape Crisis centre in Aberdeen, looking at funding issues as well, and one of these women, Elizabeth Shiach, worked in the same building as I worked in in Aberdeen…St Catherine's Centre, where a number of voluntary organisations were located…Elizabeth was talking about her involvement, and I felt strongly that there was a need for a Rape Crisis centre in Aberdeen and that I wanted to be involved…" [Isla Laing]

"I stayed about a two minute walk from where the line operated…which brought its own dynamics… Living so close…it meant that any time other members weren't able to cover, I got a phone call…the line was only open at night and if I remember it was only open two evenings a week, because we were a small group – that's all that we could manage, because we wanted to be able to retain the ability to meet women face to face because we found that that was what an awful lot of women wanted… particularly women who were talking about their experiences for the first time – they really wanted to meet, and we wanted to be able to offer that flexibility…so it was open I think from 7 to 9, two nights a week…" [Isla Laing]

Isabelle Kerr, who had already experience of a Rape Crisis centre in its infancy arrived in Aberdeen from Glasgow early in 1982 and was invited to take part in the development of the new centre in Aberdeen:

"I had decided I was moving up to Aberdeen…cos my partner had got a job up there… I cannae remember who it was but somebody…in fact it was Moira Kane had been in touch with the Rape Crisis Centre in Glasgow because there was a group meeting up there who were thinking about establishing a centre in Aberdeen. So she gave me Moira's telephone number…It was…early 1982 right at the beginning…obviously I didnae know a soul in Aberdeen. Very early on I got in touch with Moira and she said 'Oh we're having a meeting this week, why don't you come along?' So I went along to her house. And everybody was meeting in there. And that was how I got involved in Aberdeen. And at that time the centre was just getting …off the ground…it was Moira and me and Claire Darling was there at the time and an American woman called Diane who was doing an PhD at

Aberdeen University...Siobhan, Elizabeth Shiach and Maggie Havergill...was involved then as well. I think Maureen was involved right at the very beginning as well...I'm sure she was...and Liz Hall." [Isabelle Kerr]

"I didnae have a huge amount of experience with Rape Crisis but I have to confess my first thought when I went to Aberdeen was that I'd felt incredibly intimidated because all these women were all professional women... like Siobhan was a lecturer at the university and so on and, the woman Diane...she was doing research here. Frances...was a lawyer. And then and Liz Hall...was a psychologist...and of course Claire was...a psychiatrist, from Mousehole, in Cornwall. So...I felt really quite intimidated by everybody because they were all incredibly professional." [Isabelle Kerr]

However Isabelle, along with Morna Findlay (who had also been part of the Glasgow collective) as the only members of the collective who had worked in a Rape Crisis centre, had a lot of valuable experience to offer, and became heavily involved in the planning process:

"It was quite a lengthy period and meetings were held, sometimes in Moira's house, sometimes in mine. And the university – Siobhan often got rooms in the university for us to meet up. So that was...how I got involved in Aberdeen." [Isabelle Kerr]

Sue Hunt was doing social work training at Aberdeen University at the time, where Siobhan was one of the lecturers:

"It would have been about '81. No, about '82, '83...And I think the group had been going, probably for about a year, then, so I wasn't a founder member." [Sue Hunt]

This proved to be a challenging experience:

"I was just very naïve...I think the two things at the beginning, that I suppose were completely new to me was coming, you know, into a feminist organisation with women who had some very, very strong views...to the point of almost being separatist, and also, a fair number of the women were gay and, again, my first experience of working closely with gay women... it challenged me...there was a lot of thinking for me to do, and try and make sense, for me, of some of the views that were being expressed... I had done a sociology degree, and then a social work degree, so in a sense of, you know, how society operates...class, power, I was very familiar with those – but in the context of gender...that was very new for me." [Sue Hunt]

Brenda Flaherty also joined the Aberdeen collective through contact with Siobhan:

"It must have been about 1984 or maybe 1983 because I started university in 1984 – I went as a mature student. And she asked me then if I would like to join and I already knew Maureen Porter because she was a friend of Siobhan's already and we'd met on social occasions at Siobhan's house." [Brenda Flaherty]

Meetings at home had both positive and negative aspects that brought women closely in touch with the realities underpinning some areas of their discussion :

"That proved to be really quite both interesting – it meant that I didn't have to worry about childcare, but it also meant that I'd come out of these meetings and face... well, my ex-husband as he is now, with all these new thoughts about men and what they do to women, and they could have done to some of the women who were in that group, and it kind of brought it right up close, so that caused actually quite a lot of problems for me personally in relation to him. He didn't mind the meeting, but as soon as the meeting was over he wanted to hear nothing of it and wasn't interested and got really angry, thought the women were sometimes very rude to him, and he got on his high horse. But mind you, it didn't take much to get him on his high horse." [Liz Hall]

Collective meetings were weekly, and often very lengthy:

"Collective meetings…were every Monday evening…I think 7 or 7.30 and would last till half 11 or, you know, it'd be really late. We used to try and put a moratorium on the time or it would just go on." [Siobhan Canavan]

Aberdeen Rape Crisis' first home was in premises offered by one of the two local Women's Aid organisations, just off Crown Street in central Aberdeen. Siobhan recalls:

"At that time there was a war going on between Aberdeen Women's Aid and Grampian Women's Aid… one of them was a feminist organisation, the other one wasn't. And ironically the one that…said it wasn't a feminist organisation offered us premises…They had a tenement building in the middle of Aberdeen and they offered us a room and a back room, back cupboard, really for very little rent, a peppercorn rent of two quid a week or something, so that was our first premises. One room." [Siobhan Canavan]

"And then we got some premises down…by the station…And the phone line was run oot of there." [Isabelle Kerr]

"It was a very bare, dingy, dirty room…And no curtains…and from time to time, men who were abusive would discover where the Women's Aid hostel was. We were sort of adjacent to it, but we weren't meant to know that, and there'd be all this row outside and it'd be quite scary, A) getting there and B) going away. It was a bit like the black hole of Calcutta, as I remember." [Liz Hall]

"There was a notice board above the wall with…useful phrases, which Liz Hall had written up…Things to say…if there was silence, 'I'm still here'… and there were other telephone numbers, so there'd be a telephone list – housing department, homeless person's unit, police…" [Elizabeth Shiach]

The new service was advertised by the collective in various ways:

"Through posters…we had quite sympathetic coverage from Northsound, the local radio station…I think certainly they carried out some interviews with members of the collective which…reached a fairly wide audience…" [Isla Laing]

"Certainly on North Sound it was mentioned, you know the local radio and there was stuff in the paper… We had posters all over the place like libraries and community centres. And University, you know the loo doors you can have a little sticker on the back and we went round and did that. " [Maureen Porter]

"I remember Isabelle and I going on to a Granada, Grampian TV studios and they had this system where… voluntary organisations could go and do a little commercial for… their organisation and Isabelle was the spokesperson for us and this thing sort of lasted about a minute, two minutes and it was just sort of what we do, and who we are, and how to get in touch." [Maureen Porter]

The collective in Aberdeen also had a close relationship with a local alternative bookshop at the top of King Street, Boomtown Books:

"There was a printer's in the basement…that would have printed all our material. The bookshop was a collective I think, as well. Yes, it was a collective and one of the women who worked in there was the partner of one of the women who were involved in the Rape Crisis Group…so if folk came in and asked…she could put in touch with us." [Elizabeth Shiach]

The group started taking calls in June 1982.:

"It was such a big day and I remember feeling that at the time, but I couldn't give you a date…" [Isla Laing]

"I took the very first phone call…It was quite interesting because we'd had…a wee article in the local newspaper. Which was the Press & Journal or something. And it was, it was quite small and it was just saying that the Rape Crisis centre was opening…we did start off by presuming that it would be a waiting sort of period where there would be no calls and we would have to do a whole load of publicity around it. So I was there on the first night and I'm sure Maureen Porter was there on that very first night as well… but the centre was opening up at seven o'clock, so I went down, got myself settled in… and the first call came in at ten past seven…Which was astonishing. Because we had expected it to be like, you know weeks, months maybe before the phone rang. Because it was, you know it was a brand new service and that's just what you expect. But no, almost as soon as the phone line opened, the first call came in. I remember it was a woman from Huntly, but I don't remember a huge amount else about that. I just spoke to her for a while…that was it. " [Isabelle Kerr]

"My very first call, well I can remember my very first call was from a young woman who was a survivor. Still living at home with…her father who had abused her, and that was my first call and I continued to work with that young woman…on the telephone, for several months and then we met face to face for a year, maybe, and then she was one of the women who became the nucleus for our survivors group." [Elizabeth Shiach]

As was common practice in most of the centres, the practice was for two women to be working together on a shift:

"Just for a whole load of reasons obviously…because of where the premises were as well just personal safety sort of coming in and out…obviously a lot of the operating procedures had been taken from other centres." [Isabelle Kerr]

It became very clear to the group that they were providing a service that was badly needed:

"What did happen though was that…because people knew that the group was establishing a Rape Crisis Centre, one or two people had contacted members of the group and said you know 'I know somebody who's a survivor' or 'I'm a survivor' and one or two people had already been supporting women, but you know almost kind of like …well unofficially but you know it was just before the centre had started…I think it was really establishing it was a real need for the service…there was… a couple of women who were certainly being supported. Before the centre was officially established." [Isabelle Kerr]

"Some women would make a one-off contact, some women would want to meet, and some women would need support over a lengthy lengthy period of time and as far as I can remember we never had a sort of cut-off point for supporting women because everybody's situations are different…" [Isla Laing]

"I don't think that we imposed geographical boundaries as far as…contact with women was concerned, because we were aware of the fact that there was nothing North of Aberdeen but, obviously in terms of making contact…meeting women face to face, we really just did not have the resources to go outside

Aberdeen...and in terms of training, we could've done a lot more had we had the resources but we didn't..." [Isla Laing]

Whether or not the calls should be recorded was the subject of some debate:

"We had a diary...each week we would log the calls anonymously...we had debates about how we would keep records [laughs], we had debates about everything...We kept ...anonymised records, but not everybody kept them." [Siobhan Canavan]

"We had a book. A big A4 hardback that it was all written in, under 'Meetings'. We met once a week as well. Monday nights I think. It was all in there. Obviously not people's personal details but just logging the calls... I have the feeling it was sort of seven till nine one night and sort of six till eight another or slightly different times. But just a couple of hours." [Maureen Porter]

"We tried to log all the calls that came in ...I think we actually managed to do this, and we would record ...whether it was a first call, or a subsequent call...what the woman wanted to talk about, whether they'd been raped, whether they'd been assaulted, whether they were an incest survivor... whether there'd been a complaint made to the police...but I think that there could've been much more done with the stats in terms of trying to secure funding and the amount of calls that we were taking..." [Isla Laing]

"Women didn't want to identify themselves, so we tended not to know who women were or just have a first name, and a mixture of one off calls, regular calls, so...because we had a rota...so I could say to someone if they want to speak to me again, or the other woman who was on again, we could say...we'll next be on, I'll be on next Thursday at whatever time, you can phone me then...The criticism I always remember us getting was that it was such a short space, I think it was only four hours a week... it was always, you're only open, women get raped, you know, so that was it. So...we would defend that, saying well, if we weren't doing it, there would be no service." [Elizabeth Shiach]

"There was an answering machine, which was used occasionally by people, but often by us leaving messages for each other, but it was also used by agencies so if an agency was wanting to talk to us then we could get back to them at some other point." [Elizabeth Shiach]

Later on the centre moved to new premises ("another black hole" [Liz Hall]) on Crown Street itself, in a Quaker meeting house, next to the post office.

"We went and had a look at this place, and to get to it, you had to go through the Quaker Meeting House, and I remember the day we went to look at it, there was a Japanese tea ceremony going on in the Quaker Meeting House, and we went "Oh, this is really nice!" [laughs] and then we went out and through the cloakroom and out the back door and down some steps and down some more steps and past a slippery thing, and then into this place that they called "the cave." It was terrible. It was smaller, much smaller than the room we'd started off in...and it had bare brick walls, which we then whitewashed. So it was constantly kind of damp ...it really was freezing and... if you put a heater on then it was claustrophobic, and that was it. That's what we had." [Siobhan Canavan]

"Oh God it was in the most awful grotty little room at the back of the Quaker meeting house in Aberdeen and you had to go through...the Quaker Hall and out the back and down some really awful steps, that were in really bad repair and slippy and mossy, and then across a ...tiny little courtyard...and then into this tiny freezing cold damp fusty revolting little room that we kept everything in. Yeah, a desk and a chair, probably broken, both of them." [Brenda Flaherty]

"They were not premises where we could meet women, they were only a space to operate the line from…" [Isla Laing]

The group began offering face-to-face support some time after the helpline was established:

"Nobody ever came into the centre at that time…so we just had the PO Box and we would have went out and arranged to meet the women either at the woman's home or a place that she felt safe, something like that…it would always be in twos." [Isabelle Kerr]

"We were offering to meet women as well, but we weren't able to do it in the centre's premises. We arranged to meet women somewhere where they would feel comfortable…There was always two members of the group went to meet women…cafes where the woman felt comfortable and felt that it wouldn't be too crowded and that we would be able to talk…" [Isla Laing]

"We usually met in a public place…they couldn't have come to the Rape Crisis centre – one, it was completely unsuitable for public entry, really, and two, we didn't want to jeopardise the confidentiality of where we worked. We felt vulnerable… people must have been hostile if we felt vulnerable, although I can't remember any particular incidents, but we did feel vulnerable, we did want to keep where we met confidential. So we met in public places …It tended to be cafes – I remember a café in Union Street, and two of us sitting in the café, in the window, looking for this person who…must have been one we'd met …before, so that we knew what they looked like." [Elizabeth Shiach]

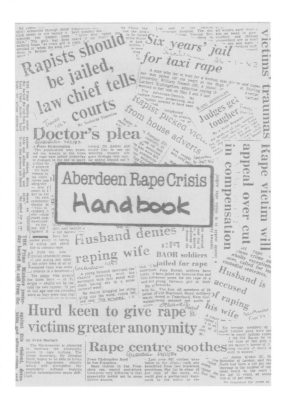

Support was also carried out by letter:

"I think there were a few letters came in…that's what women feel comfortable with…we would've written back and said do you want to make contact – this is when the lines are open, but if people didn't actually want to talk even on the phone then we provided support by whichever way we could… for some women it's hard even to get to a phone…if you don't have one in the house and you are in a remote location…" [Isla Laing]

Aberdeen Rape Crisis also started doing groupwork with survivors:

"There was a lot of time spent talking about that, and then we did establish a group in, I would say it was about 1984, '85… a survivors' group, and we did that from a family centre. There was a voluntary organisation which was called the Aberlour Childcare Trust, and they had a family centre in Old Aberdeen, which was in a lovely old house, and I can't even remember how this happened…maybe it was through the community worker…but it was through that person…that we got access to their premises…in the evening, once a month, we had the premises for about two and a half hours, and we just advertised again through the usual means – posters and the radio, I think, and stickers and all the rest of it and leaflets – and we opened…the space for women to come." [Siobhan Canavan]

"The survivors' group…I think it was maybe four women and Siobhan and I when we started, and one of the first ground rules they made was that it was an open group. They …were very keen that no-one would be turned away because it was a closed group. They said that they've had the courage and they want to meet other women, we want them to be able to do it right away, not wait for six weeks or ten weeks or three months or whatever, which meant that the type of group it was, was different from if it had worked as a closed group, so … some women came and went and some women just stayed and were a kind of stalwart part of the group. So when Siobhan and I became involved…in the the survivors' group, we pulled out of working on the line. We were still involved in the collective and went to collective meetings" [Elizabeth Shiach]

The collective's relationship with the police was very mixed, and recollections of their responses to women survivors and to the work of the group reflect both negative and positive experiences:

"We had…very much a kind of love hate, or a hate/hate relationship with the police…it's probably best described in a telephone call that I took at one point where we had been supporting a woman who had made a complaint to the police and the woman had been just put through the most awful experience by the police and finally she had withdrawn her statement. And the police had then decided that she was wasting police time and were threatening to charge her with wasting police time …

I was at my work…in the Unemployed Worker Centre in Aberdeen at that time…I got a phone call and the police officer said to me, I just wanted to let you know, that this particular woman…we've discovered that she has made false allegations about this alleged rape. And I said oh has she indeed? And he said yes, I know you girls mean well and you always believe women, but sometimes, you know you have to accept that they do make…false allegations. And I thought, just so that you could then, you know kinda offload her from your…organisation that I would let you know that she had in fact been lying…

They had put this woman through the most awful experience…I think she had been at a party and she was being walked home by a man who had then raped her on a piece of waste ground…She'd gone back to [her] accommodation and her friend had sort of looked after her and, tried to patch her up and then they had called the police.

And right away, the police latched on to the whole business about how she had been at a party, she had been drinking she had been walking home wi the guy, the whole business… And they had said, who were you at the party with?…And she said look I don't want to tell you because she was from outside Aberdeen. She says one of the girls lives close to where my mum and dad live and I don't want it getting back to them. And what they had said they would do was that if she didn't tell them to corroborate her statement, if she didn't tell them…who she'd been with…they would go to every single door, chap the door and …say that they were…investigating a rape and were they at the party with this woman?

So needless to say the woman was in such a state that she withdrew the complaint and they threatened to charge her with wasting police time. She almost had a complete breakdown after that…and that was the phone call that we had was to say that you know, you girls mean well, but sometimes we just know that they're lying." [Isabelle Kerr]

"What I remember of the police is that they quite quickly came round and that I think at that point the police were under a lot of pressure to do something cos there was that thing with Thames Valley police… so they were getting a lot of stick, but we did a lot of work. Lots of people went and saw them and did sessions with them and I think eventually got the rape suite established…and it happened fairly quickly is what I remember, so they must have been well on the way." [Liz Hall]

Some of this was possibly due to the input of a policewoman mentioned by several of the Aberdeen collective, Diane Hay:

> "I remember there was a lovely policewoman called Diane Hay… she was involved in the Child Protection Unit of the police, whatever it was called." [Liz Hall]

> "I think beginning to open up lines of communication with the Police was really important, and Diane Hay, who was absolutely outstanding, was immensely helpful in that… so we started to offer training, you know, from a position of not having a notion and having to train ourselves, then we were suddenly, you know, doing training sessions." [Siobhan Canavan]

> "I think when we set up, the police were very supportive and they were in the process of trying to humanise the way they treated rape victims as well so they sort of presented us as a learning experience. And they had women, a new innovation really at that time having women interviewing the victims. They couldn't arrange a woman doctor unfortunately. So that…they were very positive and they had our numbers and they did phone us on a number of occasions, when there was an emergency." [Maureen Porter]

Similarly supportive, to the astonishment of the group, was the local Procurator Fiscal:

> "He was very supportive. He understood what we were talking about…he felt that the legal system was wrong, that the women were very badly treated. He was excellent…very enlightened. Very surprised, we were absolutely gobsmacked, I mean, when we discovered that." [Siobhan Canavan]

And local councillor Catherine Nikodem was also extremely helpful to the under-resourced collective:

> "Catherine was a big ally in the Council…If we needed anything she would be able to push it through or support us in whatever way she could… I think we got a grant from the City Council, if I remember rightly. I mean, it wasn't much. It was like 500 quid a year. There was a Voluntary Organisations Fund. I mean, we had nothing, absolutely nothing. … We always felt like she was somebody who had power and used it very well, and she would be there if we needed it, you know?" [Siobhan Canavan]

Inevitably, the Aberdeen collective evolved, and the original 8 women were joined eventually by new members:

> "For a while it was felt that the core group should carry on for a while, and what we tried to do was to recruit new volunteers together, so that there was a proper induction, and a proper phased period for people starting to answer the phone…We did have some training materials, you know, articles from newspapers, journals, discussed how people perceived those, and tried to formalise the induction period…but I think it's true to say that we were all learning very much as we went along…" [Isla Laing]

> "Twelve was the magic number we could never get past. And we were always looking to go past it so we could have either less demands on our time on the line, or expand the hours that we were open and we never got past that magic number." [Elizabeth Shiach]

> "I think once the group started to open to new members, it became really difficult to work as a collective and there was, inevitably there was a kind of old girls, new girls thing… And…I think we probably could have found other ways of working together that weren't always about everybody having to be involved in every decision. Because it took so much time." [Siobhan Canavan]

"We were all young then weren't we? Or you know 20-30, 35. So if it had been women in their 40s we'd probably have been more settled. Those women were just going off to find the world. "
[Maureen Porter]

Aberdeen Rape Crisis actually wound down towards the end of the 1980's and eventually (for a time at least) ceased operation:

"Some people moved away like Elizabeth Shiach moved away, Isla Laing moved away. Liz Hall had already gone. Who else did that leave? Me and Maureen and Sue Hunt…I think that's about it. And I think and I might not be right on here, but I think the ritual abuse bit sort of started the end… but I mean other people might perceive that differently. Because those of us that were working with the people for that… moved sort of slightly aside from the mainstream, because we had two people that we were counselling long term and supporting. And as I said to you earlier some of the women there found it difficult to cope with that…it didn't really come to a definite end it kind of just dribbled out." [Brenda Flaherty]

"It was always an irritation that we could not secure money to get adequate funding for the service, that the money that was available was scarcely enough to keep basic costs going let alone employ staff to do fundraising, do development work, undertake training …and I left Aberdeen about 1990 to move to Glasgow for work and I think that the centre went through quite a difficult time after that, just in terms of having enough volunteers to cover the line, to provide any kind of service…the problem with that is that the service had become fairly well established in that it was well used…it's a real shame if services begin and there is a need…that cannot be maintained." [Isla Laing]

The group had a meeting to decide what to do with all of their documentation:

"We gave them to the city archivist at Aberdeen City Archives." [Brenda Flaherty]

However the need for the service its volunteers had provided remained as acute as ever, and in 1991, Leslie Brown, who was employed as Women's Officer for Aberdeen City Council at the time, was asked to look into reviving the centre:

"There'd been a spate of rapes…up in kind of the student…areas, and quite rightly people missed having a Rape Crisis, so the [*Women's and Equal Opportunities Committee*] said 'Well, let's see whether we can get an Aberdeen Rape Crisis back up and running'… There'd already been feelers out from women in the community who were interested in seeing that happen, so the Council took on the role of trying to make it happen, and the first thing we did is that we held a public meeting."
[Leslie Brown]

Any doubts they might have had about the public will to do this evaporated when the meeting took place:

"Attendance at public meetings is notoriously poor, but we had over a hundred women turn up…it was like standing room only in the Arts Centre, so…that kinda set the tone, really…" [Leslie Brown]

There was input from a variety of individuals and agencies, with equally varied responses:

"We'd also got somebody from the police along, who didn't go down that well, I have to say… it was a long time ago and attitudes in the police have changed somewhat since then. I mean, he wasn't horrendous but he wasn't… terribly enlightened either…it was just really kind of old-fashioned stuff about, you know, "women just need to be careful" and all that sort of thing and it just…it was a bit awkward, to say the least." [Leslie Brown]

However, what really mattered, was not in doubt:

> "The important thing was the kinda groundswell of opinion from women out there who... really felt that there was a need for Rape Crisis and that it was a valid thing for the Council to sort of help resurrect, and from that we got a group of women...who said that they would help and they would be part of a steering group, cos the last thing the Council wanted was some sort of Council-run Rape Crisis, because that's not what Rape Crisis is about...it was about...getting a Rape Crisis...feminist collective...organisation back up and running, with a bit of support from the Council." [Leslie Brown]

The revival of Rape Crisis in Aberdeen got quickly underway:

> "The Council gave us premises and paid the rent...put a little bit of money into ... development money for training and publicity and that sort of thing...it wasn't a huge amount of money, and unlike places like Dundee, where I think Rape Crisis was Urban Programme funded for a while and they could have paid workers and things, Aberdeen was never eligible for a huge amount of that sort of money because of its low unemployment." [Leslie Brown]

Brenda Flaherty, who had been part of the original collective and who worked for Aberdeen City Council, also took part in its resurgence:

> "She was the main contact, really, between the old and the new, if you like." [Leslie Brown]

> "Leslie basically asked me to come on to the committee to help get that going. And there was Margaret, Leslie, me and I think Connie Hadden was on that as well." [Brenda Flaherty]

> "I was glad to see it start up again and I was quite happy to do my bit on the committee, but I was fairly clear that I didn't want to be involved in the counselling side of it again. That was because I was still involved with the two women that had been ritually abused... and...was taking...phone calls at home and things from them...supporting them on a personal basis...without really much of a support network." [Brenda Flaherty]

The new, fairly basic premises were in Frederick Street, and included office, toilet and counselling facilities. Press coverage was very positive, with extensive coverage of the revived Rape Crisis service both before and after the public meeting:

> "There was a lot of press interest, and largely, for that era, it was quite appropriately written...and that was good...Later as we got going and we started recruiting volunteers for our training courses and things, we did some paid advertising, but the free advertising that we got through articles in the paper were what really got us the people, and we had great big articles regularly, on...what we were doing and what sort of people we wanted as counsellors and what we were offering and the kind of commitment. Huge great big articles. You couldn't buy that sort of publicity, and...kind of the messages that...we wanted to put out. I'm not sure that we would get that same quality of coverage ...It was both the Press & Journal and the Evening Express." [Leslie Brown]

> "We were very careful about who we recruited. Em, having said that, we had to reject very, very, very few people. Less than a handful, I recollect... and then there was a training programme, and that training programme was part of an assessment period." [Leslie Brown]

A steering group was assembled, and were assisted in their efforts by some of the women who had been involved previously:

"We'd got …steer from members of the previous Rape Crisis, who'd been really supportive, and… when they saw [we] were a kind of bona fide set-up and going along the right lines, they …handed over their …bank balance to us and things, which was nice" [Leslie Brown]

Recruitment efforts paid off:

"We ended up with a really interesting group of people…from a…wide range of backgrounds, and I think that was a real strength." [Leslie Brown]

"We had a woman, Elma…who worked in an office attached to a factory I think up in Torry, and she was slightly older than a lot of us at the time. She was maybe…about 50… and she hadn't had a background in …women's groups and things like that, but she was just really interested in doing something like this and…she was a real stalwart, really reliable…she was one of the people…if there was an emergency you really felt that … you should speak to somebody, I could phone her up and know that…she would do it, and that she would be good in that kind of sort of situation…Just a really good bunch of people with a really different mix, and generally, you know, that first group, I think, gelled really well." [Leslie Brown]

There was also a great deal of goodwill and valuable input from other sources, including a woman called Ruth:

"This fabulous woman who was well-known in the city, in terms of counselling, developing counselling and being really well-regarded in doing training and things…she did our counselling training for years for free, and…she really gave us a solid base on that." [Leslie Brown]

A police forensics expert, Ros Brown, also offered a lot of insight into this aspect of the criminal justice procedures around rape and sexual assault:

"Ros Brown from the Police – she was fabulous. It was a real bonus, getting that kind of forensic perspective, and she had a lot of experience…in court, and she just said it as it was…It was very depressing, but you were hearing it from somebody, you know, horse's mouth, and who knew it was wrong…I mean, she wasn't trying to say…that this was right and appropriate. She was just…telling us as it was, and I think that really helped people…kind of understand…what the issues were, what folk were up against…Cos… you kinda naively think the justice process is all about justice…it was quite hard for some people to realise…that oh my God, it's…far from the truth." [Leslie Brown]

"We would get the Women's Centre premises for nothing. Their lunch club would leave lunch for us and things like that." [Leslie Brown]

"Somebody donated paint and…there was a big painting weekend…I think somebody donated us money to buy the furniture and…nice cushions for the counselling room…I think the Council gave us office furniture." [Leslie Brown]

Members of the steering committee sat in on the training themselves, both to learn and to assess the suitability of prospective members of the new collective:

"The one that I remember cos I got elected to tell her "thanks, but no thanks" in the end, was a woman who just had no listening skills whatsoever. In the entire training she just argued with the trainers and everybody else, and talked over everybody all the time." [Leslie Brown]

More formal support and supervision arrangements were eventually put in place for the workers:

"After a couple of years we got an external supervisor in for the counsellors so they got one-to-one supervision. A woman called Sally Wilkins…She worked at Alcohol Advisory and Counselling Service, but she did this as her personal support to Rape Crisis… that was really solid, and she did one-to-one and group supervision." [Leslie Brown]

The newly revived helpline was opening initially for two hours a weekend was widely advertised:

"GP's surgeries, community centres…even some of the supermarkets and things like that…stickers, God knows everywhere." [Leslie Brown]

Face to face support was offered too:

"It would generally be Frederick Street but sometimes…other premises might be more appropriate… Occasionally use a…room in a community centre. It was about what was appropriate and also what was safe…we didn't want the counsellors to be going into any…awkward situations…it was getting that…balance right." [Leslie Brown]

The sensitive issue of recording data re-emerged with the service:

"We'd try to keep…some statistics, but anonymised…there was that whole thing about the kind of legalities of it all and…confidentiality…and we were very conscious of that, but we were very conscious as well, if we wanted to build up the case for more funding…We'd have to have some stats, and… we needed to sort of do a bit of monitoring anyway…to say what was happening in the service." [Leslie Brown]

Unlike its forebear, the new service in Aberdeen, at least in its initial stages, did not operate as a collective:

"It was a collective-lite, I think…I've never personally been a great fan of collectives because I think my experience of them has been an awful lot of navel-gazing and internal angst and not much getting on with it, and…I like to get on with things…so we had a constitution and… for the sake of the constitution, we had a structure." [Leslie Brown]

Leslie's involvement was mainly around the administrative and financial running of the centre at that time:

"I kept the cheque book and then the signatories would come in and sign cheques, if there was an urgent…need for it…The other kind benefit of my kind of official involvement was…when we were only providing that sort of Thursday evening 7 till 9 thing, there was people out there who knew that I had an involvement with Rape Crisis and that if they came across a woman in an emergency situation, they knew if they phoned me, I could…put them in touch with somebody without having to go through the answering machine and things." [Leslie Brown]

A Council charity shop in George Street was also occasionally used for raising funds for Rape Crisis in Aberdeen. Eventually, with improvements in technology (allowing phone diversion etc) the service re-established itself more fully, and financial support from the Council continued:

"We still pay roughly what we used to in Frederick Street towards the rent of our current premises." [Leslie Brown]

Dundee [Margaret Brown, 1982-, Florence Germain, c1983-c1985/6, Fiona Raitt, 1983-c87/88, Dorothy Degenhardt, 1985-8, Pat MacCowan 1986-88, Heather Duncan, Margaret Groves, Fiona Reid, Izzy (Sarah Robertson), Laurie Matthew, Avril Crossley, Gillian Ferguson, Catherine Baker, Jackie Christerson, Caroline Duncan]

Margaret Brown was working for Dundee Women's Aid in 1982, and it was out of DWA that Dundee Rape Crisis gradually emerged. Margaret recalls:

> "The title of my post at that time was Refuge Worker…Dundee Women's Aid were getting all their referrals from police, social work, anybody and everybody, with any woman, with any kind of need for…support…So the group were inundated and we…had hardly enough resources to be able to meet the demand where there had been an occurrence of domestic abuse. So I had 32 and a half hours per week, and what the group decided was that I would be allowed to have two and a half hours to try and pull a group of women together, with the long-term aim of setting up a Rape Crisis group that…had some form of funding. So I went about doing that by talking to various women. I also held a meeting in the Dundee Women's Aid office with as many women as I possibly could, and did a kinda wee presentation…

> Another woman in Dundee was good enough to have a benefit… we used her house, we got various films from Leeds Animation, who were the feminist…animation group in Leeds. We had hired a couple of videos from them and we were showing them and charging for entry. So we made…a very small amount of money, but it was enough money for things like postage…Eventually I was able to bring together a fairly cohesive group…Fiona Raitt, Dorothy Degenhardt…I…basically went round women that I knew. I knew Fiona Raitt…as a practising solicitor at the time, and because of my involvement in Women's Aid and accessing Fiona and taking women along to meet her for information and representation, I got to know Fiona and we had discussed many aspects of violence against women, including rape and sexual assault and incest." [Margaret Brown]

> "Rachel Scott, who still works for Rape Crisis…this would be in the nineties at some point…was going through archives and I was in the Rape Crisis office cos I was the management committee member in the nineties…and she came across a piece of paper, …and it's my handwritten note to the group, saying… this is the group way back in '82, '83, "I'm going on holiday for two weeks in about three or four weeks' time, and I wonder if this is a good time for me now to withdraw from the group?" [Margaret Brown]

The group met in the Women's Aid offices in Thompson Street.

> "Dundee Women's Aid supported the group by…agreeing to them having a telephone line in the kitchen of our office, which was like a kitchen-cum-office…so they had a telephone line which they started…I think it was one or two evenings a week. And that was really the beginning of Rape Crisis in Dundee." [Margaret Brown]

Later on, the new Dundee Rape Crisis Centre moved into its own premises in Ward Road. By the time Laurie Matthew and Avril Crossley joined Dundee Rape Crisis, the centre was at 5 Bell Street, above the Cyreneans:

> "I remember thinking with horror "This can't be it, this can't be", you know? There was big red doors, the place was stinking, it was absolutely minging. I mean, clearly people had been using it as a toilet. When you opened the door there was sort of pools of water, there was pools of vomit, there was pools of other things I wouldn't like to put a name on and you had to go up those stairs. It was dark and scary. That first night there was no men there, thankfully, but you went up the stairs and there was one room and there was no toilet." [Laurie Matthew]

Advertising the new service was done in a number of ways:

"Dundee Women's Aid at that point were producing a newsletter, a quarterly newsletter, … and that had quite a distribution, so it was advertised there. And I think eventually they took out an advert in the newspaper…although my aim was that there would be a Rape Crisis group that was funded, I withdrew before that funding" [Margaret Brown]

"We had certainly loads of leaflets…we handed those round…to GP's surgeries and the Library and stuff." [Dorothy Degenhardt]

DUNDEE EXTRA, SATURDAY, OCTOBER 11, 1986   7

RAPE > COULD YOU HELP A VICTIM?

DUNDEE WOMEN are rallying to the help of victims of that most heinous of crimes—RAPE.

And they are looking for more volunteers, with the basic capacity simply to sit and listen sympathetically, to join their ranks.

Dundee Rape Crisis Group, formed only this year and operating intially from the Women's Aid Centre in the West End, now have office space within the Dundee Resources Centre for the Unemployed.

There, within a soundproof room, they keep a 24-hour telephone-answering machine upon which calls for help are recorded—and the response is prompt.

Run entirely by women for women, the crisis group volunteers are available to any woman each Wednesday between 7 p.m. and 9 p.m. at the D.R.C.U. premises, at the foot of the Hilltown.

FRIGHTENED

"There are a lot of misconceptions about the crime of rape," a spokesperson told the Extra this week. "For many people, such attacks are thought to be things that happen outdoors in the dark between two complete strangers.

"That's just not so. Sixty per cent of these attacks take place inside a building—and over 50 per cent of women who've suffered in this way say they've had some prior contact with the man who raped them.

"And it's a stark fact, too, that 31% of these attacks take place within the woman's own home."

SYMPATHETIC

Sexual violence against women, in Dundee as elsewhere, is much more common than even the statistics, bad as they are, reflect.

"Many women subjected to sexual violence," say the crisis group, "have never told anyone. Many feel ashamed and even frightened that, if they do talk, they will not be believed.

"This may be caused by false myths concerning rape. These myths are dangerous, because they hide the truth."

The rape itself is always a horrendous experience. But it is often the aftermath, the bottling up of the emotions and failure to "talk out" the experience to someone trustworthy and sympathetic, that drives a woman to breaking point.

Rape victims come from no particular age group—they can be young or old. Sometimes the contact with the crisis group may be made, for instance, by the mother of a girl who has suffered in this way.

At other times, the victim may be a mature woman whose problem is that she just cannot find anyone to talk to.

DEPRESSION

Some women may have been through the trauma of a trial if there has been a prosecution after the rape. Others may have that attack indelibly stamped on their minds.

In either circumstance, even a long time after the event, depression can be almost overpowering.

Most difficult of all, perhaps, is the situation of the woman who has been attacked by someone she has known well. Where does she turn? Would talking automatically lead to a court case and prosecution of the man?

No such direction would ever be recommended by the Dundee Rape Crisis Group. They are there simply to listen, to extend support and sympathy.

The group can be contacted on Dundee 201291. If you consider becoming a volunteer, be assured that you won't be left on your own to deal with interviews. "There will always be an experienced member alongside," say the group.

52

The recently established Aberdeen Rape Crisis Centre was a great source of support and advice for the new centre in Dundee:

> "They were already ahead of us. And they were able to…assist us…in …some kind of framework on how they're going to operate and probably and also looking at…safety issues about not only how you deliver the service, but how you look after …your own volunteers… We had probably a couple of trips up to Aberdeen…it was a lovely mix of lightness and laughter and…very serious discussion. And obviously somebody was taking notes there because we were going to take that back…to Dundee. And I think … what was inspiring was a kind of willingness to learn from each other and because some groups were ahead of us and took too long, maybe some mistakes or things to try and avoid, things that had worked, and then basically we had to put into, sort of into practice ourselves." [Florence Germain]

The Aberdeen workers were also a great source of support in terms of the new Incest Survivors group at Dundee:

> "That's when it was very useful speaking to the Aberdeen group because that's how they started … I remember the day we went up to Aberdeen and we met with them… I can't remember if it was Siobhan's house or Elizabeth's house. And sharing and realising, hearing from them how there was so much more involved than…we'd originally thought. And that they seemed so experienced compared to us groups of people." [Dorothy Degenhardt]

The calls started coming in as soon as the new centre was established:

> "I think as soon as the word hit the street, it came in immediately, because the demand was already there on Woman's Aid, so we were able to transfer it over to Rape Crisis." [Margaret Brown]

Margaret withdrew when the Dundee centre became established, but a lengthy period of preparation had provided a solid foundation from which the service could flourish, both in terms of awareness-raising within the group, and also in terms of mutual support:

> "It's as if we, we wouldn't leave any sort of stone unturned so we were doing, we went on for months and months and months before we went on line…we wanted to be…quite aware and I suppose also for some kind of consistent understanding and approach to the service…From the outside…particularly from a…patriarchal point of view, it looked like there was no structure, but in fact, looking back, the discussions were very thorough…we were looking at so many issues…practical as well as …philosophical or ideological…so I felt we were given an extremely good grounding. And…also in a way trying to look after sort of each other…So there was a, a tremendous sense of support within the group." [Florence Germain]

Florence became involved through Lily Greenan, who was one of her lodgers in Dundee at the time:

> "For me it was still keeping the balance of not …almost being taken over by hatred at times, because when you're dealing with these issues and concentrating on that, there is a danger of cutting off all the goodness as well and that was hard. Maybe I think it helped me and maybe why I actually became involved because I was actually living abroad, and it was in a different language and that has always helped me at an emotional level to express that…It's almost as if there is a…little protection somewhere like an invisible wall that has protected me…I think I was able to do it because it was in English." [Florence Germain]

Fiona Raitt had arrived in Dundee around 1981 as a young lawyer, to run the Legal Advice Centre. By 1983, she had set up a law firm with a partner, Liz Wilson, and was also building networks with what was at the time a very strong voluntary advice network throughout the city. The work she became involved in opened her eyes:

> "The work we were doing in the law firm involved dealing with lots of women and children who were dealing with abuse and in a sense, that was a bit new to me …I was thinking, why are all these women coming to me and they've either been domestically abused, or the children have been assaulted?…And then we were dealing with cases where women had been sexually assaulted …I was in my early 20s still or maybe my mid 20s…and it sounds a bit naïve and pathetic now but I really hadn't …understood the extent of what that was to people's daily lives. So, I suppose part of trying to be involved a bit more, find out a bit more and try to offer whatever I could was to…get in touch with the local Rape Crisis group which… I don't think would have been long set up at that point." [Fiona Raitt]

Dorothy Degenhardt had been living and working in Edinburgh for 15 years when she moved to Dundee in April 1985. The previous year she had been in Liverpool to do a 3-month placement as part of a year's course she was doing and had gone along to Liverpool Rape Crisis, which inspired her to get in touch with Edinburgh Rape Crisis when she got back:

> "For a few months I'd gone to some of their training…with the expectation I'd become a volunteer there but then I had got this job in Dundee and moved up in April '85." [Dorothy Degenhardt]

Shortly after Dorothy Degenhardt arrived in Dundee, where she was training as a practise teacher for residential and day care establishments in Tayside, the Rape Crisis centre moved from the premises in Thompson Street, to a new location in Ward Road. Once again, there were still many practical issues to be dealt with:

> "There was…ongoing training then – I think we did that in people's houses, just to inform ourselves, consciousness raising and all that sort of stuff. And then there were the practicalities…about how do we get a phone line, how do we get a post office box and then the finances… the crux was getting the phone lines and getting the funding to pay for the phone lines… I remember the hassle of getting into the premises and often setting the alarm off and then not being able to get the alarm to go off… remembering the key to stop the alarm. I'm trying to think what the building was…I think it was owned by community education." [Dorothy Degenhardt]

The Rape Crisis line itself was the most important resource of all:

> "Getting people to, actually do the line was a, was our single most… important thing…we weren't opened as much as we wanted to be … cos it was an answering machine for the rest of the time and of course people had to pick up the messages and respond to them and…if you can't respond for five days or something, it's hopeless and we were very conscious that we needed some kind of regular system… so I know the money would have gone into getting funding for the line itself to go to actually have somebody operating at the end of it as much as possible. But …my recollection is it was mostly on a shoe string for a long time." [Fiona Raitt]

When the line began operating, calls were taken during the evening, and sometimes face to face meetings with women were arranged for during the day:

> "Usually it would have to be a kind of a fairly mutual space. So it could be a, I suppose a quiet sort of café where you could talk without too much noise at the same time and also you won't be overheard too much either." [Florence Germain]

Dedication among the volunteers to keeping the phone lines covered was absolute – Laurie Matthew and Avril Crossley recalled another former worker, Gillian:

"Her baby would have been three or four days old and she came out of the hospital into the phone lines, cos there was nobody else to do it." [Laurie Matthew]

The Dundee centre covered quite a wide geographical area, including Perth. Resources were very limited – the group applied to funding bodies like Dundee Voluntary Action, and also applied for Urban Aid funding when they could. The women involved in the new Rape Crisis centre were part of a small but very active network of women in Dundee, who were committed to campaigning for change to benefit women's lives across a range of issues:

"The pro-choice movement was also very much around at that time, and what you'll …find is, I mean, for example…Margaret Groves was involved in Dundee Women's Aid. I was involved in Dundee Women's Aid…Margaret became involved in Rape Crisis. I think that there'll be a crossover of some of the names in the Young Women's Project. There'll be a crossover of names in the pro-choice movement. So… it was all kinda out there. I think that what at that time… it was…actually, a fairly small number of women that were taking it all forward." [Margaret Brown]

Although Women's Aid were instrumental in getting the new Rape Crisis centre off the ground, and very generous in their support after it was established, some tensions did emerge:

"I am aware, although I was away from Women's Aid by this time, that there was some friction between Women's Aid and Rape Crisis at some point…And for me that's very much the mother/child scenario where you've got the mother and you've got the child, and the child grows up and starts to want to be independent and autonomous and all the rest of it, and although they were autonomous, it really needed – it's like me having to withdraw from the group because that's what was best for the group – the group needed to withdraw completely from Women's Aid, because that's what was best for the group…there was that period of conflict…which is…well, almost natural, you know, to have that bit of friction…The mother wants to be protective and wants to help…but then if we're using the kind of analysis where is it the protective parent or is it the controlling parent? If we're using transactional analysis, for example… is it an adult-to-adult relationship?" [Margaret Brown]

Support from other workers in more established centres was always important:

"Every now and then we'd get a letter from Lily Greenan in Edinburgh Rape Crisis, and what a boost it gave us, you know?…'Are you still there? Hey women, are you still out there?', you know, and things like that. And of course, we didn't have the energy to write back, you know? But later, in time, we did… and somewhere in there we got involved with the network as well, with trying to start up the Scottish Rape Crisis Network." [Laurie Matthew]

The Young Women's Project emerged from Dundee Rape Crisis in 1994 with funding from the Unemployed Voluntary Aid Foundation and an Urban Aid application which workers from Edinburgh and Strathclyde Rape Crisis had supported the Dundee women in putting together. The two posts that the funding created were the first ever Rape Crisis paid posts in Dundee. Laurie Matthew explains the background to the new initiative:

"I'd been doing support for a long time and everything I was hearing, all these women were telling me it was the same thing, you know? They were assaulted in their childhood, this had happened when they were children. I was listening to broken lives, you know? It wasn't that what we were doing was ineffective. What we were doing was very necessary for those women, but I just kept thinking 'This should have been sooner', you know? 'There should have been intervention when she was 12', you know? 'There should have been intervention when she was 7', you know?" [Laurie Matthew]

Highland Rape Crisis [Gale Chrisman, 1982-, Sue Owen, 1982-84, Frances Hunter, May Johnson, Fiona Peace, Sandra Macdonnell, Cath McMahon, Tiana, Pat]

Like Glasgow Rape Crisis, the Highland Rape Crisis Centre that was set up in Inverness in 1982, came out of a pre-existing Women's Group. Sue Owen describes what led to this development:

"My memory of it was that there was a woman who, it was in the Courier, the local Paper... who had been sexually assaulted...in the Ferry, which is a part of Inverness...thought of as a bit rough...it had been a weekend night, perhaps a Friday or a Saturday...and the media coverage...subtext was she was a woman, she was on her own at night on a weekend, out late, in a rough part of town, had probably... been drinking in a local place or whatever, but you know, that was the implication, and it was reported in that extremely unsympathetic way, you know, that ...women who go out late at night in such a place are asking for it, really. So I think that some of us had some correspondence with the Courier about that... but certainly what it galvanised was the women who were already in the Women's Group talking about it and thinking this was... enough was enough, and...that perhaps we should set something up. And as far as I remember, that led us to talking to Glasgow and Dundee about their lines...Aberdeen... and Edinburgh as well and, yeah, I think we talked to all the places in Scotland who already had lines, and had lots of help and support from them in setting up our own with women coming up to talk to us." [Sue Owen]

Gale Chrisman takes up the story:

"We...invited up representatives of Aberdeen and Glasgow to talk to us about how you set up a Rape Crisis Centre, and...we relied very, very heavily on the experiences of ones that were already up and running...we got hold of the Edinburgh Rape Crisis Centre report, which was extremely good, very, very detailed, and used that as a kind of a template for what we were going to do, and ...we spent sixteen months training ourselves...We did not leap into anything. We wanted to do it properly, and that involved thinking about, discussing funding and also talking about training so that the kind of counselling we gave was useful and helpful to people, and not...off the top of our heads...None of us had training in counselling. So... that was how we went about it. We took a long time. We got the training under our belts. We consulted those who had already set up things, and I was very interested in it for lots of reasons, but partly because I was interested in...answering questions like what would it be like to... [laughs] set up a Rape Crisis Centre? [Gale Chrisman]

The group maintained a steady number at the beginning, and:

"People would go and then other people would come and it always seemed to be around seven or eight people." [Gale Chrisman]

They even hired someone to give them training in counselling:

We had a guy come up who was very good...he... had been involved...in... counselling training, so we hired him. He came up from down south somewhere... I've no idea where we got the money to hire him, because we wouldn't have been up and running...but we did have the money somewhere, somehow." [Gale Chrisman]

Many ingenious fundraising methods were explored in these early days:

"We had a lot of films in my house [laughs], in my living room...

We had video parties, we had parties...I made...40 gallons of wine a year...Honestly, that was my big hobby. And we would have a party and sell wine at, I dunno, 25p a glass or 50p a glass or something." [Gale Chrisman]

The group were eventually successful in obtaining funding (in 1983 to the tune of £365) from the Highland Regional Council, Western Isles, Shetland Isles, Inverness District and Caithness District Councils, which reflects the size of the area they were trying to cover (in origin if not in financial terms!)

Gale's house was also the base from which the Rape Crisis line was operated, and the group made sure they got a very thorough grounding in as many relevant areas as possible:

> "We needed to become informed on police and courtroom procedures, the law regarding sexual crimes, relevant medical matters, criminal injuries compensation, et cetera, so we called upon the professionals to address us. We had the police come and talk, a solicitor come and talk, the police surgeon come and talk to us. This was the guy who ran the workshop. We developed our understanding of counselling through a workshop session with Dr Graham Cooper, a former BPAS trainer of counsellors. That was his background. Ran a workshop on the principles and techniques of counselling. Some HRCC members continued self-development in this area through a correspondence course and weekend workshops run by the Community Education Department." [Gale Chrisman]

The Highland Rape Crisis Centre's very first call led them into a brutal but instructive encounter with the realities of the way the judicial process operated in cases of rape and sexual assault:

> "I remember the first call we got, which was a very, very demanding call…and it was quite clear she had been raped. Now, I don't remember how she heard about us, but …the case came to trial here… and she came down and she stayed here and… we supported her through……that court case… And I think my own…naïvete was exposed to me when… it was very clear she had been raped. She had been beaten up, she was bruised, she was unable to eat, she had psychological problems following that… when the jury…found him not guilty…That was …as a Rape Crisis Centre, the very first call we had and our first experience with what was likely to happen, and continues to happen to us now… we could see absolutely no reason why he was not found guilty, none at all. I remember thinking that. That was an eye-opener, and the reason … she had been in a bar drinking and she had … continued to drink with this guy outside the bar, and, he had dragged her onto wasteland and raped her…But she must have asked for it is what I think the jury thought, you know?…They found the guy guilty of having beaten her up…But not of raping her. That was so strange, you know? If she had consented, why was he beating her up? You know, there was no consistency or logic in their decision about the situation." [Gale Chrisman]

This case apart, the group found eventually, in common with other centres, that most of what they were dealing with related to childhood sexual abuse:

> "By the time I joined…I think almost all the calls were… were incest-related." [Frances Hunter]

The Highland Centre also had contact with women in Skye who were anxious to get their own service off the ground:

> "I think it came about as one or two women from Skye who were interested in setting up, contacting the Centre and wanting to… find out from established centres how to get going, so we got a Centre going in Skye then… I can't remember how they recruited their volunteers but they knew one or two people to start with and then went through a process of recruitment, and they … trained their volunteers and supported them as well." [Frances Hunter]

The evolution of Highland Rape Crisis
Towards the end of the 1980's, Highland Rape Crisis underwent a change:

"A lot of people who had been active in the Rape Crisis Centre just weren't prepared to do it any more and it moved to Dingwall and it ceased to be a feminist organisation… it became something entirely different… They invited me, the Rape Crisis Centre, once, to come. This was the new-look, the new non-feminist Rape Crisis Centre – and they wanted somebody to speak from the old Rape Crisis Centre because they were very perplexed about this not having any men in the Rape Crisis Centre as counsellors… They had men. They had obviously come into some flak from other Rape Crisis Centres, and they didn't understand why. I think they were genuinely perplexed, and I tried to explain the feminist basis …They still couldn't understand, after I had been there for hours and hours talking to them about it, that… they couldn't understand it." [Gale Chrisman]

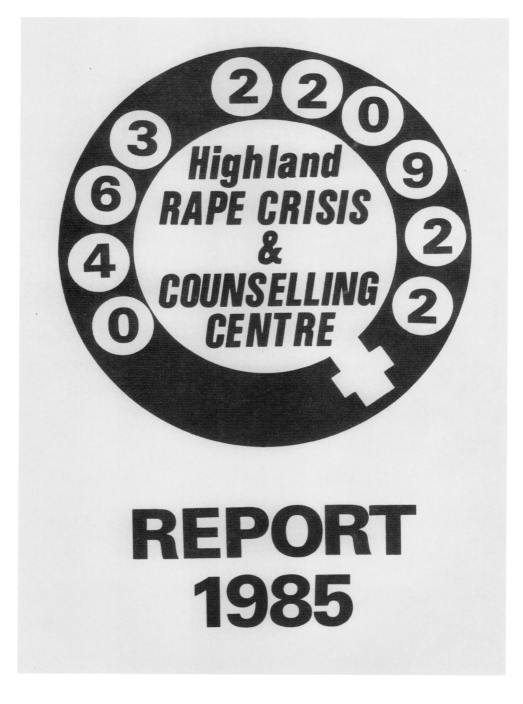

Kilmarnock [Sandra Osborne, Sandra Paton, Norma Benzie, Anne Thomson, Maggie Boyd, Linda, Liz McMahon, Mandy McKerl, Kirsty, Tanya, Margaret Montgomery, Gina Simpson, Helen Simpson]

A Rape Crisis service was set up in Kilmarnock in the autumn of 1987:

> "We started out when Sandra Osborne, who was the Development Worker with Kilmarnock Women's Aid, identified as part of her job…there were a lot of women disclosing and that Kilmarnock Women's Aid wasn't set up to deal with it really. Women's Aid…maybe present a more practical form of help for women, and long-term hourly sessions with women on abuse just didn't fit in. So she thought that instituting a Rape Crisis group might be successful so…I was around at that time as a volunteer and thought that I would like to get involved in that." [Norma Benzie]

The group operated on a shoestring for several years:

> "We worked for a little while before we ever applied for any kind of grant. I think we got £1500 from Social Work – eventually along the way. But we worked for about 4 years on a voluntary basis before we ever applied for funding." [Norma Benzie]

Plans to submit a larger application which covered a larger part of Ayrshire were superseded by the decision of women elsewhere in the district to submit an application separately, and earlier than had been understood by the Kilmarnock group:

> "It was a funny one this because…**we** thought we'd all decided that…we wouldn't apply for funding until we'd really established our working practices, and that there was a need for it – that people were gonna call…So we were working towards that, and the idea had been that…there was two women from Ayr Women's Aid who wanted to become involved and…I don't know if we'd started the application or not, but Ayr jumped the gun, and they went ahead and submitted their application, but we had thought we were gonna go for a whole big…effort, so it complicated things a bit…In the meantime, we just ploughed ahead, and then we asked for another worker, because by this time we were getting very busy." [Norma Benzie]

However when they did make an application, it met with great success:

> "We presented an application for Urban Aid. And that was – I think – 4 years funding and an additional 3. It was wonderful …there was so little bureaucracy involved. It was mainly left to the councils who administered these things…we got three workers…that was 1990. We had actually started before 1987 but that was when we were being rookies…or was it '91?" [Norma Benzie]

Boundary changes created great difficulties for the centre:

> "We got caught up in that, but at that time we did Kilmarnock and Loudon, and Cunninghame district… the three towns, and it was a wonderful dynamic place to work…great. All the workers in that area were…enthusiastic about women's issues, getting things going and then they changed the boundaries – and we lost it. They took their money with them as well! And we lost the post because of it. But… East Ayrshire Finance – lovely man called Alan MacDougall – he managed to find us money…we only needed enough money for two workers, because they'd halved the project, so we did manage to get the money for three. So we got kind of stuck there – in fact we're still stuck there – it's just three posts for East Ayrshire…" [Norma Benzie]

Training in the early days at Kilmarnock in 1987 followed much the same pattern as in other centres, with the women in the collective identifying resources that would enable them to progress in many different forms and in many different geographical locations:

Along the way we had thought well…we'll have to find some kind of training…there wasn't a training course offered by anyone at that particular time. So we went to anything that had the words women, violence, rape, sexual abuse, anything at all that suggested itself – conferences or training courses so we would go along. And we met some really good people in those early days – Ouaine Bain, who wrote "Out in the Open" – that's a wonderful little book…and the woman who worked with her…Maureen Sanders…she was working in Glasgow at the time and we went up and visited the project she was working in at that time – things like that…

In those early days we went to Glasgow, and we sat around watching what went on…we were shown "the book" of the calls that were recorded, we got all kinds of handouts on things not to say and things that were ok to say, open-ended questions – it all seems quite babyish now, you know, but…it was all dead helpful at the time…They were very patient with us…we were able to go up in twos on different nights over quite a period of time until we'd all gone and sort of saw what was going on. And then they had a volunteers training, and they let us attend that…it was good…they set out to help us." [Norma Benzie]

The Kilmarnock women also went further afield in their efforts to prepare themselves:

"There wasn't a lot…on offer…We asked for a speaker from Female and Child Unit…We went to a conference… in Aberdeen…it's a group that no longer exists I think…but then I think that they re-instituted themselves recently… Scottish Women Against Sexual Abuse – something like that. And exercises that we did for ourselves were…like Mother Daughter Child groups…language…becoming comfortable with words and language that might be used…things like race…racist issues…real-play, on a telephone…stuff like that…That's what we instituted for ourselves, that's what we came up with, and we took bits from Women's Aid, and bits from places we had been." [Norma Benzie]

About 6 months passed while the volunteers did their training before opening the service:

"There came a time when Sandra decided – 'Right – we've got to go public now' and then we had one final training day because we all panicked (laughs)…and…began the following week. We had one phone line and we offered…one day a week…When the calls began to get more numerous, we added…a daytime helpline from the Women's Centre." [Norma Benzie]

"I remember the very first night that we had the…crisis line on…we were doing it in twos, and we've actually still got that set-up. You've got a handset and an earpiece…it rang, and we jumped, and were like "You answer it!" "No you answer it!" and we were nervous because we thought that we were gonna get "crisises"…proper crisis-type things, and it wasn't like that at all…and that was a big surprise… although I reckon that we must've been told that…working with Glasgow and such like, but I think we kind of still expected that …" [Norma Benzie]

60

Facilities at Kilmarnock were pretty Spartan:

> "In those early days …I sat on these milk cartons in front of a little fridge with a typewriter on top – that was my desk!" [Norma Benzie]

But the team of women was extremely committed, with some travelling considerable distances in spite of commitments in their own lives:

> "Kirsty…worked for NHS, Tanya…she was the Ayr Women's Worker, and…Margaret Montgomery – she travelled all the way from Ardrossan or Stevenston or somewhere every week and it was no problem to her and she'd all these wee children to take care of …but nevertheless she was there every single time. These women had … such dedication, it was really great…Gina Simpson and…Liz McMahon…And there was Helen Simpson…everybody was just so reliable…
>
> It was so active and dynamic and there was always fun and at the same time a terrific approach – a constructive approach…"That's not working – what do we need to do to change it?" – It was great. There was Linda, and…two of our workers just now had been volunteers as well, that's Maggie and Anne…a lot of people did a lot of good work…" [Norma Benzie]

The notion that support and counselling was something that might involve formal training was largely unheard of at the time:

> "We all were amazed that…Tanya [who was from Gateshead]…when she'd been a younger thing than she was then…she's been able to go to a college who offered counselling training, and she'd been able to get her diploma, and all the rest of it, and that was so unheard of…on our West coast here…" [Norma Benzie]

The group publicised the new service in a number of different ways:

> "We would do things like outreach…proper outreach – we would go to speak to people and then other times we would go out with stickers – round stickers, and put them on every lamp post…all sorts of things…" [Norma Benzie]

Like other centres, Kilmarnock collective moved around a great deal over the years:

> "We started out in John Finnie Street with Women's Aid…they gave us two rooms…an office and a counselling room. And then…we wanted to strike out on our own, because we were an autonomous group…their Admin worker – she was still doing our book-keeping and that was wrong, so when we employed workers…we did our own, so we decided…that we really needed a bit more space, and we didn't need to be babied any more (laughs) and we actually moved up the stairs in John Finnie Street …

Some of the accommodation the group worked from over the years was far from ideal and sometimes posed serious problems:

> "We then moved to a shop in a part of Kilmarnock called Bellfield – it was just like three shops, maybe, in a little island of housing scheme, and that soon became quite unworkable because the school kids would go past, and throw the door open, and shout "Rape!" or some other unsuitable language…It was really bad, and …getting women to the premises was quite a big problem. We would finish up getting a taxi, going down and picking the woman up, say from the bus station and taking her to the premises – that was awful…Titchfield Street – it was far too small. We had to move out of John Finnie Street because the ceiling caved in, and we were absolutely flooded, so we were out of operation for a couple of months trying to get that in order and then we got this place. " [Norma Benzie]

There is still no waiting list at Kilmarnock:

> "We've always been able to keep it turning over. We can always see a woman the next week, and we've never, fortunately, had to say "I'm sorry, you're gonna have to wait two weeks, or three weeks or whatever – heaven forbid. We can always offer them something, and we offer, for example – well, we can send them packs or we could offer them telephone support, if they can't manage to come in…" [Norma Benzie]

One major achievement that demonstrates the persistence of the Rape Crisis workers in Kilmarnock, and the respect they have gained through their work, has been the willingness (following initial extreme reluctance) of some schools in the area to have them in to train guidance teachers and (more recently) pupils. This, however, did not happen overnight. Norma Benzie recounts the group's efforts to secure the cooperation of the Deputy Director of Education:

> "The schools would not entertain us…in any size shape or form…we even went to…the Education Department…we asked could we go do training to Guidance teachers and he said…certainly not! And he wrote us…I don't know how to describe this letter but it was beyond what had been called for, you know, there was a message running through it behind the actual typewritten words…so we asked could we go speak to him, and we did, and…he let us speak, but he said that he would not allow our group anywhere near his teachers because a little learning can be a dangerous thing…He must have seen our faces, because he kind of added some words to the effect that…something about people running away with themselves…maybe they'd had an incident where a teacher had maybe ventured too far and got into trouble, I don't know. He never really did explain it, so we then complained to his boss…and he sent us a copy of the letter saying "do something about this – let the guidance teachers have this training". But we never ever got it…it was kinda obstacles in the way and what not…
>
> The schools themselves weren't …willing to take the initiative to invite us until maybe about 5 years ago…one of the secondary school guidance teachers – and I have to give him a lot of credit for that, cos he was really stepping outside there – and…he invited us several years running, to come and speak to his 5th and 6th year pupils…But now …they can't get enough of us! …they're wanting 2 sessions – 2 classes, one after the other maybe three times a week…it's just all running mad! It's really good…we've done one in Ayr…two schools in Cumnock…" [Norma Benzie]

Central Scotland Rape Crisis [Kate Arnot [1983-84], Che, Kim, Josie Crockett]

Central Scotland Rape Crisis was set up in 1982 following recognition by local Women's Aid groups (Falkirk, Stirling and Clackmannanshire) that there was a need for the service, and an acknowledgement by them also that they did not have the capacity to meet that need.

> "Certainly the Women's Aid groups felt that they couldn't take on this other area of need — we were struggling to do what we were meant to do, so we were not prepared to take this on...I know in other countries, groups formed took on everything to do with violence against women, but we were certainly not prepared to take it on ...the networking in Scotland has always been good...there was a need in Central Scotland, so that's why it was set up." [Kate Arnot]

A public meeting was held to discuss the way forward. Kate Arnot, who was a worker with Falkirk Women's Aid at the time, recalls:

> "I chaired the public meeting that was called to discuss setting up a Rape Crisis centre in Central Scotland...Stirling is a better venue for the three councils because there's direct public transport links by both Falkirk and Clackmannanshire into Stirling, whereas from Falkirk to go to Clackmannanshire or vice versa is difficult, and public transport isn't good. So I have a vague memory that it was in the Cowane Centre in Stirling..." [Kate Arnot]

Central Scotland Rape Crisis Centre was initially based in the office of Falkirk Women's Aid:

> "That was in Leslie Place, opposite the bus station in Falkirk...So there must've been several Women's Aid workers involved, because the helpline was open two nights a week — it was open Tuesday and Thursday...I'd be guessing the hours, but it would've been 7 to 9, 8 to 10, and there were always two women on the line." [Kate Arnot]

With a two-year-old son, and being already heavily involved with the Women's Aid collective in Falkirk, Kate did not feel able immediately to join the new Rape Crisis collective that emerged following the public meeting:

> "After I chaired the public meeting, then other Women's Aid workers were involved in going on to form the collective, but I decided not to do that, partly cos my son was two, and getting childcare at nights for the collective for Women's Aid was difficult enough...putting on more nights would've been even more difficult." [Kate Arnot]

The following year, however, she decided to get involved with the new Rape Crisis centre, although with virtually no resources, things were far from easy:

> I did get involved in the collective in 1983, and found it very difficult. The collective met on a Thursday night in the Women's Aid office. There must've been a separate, dedicated phone line, but there would've been almost no money. I think Rape Crisis has always had a much harder job than Women's Aid in getting funding, because really Women's Aid for many years has run off the back of refuges, because they're classed as homeless provision, and therefore women, almost from the beginning, could claim some for of allowance for staying there, and that, in effect, enabled women to access refuge, which enabled offices.
>
> But because Rape Crisis was providing a direct service but without accommodation, there was very very little money about." [Kate Arnot]

As for other centres, recruitment of volunteers was a priority:

> "There was no paid staff at all, and no likelihood of any, I don't think, because…it was difficult to get that from the Region, and the District was hopeless…There must've been some funding, but where it came from, I can't remember. It must've been minimal, because…there was no office rent and associated costs…the only expenses really would've been the phone line, and costs…Women would've got expenses for travel and childcare…so there would've been costs, but how they were met I don't know…" [Kate Arnot]

Publicity was managed mainly through the local press:

> "Advertising and publicity…would've been expensive…but there would've had to have been advertising in the local papers…Falkirk Herald and Stirling and Alloa Advertisers…as well as posters…" [Kate Arnot]

Support was offered principally over the phone, although this took some time to get off the ground:

> "There was a long time…not just weeks, but months in which it had been advertised, but the phone never rang…and I think I might have got involved at the point at which the phone was beginning to ring….and I think that's not unusual for helplines." [Kate Arnot]

Although the work could be challenging, many aspects of Rape Crisis work, in particular the way in which the collective worked, were very positive:

> "That was fine, if I remember – much less fraught than Women's Aid, because you didn't have the same range of responsibilities, you weren't an employer, you weren't running accommodation…it was much easier in many ways, but there was much bigger turnover…I think because it's so difficult to do to be absorbing that pain and grief and cruelty without having the balance of children in refuge, without hearing about the other parts of women's life." [Kate Arnot]

Central Scotland Rape Crisis also offered face to face support:

> "Anywhere but in the Women's Aid office…so I remember one night after the phone lines closed going out to…a woman's house, it was a parent's house…and being there till one in the morning…Her mother was in the room with us, and I remember …her presence not being particularly helpful – in that she was trying to be helpful, but wasnae really…
>
> I remember once meeting a woman and walking round Callendar Park with her…in Falkirk, and there were two of us…I think we were always in pairs." [Kate Arnot]

Kate Arnot wound down her involvement in the centre after around a year:

> "It was just too much, because you had the collective on the Thursday night, you were often on the line on the Tuesday night, and then you were also seeing women outwith…because I was in paid work with Women's Aid, you were often meeting women at night or over the weekend, and childcare was very difficult for me to …so…it just became too much – both in terms of time, and in terms of what you were listening to – you know, doing Women's Aid all day, and then doing more violence against women at night…" [Kate Arnot]

Central Scotland Rape Crisis fell into abeyance in the early 1990's, but was revived in 1995 after Central Region gave funding for a worker for 6 months to set up the Rape Crisis centre again.

Recruitment

Recruitment was an ongoing concern for every centre. Pressures on volunteers created by family, formal employment, education and health and many other areas of their lives meant that it could be increasingly difficult to satisfy an increasing demand for the services centres were offering. Whereas now recruitment usually takes place annually within centres, in their formative years, this was much more likely to take place on an ad hoc basis:

"We would go into our workplaces and we would be chatting about …what did you do at the weekend, do you know, oh, I was at the Rape Crisis Centre, we had a laugh, or we were at a disco and, that sounds, what are you doing? I wanna come along and see…

And actually, it was by…word of mouth and motivation…because people wanted to be part of something. People always want to be part of something that is successful, I think, or forward thinking and different. So I think, because we were forward thinking and were different, we attracted different and forward thinking people." [Jane Dorby]

"There was an alternative café, Jaws, which was in the Community Centre in the town. There was an alternative book shop, Boomtown Books, so we'd advertise in those places, community centres, and in the paper." [Elizabeth Shiach]

"It was always just who came in the door, who volunteered, who rang up." [Aileen Christianson]

"I think they were Shanghai'd, weren't they?" [Sue Owen]

"I twisted her arm. 'You wanna be helpful and useful in the world, don't you? Do something good?'" [Gale Chrisman]

"I remember going out to colleges to talk about the centre… we went somewhere like Greenock…to talk…or do things like open days or things like that to hand out the information and what have you, try and encourage a few people to become volunteers." [Sheila Brodie]

Sometimes centres used the newspapers to advertise for new members. Glasgow Rape Crisis submitted a small piece to the Glasgow Herald, which appeared on 12th July 1978 under the heading "Helpers wanted":

"The Glasgow Rape Crisis Group, an organisation set up by women to help victims of rape and sexual assault, is now in operation. Our aim is to provide a 24-hour counselling service but we find we are unable to do so at present due to a lack of volunteers. Any reader interested in providing help, either practical or financial, can contact us at 041-331 2811 from Monday to Friday between 6pm and 10.30 pm. **F.M. Shepherd, Glasgow Rape Crisis Group**" [The Glasgow Herald, July 12th 1978]

All sorts of women put themselves forward to join the collectives, and sometimes the backgrounds of those who wanted to join posed issues that had to be debated within the group:

"One time a woman asked to speak to me outside of the meeting, and she said 'I have to tell you this because…I'm a policewoman, and my boss thinks you won't let me join.' And of course, that was a red rag to the bull…but in her case, I said ok, stay in the meeting and then I'll bring it up at the next collective meeting and we'll let you know, and of course, we discussed it and we did let her join and she was terrific." [Aileen Christianson]

"In my experience it was like-minded women who tended to come and you would, it's not so much screening as talking through the issues with them and you'd know they were on board." [Sue Owen]

"We also met with and talked with them individually. 'Cause what we were trying to find out was what their political analysis was – whether they could accept where we were coming from. So it was very much trying to get their values. Their values and beliefs were what was important to us, and also their ability to hold confidentiality and communicate…but an awful lot of the women who came were word of mouth. I think an awful lot of them …knew people, and so…you would suggest it to people, so I think some people came from word of mouth, but other people just came from notices or people who had seen the Rape Crisis advertised and getting in touch and saying I want to be involved." [Elizabeth Shiach]

Very occasionally, the collective would decide that a prospective recruit was not cut out for it:

"There were women that we asked to leave. That was always tremendously difficult. Not very often, because…there were never so many women offering to join, and most women self selected themselves out if it wasn't gonna be for them…there would have been the odd one where we just said 'I'm sorry, it's not for you.'" [Aileen Christianson]

"I've got these memories of maybe talking to people on the telephone who might have wanted to volunteer… and they would start off OK but then you'd get to the point where 'Well, some women do ask for it, you know?'" [Sue Owen]

This was not something that was ever done casually or taken lightly:

"The emphasis would always be on thinking positively about someone, and it would take quite a lot to make us…I mean if somebody was…clearly not suitable, then we would grit our teeth and tell them, but that very rarely happened, that I remember." [Aileen Christianson]

Very often, the women who volunteered already knew and shared other activities with members of the collective:

"They could have come to other … Inverness Women's Group activities like the reading group or the consciousness-raising group or something." [Gale Chrisman]

"I can't remember whether we had pregnancy testing and abortion counselling before Rape Crisis. I think we did… So that was another route that women might have come." [Sue Owen]

Later on, as centres received more substantial and sustainable funding, it became possible to take on some paid workers to manage and develop the service. However, a debate about the impact this would have on Rape Crisis centres, their ethos and the way they operated went on for a considerable time, as the pros and cons of having paid and unpaid workers was debated:

"I'm sure that's because of that experience of Leeds, you know it's like everybody that got money after that's like, don't let your workers answer the phone cos you'll lose your collective do you know what I mean? And it'll all fall apart…But it went on for like about twenty years after that without revision and I think it's not really sustainable now you know. If you've got paid workers, the people that fund you do really expect your paid workers to be providing some sort of direct service." [Jan Macleod]

"Having a part time worker meant that you know, the collective could decide, you know up the ante a bit in terms of being proactive about publicity or fundraising or whatever, so yeah, it did make a difference. Don't know if it's necessarily a particularly easy job to have at first you know. Quite a lot of admin and sometimes the more resources you've got the more arguments it causes you know. But yes it did make a difference." [Jan Macleod]

Discussion on whether or not to make formal application for funding and the impact that would have became a major topic of discussion, particularly within the Edinburgh collective:

"I remember a big discussion when I went back in the mid '80s about paid workers, you know should we have paid workers and… would that undermine the collective? That was a huge issue in Edinburgh… That was '85/'86 in Edinburgh… I think we…were just beginning to agree that maybe, maybe, maybe that might have to be the way forward…It felt like, you know this was a collective in order, once you get into funding and paid workers, you then had this…compromise and then it was a division…so it was [a] hugely fought issue. But I'd just come from Glasgow where we just set up the Women's Support Project, and that actually wasn't easy in its own, I mean there were issues, but nevertheless you had funding and you could do things and people could mainstream and it meant that women didn't have to do day jobs and spend every night doing a night job as well, they could actually sit by the fire on two of those nights." [Helen Mackinnon]

"My recollection…is that if anything, the group resisted going down that road for quite a long time. I mean, not that necessarily money is just as easy to get, but it wasn't necessarily the first choice of the group, and people were concerned at that time, and I think they were right to be concerned, because I think it does change the dynamic of an organisation. And I mean, now…probably groups like that are much more used to having paid workers, who'd be surprised that you even had the discussion…But it was quite a big debate." [Sheila Gilmore]

"In a way, we'd always been worried about paid workers because we thought well, you don't get to rely on them and so you don't manage to do all the things collectively, and so on, and to an extent that happened – but the change, by then, was women expected us to be there more. They saw it as a service. We still saw it as a feminist collective." [Aileen Christianson]

"The irony is, I think it's often easier to get that commitment when it is a purely 100% volunteer thing, even though that has its sort of limitations and you are totally dependant on that commitment if it's not kept up, but I think my observation of both that group and maybe other sorts of organisations is that it changes the dynamics when you actually have suddenly got the money to employ paid people and then, more and more, I suppose gets left to them, and it can be quite a different, I don't want to say impossible, but it does change the dynamic, and perhaps people think, well, you know, I don't really need to do that, or I don't need to go to that meeting or I don't need to do that because they've got somebody there to do it… it's an issue for voluntary organisations really, how you get that balance right." [Sheila Gilmore]

But elsewhere, such funding, and the paid workers it brought was welcomed with open arms:

"Once we got that money, we could fly, because we had the money to pay somebody and…she was responsible for everything, for…training the volunteers, because…it would be a woman plus volunteers writing the letters and doing all that stuff to get into nursery schools and kindergartens. So that was great." [Gale Chrisman]

Women supporting women –
Learning to support & developing support skills

At the very beginning, workers were engaged in learning about the issues at the same time as they were supporting the women whose experiences underpinned that learning process. They did not, either then or later, see or present themselves as "experts" in sexual violence – but simply as women offering support to other women:

> "We were always clear that we wouldn't call ourselves experts…that we were doing it because we as women could relate to the experiences of women who'd been raped and sexually abused… that we were doing it because we felt that it had to be done, that there was a need for the service and there was nobody else doing it…" [Isla Laing]

> "A lot of the women who made contact were talking about things that had happened a long time ago…I think the main thing…was just how much women who contacted valued the support…just the relief that women felt about being able to talk about these experiences and realise that they weren't alone, and that what had happened to them wasn't their fault…" [Isla Laing]

> "I've never been subject to rape or sexual violence, so it was quite difficult for me, personally, to understand what had happened to someone, but it was quite harrowing, I have to say, listening to that. It actually made me realise just how, you know, all the myths around rape were so very real, because it was always people that they knew and people that they trusted…And supporting women, I found it quite difficult to support them when I was so angry." [Jane Dorby]

> "Now, I mean, everybody's got paid workers, you know? They've all got management structures, they've all got…line management and supervision and support, and back then, I mean, we were just going from…seeing one woman to another woman and trying ourselves to – it really was women supporting women supporting women, because you know, a lot of us were survivors as well." [Laurie Matthew]

> Because it was something that I had a lot of empathy with, I didn't find it particularly difficult to do or to get up to speed with…the counselling skills…if you'd been the first to see somebody you tended to carry on seeing that person…you'd get…a couple of really long term people. So you kind of…get to know them in a completely different way…I mean some, some of the women…really it was a phone call and that was it….And that was all they needed or wanted at that time, but others you had really quite a long term relationship with." [Brenda Flaherty]

> "I think I was very much fired by…the belief that women could help women and that if it wasn't for women helping women nothing much was happening actually because when you looked around… the reality was rather hard and women seems to be punished you know over and over for…for what happened." [Florence Germain]

The extent of the service these volunteers provided, even very early on and with very few resources, showed the depth of their commitment:

> "It was very flexible what the centre could offer, because I mean they did like home visits and they covered a really wide area, just got calls from all over, you know the south west Scotland and beyond. We would do home visits and so on and there was no sort of limits on how long you could come for support and you know all this sort of stuff, so I suppose in a sense, there wasn't really a lot of monitoring or accountability, but on the other hand, people were there doing it unpaid and were highly committed to it." [Jan Macleod]

Most collectives operated a sort of "buddy" system, with support work undertaken in pairs. A woman who was new to the collective would sit in with a more experienced worker:

> "Always together…an earpiece at one stage I believe…not immediately…we did some training and we talked a lot always the system being that we would try and be on with someone more experienced – that actually might be comparatively inexperienced as well…I don't think it could be termed as training as such because we really were just…considering the issues and considering what support would mean… non-directive approaches and just being another woman and listening…Morna…she came with me." [Caroline Armit]

The extent to which workers ensured their own personal safety was not compromised was variable, although they would go to great lengths to preserve the confidentiality of the centre's location:

> "I remember once going out to meet a women and three of us went actually because we weren't 100% sure on the phone that it was a woman…she'd…quite a deep gruff voice, so you would sort of go out and meet people on strange arrangements you know like some phone box underneath a tower block or something like that…thinking about it now, I don't know if you would do that." [Jan Macleod]

> "If a woman phoned when you were on the phone, and you had the ability to see her, you just went ahead and arranged to meet her. We had no checking in thing, you would arrange to meet her and put in the phone book that you had arranged to meet this woman who, you had no idea who she was…there was no safety policy…we went, often, to various dark depths of Edinburgh, without really thinking about what we were doing…we nearly always met them outside. I don't remember ever meeting a woman at the women's centre, because the premises were confidential…we met them either at their own home, or we would meet them in a café. We met women in railway stations, we met them in pubs, cafés, we had favourite cafes that were quite useful – we had a list of places that were useful…this place was quite good 'cause, you know, the tables were far enough apart but it was busy and there was music on and you could have a quiet conversation and you could drink one cup of coffee for two hours and the waitress wouldn't bother you." [Lily Greenan]

> "We used to go in twos to meet women…we would meet them, well basically wherever they felt comfortable so sometimes that would be somewhere fairly public and sometimes it would be somewhere very private, we never took them back to the place. And the address of the room was very secret…we kept that very confidential…" [Brenda Flaherty]

> "In those days…there was this secrecy thing – we didn't give out our premises address and we would meet a woman somewhere that the woman knew like the picture hall…and we would go, collect her, and take her to our premises…so cumbersome and ridiculous, when we look at it now, but then we were just trying to protect ourselves and the women… it took quite a while to get rid of that way of working." [Norma Benzie]

Occasionally, in the early days, in their efforts to reach women who needed support, Rape Crisis workers unwittingly compromised their own safety in a serious way:

> "I remember going to see a woman out in Kirriemuir and she'd phoned several times and there was messages and she'd said that she couldn't come cos she'd broken her leg, so two of us went. I took along a new volunteer, quite a young girl, walked into the house and as I walked into the house there was about ten men behind us, and when we got in there was alcohol, there was a woman with a broken leg, but to say that we were at risk is an understatement, right? …Well, what I did was…I says 'Oh, sorry, I've forgotten my diary, we'll just nip out and get it', and because we moved so fast…I grabbed the girl and we moved…But that woman must have set us up…

Another occasion…it was a woman that said she was pregnant, heavily pregnant, could I go to her house, and I went to her house by myself, rung the doorbell and I almost caught something in the corner of my eye, so I turned slightly and somebody pushed me, and what there was was a man behind me. Now, I would have gone flying in that house if I hadn't turned ever so slightly, you know?..

I remember me and Caroline we went up to a house up in the multis…poor woman's dead now, but we'd gone to see her and we'd known her a while. She was just a really tragic, tragic woman, and we'd got up there and her son had a drugs problem and that, and Caroline had gone in her house and at the last minute she'd shouted to me "run, Laurie!", right? And I was like blown away, I was like what's going on? And the door was shut on me…She was inside and I was outside, and then I heard a commotion, right, and I was trying to look through the letterbox. I'm thinking what do I do, what do I do, right? And what I did was I thought well, to hell with this, and I ran and phoned the police… I got out, I broke my ankle actually that day, running to phone the police, cos of the way the slabs were… The police came and what had happened was the woman was being held captive in the house by her son and his mates, and when we'd got to the door, the door had been opened because one of the young lads had thought it was another mate, so Caroline had walked in…realised that there was something, and shut the door… Now it could have easily been both of us, you know…

Well, when the police came they refused to go up initially until there was reinforcements, but once I said the address…I was in the back of a police van because I was shouting 'Caroline's up there', you know, 'we have to do something!' To cut a long story short, the police went up, they broke into the house, the woman was an absolute mess. She'd been slashed with a Stanley knife. She was admitted to hospital and Caroline was taken along for a check but she was actually, physically, she was OK, thankfully." [Laurie Matthew]

What women were looking for from Rape Crisis centres when they got in touch varied a great deal, but there was one thing that most of them had in common:

"What they want to do is not feel it's a normal experience, but they want to feel that they're being treated as ok …with that history, and helped through it…and that it's ok to feel all those things you feel, and that it's ok to talk about it…so many people do have a history of that, and so many people feel that they can't discuss it…" [Kathy Litteljohn]

And the chance to communicate, very often for the first time, about what had happened, was the key for many women to beginning to heal:

"I think it was the opportunity to talk. It was non judgemental. Nobody was saying it was your fault. Letting them know that it happened to lots of women, that they weren't the only ones. Letting them know that it wasn't their fault that it had happened…because quite often it was somebody they knew… it wasn't just a guy jumping out from behind a bush… neighbours, somebody who'd lived across the road, a friend's husband you know things like that…that was even more shocking because they didn't really know what to do about the friend…what do you do? It's a really difficult situation…

Some women wanted to tell you in great detail what exactly had happened to them and you just listened. And I think sometimes because they'd been so shocked by what had happened they wanted you to be shocked as well and the fact you weren't and you said 'yes, these things happen, you're not the only one', then it helped in some way to feel 'yeah well it does happen to other people, I didn't do it.'…The fact maybe they didn't fight somebody off. You can explain how fear, some people go totally rigid and… they just can't do anything. And to understand that because it may have happened to them…That that was ok to do that, it was ok to fight back, it was ok not to…" [Sheila Brodie]

Morna Findlay's first experience of offering support in Glasgow, shortly after she joined the collective there as an 18-year-old volunteer in 1979, came as something of a baptism of fire:

> "I still think about it now because I had gone into the office – we had this horrible little dingy office at the time…it was a street that was near the…King's Theatre in Glasgow…it's the same street I think as the Griffin Bar…it was a little tiny office off a kind of nasty close, and I think I had gone there to get something – to pick up some leaflets to distribute or something – I wasn't meant to be on the rota.
>
> And when I got there whoever was meant to be on the rota hadn't turned up and so I got my leaflets and the phone rang and I thought should I answer it, and I did answer it and the person who had phoned up turned out to be somebody that I had known at school…I initially spoke to her mother and in the course of the conversation I realised I know this girl – then – she was the same age as me – 18…
>
> I made an arrangement to go and visit her…I thought I have to find somebody to go with me…I know nothing about this…I went to see her by myself, I couldn't get anybody to go with me. The second time I went to visit her Caroline Armit came with me and she was much more able to deal with this…I think I just thought… I'll do my duty – I'll turn up and let this woman talk but I really didn't have much idea what I was doing at all…it preys on my mind sometimes cos I still wonder how this woman got on… After a period of visits her mother phoned us and said…her doctor had advised that she shouldn't … keep in contact with us because it was 'dragging things up'…Looking back, I certainly question how much it was worth her talking to me." [Morna Findlay]
>
> "I didn't have training of any sort…I don't think that we had that clear an idea at the time or I didn't, not being a professional, not having gone through training, didn't have that clear an idea of what to do…and I still think about that now. I sometimes think about some of the other people that I went to visit…I remember some of the other women in Glasgow at the time talking about how I hadn't been on the rota and I'd just picked up the phone and someone said 'Oh well it's alright – she's an experienced feminist' because …certainly when I was younger, I've always looked older than I was and people used to think that I was quite a bit older than I was…I was 18 and didn't know anything, and I remember for example, going to visit people that had phoned us up in the Glasgow area, and I sometimes think back at it now and think where was that? Cos I was so green, I couldn't tell you where I'd been. I remember… Caroline Armit and I went to speak to the CID – take on the CID really. I sometimes think about that and I think where was it?…Somebody would just tell us which train to get on, then we'd get a taxi…I didn't have a clue where I was going, just – really green. And bolshie." [Morna Findlay]

Sometimes a call would require unusual or creative handling, in addition the extreme sensitivity with which every call was treated:

> "A call came in from a woman…it was quite a difficult call because it was a silent one to begin with, and I had to set up the code with her. 'If I ask you a question and it's 'yes', will you indicate by just making a noise, an if it's 'no', then remain silent.' And as it turned out…I thought, the scenario that I had in my head from the coding of, you know, 'yes', 'no', was that she had actually killed a violent partner, but what it turned out to be after a number of calls back and forward was that she had discovered that her… grandfather was her father…and that he had sexually abused her as well as her mother, but the grandmother and grandfather and mother and herself had all lived in the house together, and their grandfather had died. So you can see why… with a 'yes', 'no' coding, that… I would think that it was a violent partner that she had… or somebody who had raped her, that she had then subsequently killed. So that was the kind of calls that would be coming in at that stage, and again that was very much in the early days of really looking at incest and child sexual abuse." [Margaret Brown]

Workers were keen to build on the enormous progress that a first call very often signified:

"When they plucked up the courage to phone…they would often be blaming themselves… It would very much be around, you're not to blame. That was the first key thing. But also are you in a position now…where you are safe? Is there anyone else you need to tell to feel safe? Are you …putting yourself back into a position where you're still gonna be unsafe? And then trying to work out with her how… what else she might to do get support…the internal training… was all about making sure we tried to encourage people to phone back. Because often, it would be a very short first phone call because they managed to get to the phone, but then maybe when they started to talk about it, it was too awful. So it was all about I suppose encouragement, keeping them on long enough so that you could build up some kind of rapport so they felt safe enough calling back." [Fiona Raitt]

"Women talking about…how they'd survived, what they'd done, what made them feel better…some people talked about confrontation, you know if they'd been abused as a child, or writing letters and things like that. Others it was…'I just want to forget about it, forget about it', and you're having to say 'well, that maybe fine for just now, but it, you know it won't necessarily go away forever'. You know it's difficult…people wanted like, tell me what to do, to make me better and that's nothing you can do." [Sheila Brodie]

Survivors were not the only callers:

"And sometimes you found yourself speaking to whole families. You know the phone would be handed round. I remember one particular family that it was a nephew that had raped, he'd raped his cousin… they were devastated, they just couldn't understand it." [Sheila Brodie]

The reasons for women getting in touch with Rape Crisis were many, and what they hoped to receive in terms of help varied enormously. Some would be looking for emotional support while others would be looking for more practical support:

"It was very varied. Some women were exceptionally angry, some…devastated…it was different stages…of the process. Some wanted to kill people…and it was really trying to help them talk through all those issues. Not necessarily the issues about physical things, but…there was lots of questions… about resuming sexual relationships and things like that that…maybe…a woman had been raped and her partner was not able to understand what had happened to her – to get their head round. Some were… totally fine and quite often men would phone up whose partners had been raped…'what should I say to her and what can I do?' and we used to do that as well…" [Sheila Brodie]

"I do remember that apart from the fact that a lot of people have been abused as children, one of the things that we sometimes talked about in the early days was that often people who contacted you – the fact that they had been raped was not their only problem…they could have multiple issues. Maybe people who had a perfectly balanced life and then this bad thing had happened to them maybe they were able to cope with it with their supportive family and friends without coming to us. That woman that I mentioned that was interested in taking out private prosecution for example, she was angry the guys had got off, but she seemed to have her family and friends behind her and that's all she wanted from us – you know – can you help me find out if I can do anything?…I remember someone who was very agoraphobic and was in her house all the time…I think she'd actually been preyed on by a guy who knew she was agoraphobic…the main thing she seemed to want us to do was to go and get her shopping cos she didn't want to go outside…it wasn't always obvious how people needed to be helped…maybe a mental health problem or…a problem with their children, their housing." [Morna Findlay]

"What is really significant – I did find as a social worker – well I mean it's been in the papers lots recently… all these women who end up in prison…nine out of ten of them have had an abusive background…and I worked for a while in a hostel in Edinburgh, it was like a halfway house I suppose, people were coming from Cornton Vale to this place – women who'd been abused – seriously abused. And they were being put in prison and then they were coming to us, and then if they had any kind of a breakdown or that… the hospital were saying oh well – it's a personality disorder… we can't help…At that time I remember referring people to Rape Crisis." [Moira Kane]

The practicalities and safety aspects around the support they were offering raised much heated discussion within collectives:

"Some of us we got really involved…I remember…we'd…get very heated in the group and saying, 'but this woman needs our help and we have to work with that'… And others will say 'No you've got to back off cause there's another 6 waiting here'…not calling it boundaries but saying 'Look you're too involved… step back'. But also this whole thing about how long, how often we should see them, whether we should go out to people's houses… I think we said initially we shouldn't, I think we always met on common ground but I think once or twice people did and I think that was an issue. I can't actually remember ever going to someone's house…I came from a social work background so I suppose I was bringing social work things about confidentiality and boundaries and stuff like that. As well as presumably Pat and Heather whereas people like Fiona and Florence and some of the others didn't have that background…so I was probably a bit more cautious than some of the others about…risk assessment and going to people's houses and …up people's closes and whatever." [Dorothy Degenhardt]

Confidentiality was paramount:

"In terms of recording…the minimum…it was actually a big log book…that was discussed quite a lot, and what confidentiality actually meant and could you secure your office…why does it need to be written down anyway…there was a lot of that going around because these kinds of discussions did…we weren't "proper" counsellors in the sense that we were counselling in the strictest sense…there wasn't much recording… Documentation…there really wasn't a lot of that either…women would keep their own paperwork…" [Caroline Armit]

"We never recorded personal de[tails] in fact we don't record anything even to this day – we never kept addresses, phone numbers, anything like that, for the women." [Norma Benzie]

New members of the collective learned support skills from the more experienced women:

"She answered the phone and you listened. And I mean you literally just sat in the room while she took the call, and we didn't have an earpiece or anything…so you were listening to one side of the conversation and most of the face-to-face work that happened – there wasn't a lot of face-to-face work that happened, but when it did happen, it happened in twos, so two volunteers would go and meet a woman. So that was a way that you began to get to learn of what was going on. It was very, very, very women supporting women. It was very activist…there was no discussion about counselling or support skills…it was still very much coming from a position of as women, we understand what it is to live with the fear of rape, and that's where we act from. That's where our support of other women comes from. We didn't even really see it as supporting women – we talked about seeing women, or meeting women." [Lily Greenan]

"The prevailing thing was 'Oh you've to be non-judgemental and non directive', and I think that was often misunderstood as well and interpreted as you shouldn't offer an opinion. But if you once you come to understand that the sort of status quo in society is that there's an awful lot of myths and stereotypes round about rape and women who get raped and sort of men who rape and why they do it, then…if you don't offer any comment, you're basically withholding an alternative view of the world, from that woman… there's a difference between not telling her what she should be doing and giving her information which gives her options about what she could do." [Jan Macleod]

"You usually chose who you worked with really. So even though we didn't know each other well at the beginning you would suss out who you felt comfortable working with. So I suppose that was someone that had similar values and a similar way of working to yourself. Cause obviously we're all different."
[Dorothy Degenhardt]

The support offered by Rape Crisis workers was very firmly rooted in the idea of women supporting other women, and to some extent at odds with more formal and "professionalised" methods of support:

"I think there's…a huge difference between sort of a formal therapeutic counselling where my understanding of that is that you've got a person who has made a decision that there's something in their life that they want to address, so they decide to come to you and they tell you what it is…and then it's up to them to bring that to you… if you like. And it's up to you to create a safe environment for them to speak to you about that. But if something's happened to the person like, you've been raped, like you didn't want it, you couldn't stop it, you canny make it go away, that's quite different…You do need support and information much more than therapeutic counselling."[Jan Macleod]

"I think you've got to be able to listen. And understand and empathise to a certain extent, but not allow that to overwhelm you. And you've got to be able to leave it…to go home…you've got to be able to relax and not spend your time thinking constantly about it. Because you get exhausted, you get burnt out if you do that." [Sheila Brodie]

This rejection of the formal model, although not always made explicit within the collective, could sometimes place workers whose professional backgrounds lay within it, in a difficult position, in terms of their contribution to training and support within Rape Crisis:

"I was a trained counsellor at that time…a mental health nurse and I'd done various courses and programmes and I'd quite a lot of experience of dealing with folk with depression…I'd…done quite a lot of therapeutic work. I did feel that that probably at the time wasn't particularly valued…and I can see why people probably felt you had to be deprogrammed. I didn't think I had any fancy ideas about myself…But I did feel that I had to almost…play that down hugely in order to be accepted by the collective. And it meant that sometimes in training sessions, you know it might be somebody who had been working with somebody that had been depressed that was actually leading that discussion…I didn't feel at that time I would have been able to say well this is how I would deal with somebody with depression. I do remember Nadine Harrison who had been a collective member and had moved on and was a GP… I think she came along and gave a sort of talk on health issues. But I didn't feel in that first six months that my expertise was particularly…I remember feeling a little bit hurt about that, that I had to play things down… I did feel that, but…and I was aware of this myself, coming sort of from the NHS and being a mental health nurse, it was not necessarily something to be hugely proud of… I had thought through things as well and I knew about, if you like, a victim mentality and I knew about objectifying and not, and I was aware of some of the things about the health service that played into that." [Helen Mackinnon]

Conversely, workers coming to support for the first time could sometimes experience extreme apprehension:

"I've seen a lot of people panic, because they feel … they won't know what to do. Or that there are no resources, but…sometimes it's enough just to believe the person or let them speak…I think we tend to have that problem about we must do something, and it's almost like we want to feel better because we've done something tangible. And, the skill…is about – unless obviously the person is in danger, in which case you had to intervene – it's about where is that person, what does the person want? What does she want? And then follow that up as opposed to jump in." [Florence Germain]

74

"We were working in pairs, that…was quite scary because you didn't know who was going to phone in and you felt, even though we'd done some training…quite unprepared as to dealing with the phone line. And we did offer to meet with people and again in 2's. And for me that felt a bit better because like my social work training was about you know, communicating with people and supporting them through that. I wasn't used to doing it on the phone. So it was the phone line, it was the phone counselling bit that felt quite scary. And also you know, whether we were going to be inundated and how long they were going to take on the phone and what we would do if they're obviously greatly distressed and so on." [Dorothy Degenhardt]

"It wasn't counselling, but it was what you do before you learn to do counselling, so really attentive listening and writing things down if necessary, and not doing the sort of 'if I were you' kind of stuff…I think I had some BBC counselling skills tapes, and there were a couple of things on there about what not to do, and I think I used some of those. I remember doing role-plays…a lot of it was getting people to take a back seat as far as their own view… and just really, really listening to what women wanted, and not being in too much of a hurry to rush in and rescue…Slowing down how much they needed to know, and also finding ways of ending the conversation as well, cos that can be quite difficult." [Liz Hall]

Helen Mackinnon offered similar help to workers in the Glasgow collective:

"When Helen got involved, because she was a trained counsellor…she did some training sessions on that… not that I'm saying that what we did beforehand wasn't as good, but certainly, you know… it confirmed what we'd been doing, that our practice was good practice." [Rona Clarke]

"That was really the very first time that people were talking about this…and the enduring effects… it certainly wasn't in my knowledge…Helen was…absolutely so strong for me because she …did have sort of some experience of groupwork…with people …that were very distressed in a group… she was a psychiatric nurse and she was tutoring at that stage…so that brought…quite a bit…of excellent expertise…because you are just…following the women…and it is to be what they need it to be, so you have to just kind of follow it to some extent…no prescriptions…nothing written." [Caroline Armit]

As a health professional, she was in a good position to draw comparisons between what a Rape Crisis centre could offer to women, and the far more formal systems that characterised the health service:

"One of the things I liked about the Rape Crisis centre was its confidentiality. And that …the woman was in control and you only went…to see the woman if she wanted you to see her…you saw her in her home or at her convenience and her location…it was never gossiped about ever…It was very, very carefully handled by the collective…it's not to say that patients' issues weren't in the NHS system but quite often you've got 20 people on a case conference…students and observers and…you had to go through details of that person's life…in [the] NHS at that time…whereas here it was like a group of about 18 women and it was maybe you and the other person that had gone out. And if you did want to talk it through with other people, you could, but you did it in…a very, very careful way. So I really liked that. And I also liked the way that you could sort of walk through the red tape…you could actually go out and sort of be quite helpful in a number of ways. I mean nobody said you hadn't ever to run out and get a pint of milk or nobody said that you couldn't chum that woman the next day. To something that she wanted, needed to go to, whether it was housing or whatever. So I liked the way it was…for me working in health, which was so compartmentalised in those days, and it still is." [Helen Mackinnon]

Opening hours for the helplines varied, with many women committing a great deal of time to support:

"I was in three sessions a week – it was Monday, Wednesday and Friday…It was from seven 'til ten, you know? So it's quite a long time…And then…your follow-ups from there, so I mean, sometimes it could be really, really busy, sometimes not at all, and you always dreaded getting a call at five to ten…the policy was that you didn't ever say to somebody, well will you hurry and you've got to go or anything like that, because, you know, it had taken somebody a huge amount of courage just to make that phone call…So yeah, it was quite a big commitment and…you tried to do rota at least twice a month." [Rona Clarke]

This could be a daunting process at the start, and made a deep impression on the women on the helpline:

"Very, very nervous and very, got very, very upset on behalf of women. I mean, not that they would have known that – I wasn't crying on the phone, but you know, just took an awful lot on board…I went through a period of being very, very scared of men. Just very, very scared of them in general, you know, because I was hearing all this stuff all the time, and of course…I was aware of it all, obviously, you know, being a feminist and wanting to be involved – but I think hearing about those experiences in detail, and…everywhere these things happen, just in general…just felt very, very uneasy in the company of men, …for quite a long time." [Rona Clarke]

Sadly, very occasionally, there were hoax calls:

"They were really upsetting…partly as well because it was very much about believing women." [Margaret McCutcheon]

"I remember one specific hoax call… it wasn't a man pretending to be a woman, it was a woman on the phone and she was talking about…a situation where she had been raped and of course, you…used… the listening techniques of reflecting back and this is what you're saying to me and yeah, and she said 'oh you know I need to talk to somebody about it, I need to tell you about what happened' and of course you say 'yeah absolutely if you want to talk about that'. So then it became to the graphic stage where it was I thought…this is not quite, there's something not right about this and then of course then it devolved into – it sounded as though there was a woman and a guy getting off on the phone basically." [Margaret McCutcheon]

But the importance of the service they were offering was often reinforced very powerfully:

"I can remember speaking to one woman, I'm sure it's as common now, a woman in her seventies or eighties I think, who wanted to just tell someone how she'd been raped before she died, and her phoning up…and just her memory…and her talking about it. I just remember that. How powerful that was to me, that she'd been carrying this secret for, you know… fifty, sixty years and she'd never been able to tell anyone. So she'd been carrying that level of shame and guilt, and that she finally had somewhere to go with that and that, hopefully, just having been able to let go, you know, just talk about it, would have let some of that stuff go. But just criminal that that happened." [Elizabeth Shiach]

Face to face support was also an important aspect of the work undertaken by Rape Crisis centres:

"Sometimes we'd bring them to our office, but we weren't that keen at that stage…we'd meet people at Central Station underneath the clock…it was quite kind of funny in some ways… people would be wearing like a carnation or a brooch with a thistle on it…was like a spy movie in some ways." [Heather Forrest]

"As well as the phones we did face to face counselling… it was quite complicated to arrange, because we were very, very careful about confidentiality…there was the whole issue about keeping the address of the centre confidential, secret and other issues about women…who were coming to meet us who didn't want to make it known to other people about who they were meeting…And we used to arrange to meet in Central Station…and people would kind of circle around to work out if it was the right person…It was a bit strange, and we used to say to the women that, you know well these are some rooms that… we get the loan of, and we never give out the address because there were fears of the rapists or, maybe if it was a women's partner that had raped her finding out where she was and …following her and you know attacking her there and all these kind of issues.

And the rooms were like the centre, but we never said that. And you know you just talk, usually, quite often there was two of us and that was for support and for safety as well and on the phones as well, quite often there was two people on the phones that you would provide a bit of support for each other. But latterly, quite often there was just one. I think it was just numbers as well." [Sheila Brodie]

Sometimes support was also given by letter:

"People actually wrote, we used to do a kind of a counselling thing by letter…they would write to us and we'd reply, but you had to have your letter looked over by somebody else in case you'd said something untoward in it (laughs)…and sometimes quite long correspondences and long letters as well. From all over the place." [Sheila Brodie]

"I wrote a lot of letters, actually…there was quite a lot of that at the time, and I suppose now people don't write letters to one another…And at that time a lot of letters used to come into the centre…people maybe couldn't get through on the phone, and so they would write…it would be a kind of ongoing… We were doing a big clearout … And it was quite emotional, reading through some …you'd forgotten… though I wonder whatever happened to these women…you feel like a bit of a dinosaur saying that, cos folk don't write letters any more…" [Linda Reid]

Groupwork with survivors became another valuable part of the service developed by Glasgow Rape Crisis, and something that had to be very carefully managed.

"There's always the benefit of 'It's no just me', and all the stuff around that which is very complex as we know…it wouldn't necessarily always be a place for somebody to work through their distress…women are very conscious of each other's distress and sensitivities, so that was at play as well… to be careful that there was a balance…it was really really delicate…

Make sure that everybody was welcomed…there would be a seat left if someone couldn't manage…I think a lot of the time women really led…it was what they were wanting to talk about…I do remember some things being more structured in terms of responding to what the women were coming with – anxiety, panics – how to manage panic, sleeplessness…compulsives…" [Caroline Armit]

What workers learned from women within the groups helped greatly in advancing their knowledge of sexual violence and how to respond to the calls they received. Several other centres set up support groups, which were run by survivors from the collective:

"In 1987 we then set up the… self-help group for rape survivors, coordinated by women from the collective who had been raped." [Edinburgh Rape Crisis workers in Grit and Diamonds – (Stramullion, 1990)]

Support for supporters

As the supportive work they undertook could often take its toll, it was very important for women on the helplines that they themselves had somewhere to go for support, and in the early days of the Rape Crisis centres, the workers looked to one another:

"It was each other, really…that was the support. You could talk to somebody else about how you felt. It wasn't great, you know, because you were coming off the lines at ten, ten thirty at night, and you had each other – the two people who were there – and that wasn't great, you know, because you actually needed somebody else. So, if it was a Friday night, you could end up holding a whole pile of stuff 'til the next collective meeting on a Wednesday. Or if you'd a personal relationship with people within the collective, you could phone somebody up, but you know, you don't always want to do that…we did acknowledge that that was there, and there was a need for it, and we should delineate somebody, eventually, who would be there, but I can't quite remember how that worked. So I think, just a lot of drink was the solution." (laughs) [Rona Clarke]

"The group were very very supportive to each other…we tried always to have two women answering the phones on the nights that the centre was open. That didn't always happen, but certainly, there was always other members of the group prepared to make themselves available to support women who had taken calls that they found difficult, and that was very important…" [Isla Laing]

"You're listening to dreadful stories and supporting women through some very difficult things…that obviously has an impact on yourself…we always felt that we could contact other members of the collective when we were really feeling that we needed to talk something through…I think we all did it, I think it was the only way that we managed to deal with some of the issues and stories that we heard…" [Isla Laing]

"We were doing that with very little supervision…because we were offering supervision to each other and then…Joyce Agnew [*a consultant*] offered it as group supervision. Whereas now of course you wouldn't be doing counselling without inbuilt supervision." [Dorothy Degenhardt]

"Always we'd have somebody to phone…you would have a number that you could definitely phone so-and-so if you were concerned or you wanted to talk it over, you know if you'd been to see someone…" [Caroline Armit]

"Looking back, what I identify as supporting co-workers and colleagues and staff now, is very, very, very different to what we did then. I think that what happened was the service took over, and the demand on the service took over…and that's why a lot of us got burnt out very, very quickly. The other thing that was happening, for some of the women in the organisation were they were still dealing with having to see members of their family who had abused them. So they were out there, talking the talk, you know… doing that thing where you're being really strong and really focused and really inspirational, and then… they would leave that platform where they were doing that speech…and say "Oh God, I'm seeing my granddad at the weekend. My mum's invited him over, because it's a family party. I haven't seen him for three years, oh, oh, oh, oh, oh."…it was almost like, when you did start to talk about how it was personally affecting you, it felt really selfish and really overindulgent, so we would often just not do it… that's where you can see the change, over the years, in that women's organisations now recognise the impact that working with the issues has on us, and we've become much more, I suppose, fine tuned when it comes to looking at the service providers, in order to maintain a good service provision to service users. You have to, to a degree, look at the service providers as well." [Frances Monaghan]

"I guess we saw the collective meeting as a way of doing that. And discussing things that had happened. The fact that we were meant to have two people on the phones that you could either listen…or you could…discuss something that had happened that maybe had upset you or that you just needed to talk about. When we started to…get the training a lot more structured, we used to put in sessions on relaxation and things like that so people could know have some techniques to release the stress." [Sheila Brodie]

And it was also very important for workers to recognise their own limitations in terms of offering support, and balance what they were offering with needs within themselves and their own lives:

"There was one woman I was involved with which was quite scary really and I just sort of felt…I can't handle this, there's too many other things in my life. I wanted to back off, and I knew that was selfish but I kind of wanted to protect myself… She was a schizophrenic and I just really …didn't feel I was behaving the way I should and wasn't able to handle it… I dropped out of helping her…at the time I'd had a bit of postnatal depression…it was just sort of trying to handle this woman's problems whilst handling my own. Everybody was very supportive and said I think you should back off from this. Sort of get yourself better first… I realised that I had limits. So I could only do so much." [Maureen Porter]

For most Rape Crisis centres, the idea of support extended well beyond emotional support over the phone or face to face, and encompassed a whole range of practical activities relating to women's experiences and the difficulties they faced in accessing in confidence the services they needed. The lengths women had to go to for things which were a basic human right had already been established sometimes before the centre set up. The Women's Group from which Highland Rape Crisis emerged, for example, very proactively acquired the means to help women do their own pregnancy testing:

"In those days you couldn't buy a kit in Boots…you could only have one from your doctor, and many doctors wouldn't do it until after six weeks, but we had to, we went to a chemical company, a pharmaceutical company, and bought the kind of kits that…the hospital would have been using at that time… And there were these, like, raised circles of patterned glass around it that held it, and you put the chemicals and you had to keep tilting it back and forward until a wee ring appeared…if it was a positive test." [Sue Owen]

Training

Undergoing a comprehensive training programme is now an integral part of a Rape Crisis worker's development. However, for the pioneers of the movement in Scotland there were no such programmes in place, and they had to rely on one anothers' experience, on what they learned from the work they were doing, and on any other information or resources they were able to acquire from elsewhere:

> "You had to listen and watch and learn by doing. And then, once somebody had joined…if they were on the phone lines, say, but they weren't answering the phone 'cause they were new, they were allowed to read the phone books, 'cause…when a call came in…you would take notes and there would be… minutes of past collective meetings… notes of phone calls and what action was gonna be taken and so on, and so you would read past books, and after a while, of course, there were quite a lot of those, so that was a very good training thing." [Aileen Christianson]

> "You used to listen in to calls with other women that were there and some of the women were just quite awe-inspiring – they were so good, you know, in the way that they handled calls, and I don't think you ever forget…the first time you listen into a call…it's the impact of it, you know? And I remember that call still to this day, and the woman that I was on with, and she just handled it so well, and I remember thinking oh I'll never be able to do this and handle it like that…but of course over time, you kind of build up your confidence a bit…" [Linda Reid]

> "Then if you'd been on a call, talking about how that call had been and what it felt like, and discussing with other women about…how you'd found that experience, and especially if you thought you hadn't done something right, if it felt like 'I didn't get that one right', sort of thing." [Sue Owen]

> "I think every… every contact was discussed with the group…I think that took place every single time." [Gale Chrisman]

A chronic lack of resources, and the fact that they really were pioneers and covering ground that, in this country at least, had never been covered before, meant that workers had to take whatever opportunities they could, in their efforts to train themselves:

> "We were starting to get…all day Saturday training and things like this. And that was very much to do with money. It was just trying to source the right people to get money, basically – to hire the premises for a day and to get reasonable speakers, etc…We had one on the law, which was run by a woman who'd just qualified as a solicitor – I think it was Frances McMenemy, might be her name…and I'm sure somebody like Sheila Gilmore, somebody from Edinburgh came through as well to talk about the politics of sexual violence… and I remember going through to Edinburgh and that was very, very interesting, 'cause there was an American woman there, and they always seemed to be a little bit more advanced than we were in terms of ideas and she was, again, just talking about perspectives in violence against women." [Rona Clarke]

> "I think it's actually incredible, that volunteers, by and large…pulled that off, and it took, you know, over three months for the training to go ahead, plus there was the two-day training – people were all doing this in their free time…the workers were there and they were great as well…but the bulk of the training really came from the other volunteers, who were just a really smashing bunch of women… it worked really well, and I think there was a lot of confidence-building for people…I think they were sympathetic to knowing when the time was right…trying to get the balance of but we're here to do a job as well, so at some stage everybody needs to make that leap…" [Linda Reid]

Training programmes developed significantly over time, and gave a far more solid foundation to the later volunteers than their predecessors had had:

"It was training that we kind of developed as we went along because I was involved for quite a few intakes of volunteers…we developed and added more and more onto it. I remember that when I first came, there wasn't as much as there was when I left, because we had included lots more about like police and the legal system. And different…aspects of counselling as well and the whole range of the different types of women that we saw." [Heather Forrest]

"We then, eventually, ended up with a sort of six week training course, in which people were coming… six times in a row, to hear about different aspects of the politics of violence against women, and then…a talk on the law, and a talk on medical services, etc, and abortion and this kind of thing, so that was much more organised, and that was delivered by somebody within the collective." [Rona Clarke]

"We covered loads of issues in the training I remember, there was lots of stuff about just how to handle calls and…adapt your voice, how to listen actively, and classic things that people would do wrong, as well as things about terminations and practical advice about where people would go. I remember we went to the Family and Child unit as well…looking back it was just really helpful trying to see…where people would actually go and, kind of make connections with people…so that if you did have to phone up or phone up on someone's behalf…" [Linda Reid]

"We had people that would write in and say they want to do training and …we would write to them… usually we'd have it in the summer…we never had it in dark horrible weather. And it would be an annual thing and we'd do sort of a whole range of workshops. Some would be in the evening, some would be like a Saturday or a Sunday." [Heather Forrest]

"There was a lot of discussion about what feminism is about…the training was also about our personal experiences as well so we'd talk about our experiences as women in the world, around sexual harassment, around rape, sexual assault, about…what we wanted to do about that. So it was kind of consciousness-raising I suppose…I do remember practising listening skills so…we would do the kind of back to back listening skills exercises that you could do in terms of like trying to tune your ear into, without having a visual marker." [Margaret McCutcheon]

The need for training continues to be a vital part of the effective provision of Rape Crisis services in Scotland, and the vast majority of issues facing workers are exactly the same ones women were facing in the 70's and 80's. Rape continues in many ways to be invisible, as Margaret McCutcheon observes, in recalling a recent conference workshop:

"The case study was read out and she had also been raped by her partner and it was really interesting that nobody in the panel, including the Women's Aid worker didn't actually address the fact that the woman's case study was saying…she had been raped. And it took Sandy Brindley in fact from Rape Crisis Scotland to say, why has nobody actually addressed the fact that this woman has said that she's been raped? And I think it was one of those kind of like light bulb moments really that we still haven't joined it up yet." [Margaret McCutcheon]

The contribution of survivors to Rape Crisis

The development of the Rape Crisis movement in Scotland owes a great deal to survivors and the insight and commitment they brought – either as users of the service, or as workers – or sometimes as both:

"Sometimes there were women…you'd been supporting who then wanted to come in, or they had a break and they wanted to come back and help and that was always very good." [Fiona Raitt]

What survivors brought to Rape Crisis was undoubtedly the single most significant component to the development of the new services, ensuring that these reflected as far as was possible the truth of their experiences and the needs they themselves had identified as having emerged from that:

"The core of my belief is that the women who contact Rape Crisis and all the other survivors' groups, they are the experts in their own lives and they are the ones that teach us…I owe so much to those women. I didn't have any training, that's where I learned… if you look at the literature on rape and sexual violence, you will find that in that literature, the voice that is heard best is the voice of the survivor, and it's survivors who have told us about children, what happens to children, the children can't speak for themselves. It's adults who've told us, and out of that comes hopefully better services and better practice, you know, across the board, but it's the survivors who tell us." [Siobhan Canavan]

"Whether they knew it or not, most of the women that I've met over the years, their own experience of rape and sexual assault (I'm saying whether they knew it or not because a lot of women, myself included once they've been in the Rape Crisis Centre sort of renamed quite a number of things that had happened to me when I was growing up and things like that, but you think well yeah, that was an assault you know rather than something that just happened at a bus stop)…I think they've been incredibly powerful." [Jan Macleod]

"I think they bring a bigger level of understanding…because they've been there, they're able to kind of guide it in a way that is inclusive to more women feeling safer. And when you have positive feedback from women – I mean this woman…she just wrote an amazing poem…to me as the main counsellor that she spoke to, about how…she'd got such a lot from it and…she'd found herself again after all these years. And was able to leave her husband and stuff and just really be who she wanted to be because she'd been abused in childhood and then was emotionally abused by her husband. So getting feedback like that…which I obviously fed back into the collective as well…it helps the centre grow…this is where we're actually moving forward, this is how we're growing because this is what worked, you know like doing the person-centred thing…and asking the right questions as well. And giving people the space to say, 'I'm not sure' and just ramble through their thoughts so that you can eventually say actually I think it might be that, but I'm not sure and I'll see you next week and I might know and I might know it then…the whole thing about not judging people. I think is really important." [Heather Forrest]

"I think it's very powerful…I think this whole thing about people having endured an experience…and then putting that experience back is really, really great for women that come after, but also I think it's very, very therapeutic. I was reading in the Guardian yesterday a woman who'd been a prostitute and been on drugs and she's now been clean for a few years and for the last few years she's worked…it's a group of people …who are trying to help women out of prostitution…it must be like Routes Out…a lot of the people asked to see her. And what they got from that was the fact that…she was able to say it took her like years and years and it took lots of different starting points but to keep going and it could happen for them and so the hope that you can exchange and just being very grounded about it. And I think it's the same with Rape Crisis…actually, there's no distinction… in that continuum, people bring different things and I think that to have that is really very strong indeed. " [Helen Mackinnon]

Which is not to say that challenges didn't come up sometimes, particularly when women who were receiving support wanted to join the collective:

"I think probably early on [we] didn't have a lot of boundaries and there was a very strong thing about women who used the service, if they were interested in joining a collective, they could always join straight away cos it was a sort of self help thing as well. And I mean I think that can be very, very, very good but also it can be problematic…you do need some safeguards…or maybe a little bit of distance…we didn't think about things – well if that woman joins the collective…that changes her relationship with us including the woman that's supporting her so is she clear about that…in a way you can't have both – you can't have that same support arrangement and then also be colleagues." [Jan Macleod]

"Women who had used the service and felt that they had got an awful lot out of it, then wanted – some women wanted to be involved…if you like, give something back…we were careful to try and ensure that these women knew what they were taking on and that they were in fact ready to support other women…because it could be hard…" [Isla Laing]

It became clear that it was important both to their personal well-being and to the well-being of the collective, that survivors who wanted to join it had received any support they themselves required in order to be able to deal with their own issues, before becoming collective members:

"We had a couple of women who came into the group…ostensibly to be part of the group and to do the counselling. But actual fact it turned out that they'd come in really because they'd actually been… abused themselves and they really wanted the support. So they'd kind of come in on the wrong side of the coin as it were. And it was difficult working out how to deal with them because we couldn't let them stay part of the group because they were being destructive you know… we could help them but…not when they were part of the group…if they were being counselled by us." [Brenda Flaherty]

"One person approached us when she knew about it and she had actually been someone who had been raped…There was some training event in Dundee…I remember I went along with her…what it made me realise is that our organisation was too young at the time to deal with that kind of input – she was too…close to her experience, whether in time or in total emotion – it was hugely painful…we just hadn't, probably prepared her well enough, or chosen well enough, or got to the right stage to do those kinds of presentations…" [Kathy Litteljohn]

But the progress made by Rape Crisis centres during these early years, and the learning curve experienced by so many of the women who shaped it owed everything to survivors and the way they communicated everything that their experiences had meant to other women in the movement:

"Oh, I wouldn't know anything if it hadn't been for survivors. Without those women, and men, but mainly the women, telling their stories and telling it how it was, we would know nothing, absolutely nothing. They've given us such a huge amount of information… without those, the children that I now see wouldn't be safe, because I can say categorically to the Court 'This child needs to be removed from home because this is what's gonna happen, that's what's gonna happen, this is the long-term consequences', and I have seen many women for whom that is the long-term consequence, and so because of the knowledge that I gained from them then, I am now able to put that back into helping children now. We would know nothing." [Liz Hall]

"We didn't know anything about it. We all got a shock, you know? And without those women actually being brave enough to say 'But it happened to me and this is what he did and that's what he did and this is how I got through', you know, 'That's why I developed learning difficulties because I couldn't concentrate', you know, 'so I was branded as learning difficulties.' " [Liz Hall]

"I would say survivors had a direct voice from the women in the group who were survivors themselves, and also through the work we were doing with the survivors group coming out there. Their voice influenced…what we did, how we publicised things and certainly when we did this work with the nurseries, I think that was very much instigated through, you know, women who were survivors saying, 'We need to try and do something.'" [Elizabeth Shiach]

"It was an incredibly significant…journey, my own knowledge, and particularly in what…I learned… from women who we were seeing…who were approaching the group and meeting with them…that was also a huge learning experience for me." [Sue Hunt]

"It's the people I've worked with who've educated me…I mean, they've been through it – they know what it's like for them and how they've experienced it so…it's what's written by…people who are working very closely with women who've been abused and children who've been abused." [Sue Hunt]

"Being raped can change your views on everything. And you may never be the same person you were and it can be that the change that takes place can open your mind up to a lot of things that maybe you hadn't thought about, about the way women are treated and stuff like that, and providing support maybe for other women…Quite often, you got people who were survivors… who wanted to be involved in the centre…quite a number of the volunteers were women who were survivors of one thing or another. And I think for them, it was either a way of saying thank you or they felt that they could now contribute something and help other women. And they had a particular empathy that women who weren't survivors didn't actually have…that was I think quite useful but…we wouldn't say who was a survivor and who wasn't. Because you were quite often asked on the phone, you know has it happened to you and you didn't say yes or no, you just didn't answer that question because we didn't feel it was…appropriate to answer. Because you can get support from a lot of different people – you don't need to be a survivor to give support." [Sheila Brodie]

In some cases, particularly those involving ritual abuse, survivors took very real risks in seeking out the support they needed:

"So much was at stake for her… And she invested so much in us, by wanting to come up, you know, at great cost to herself. Of course, when she was on the streets…she knew, when she went back, that she was going to be in trouble, and of course, she'd just disappeared. So she took risks, too, to stay in contact with us, and she's a very, very special person." [Sue Hunt]

Child Sexual Abuse

One area where women really were operating, initially at least, almost completely in the dark was in supporting women who were survivors of child sexual abuse. The women who set up the new Rape Crisis services initially expected that most of what they would be dealing with would involve the recent rape of adult women. The reality was often very different:

> "I can remember the very, very first call. I wasn't on the first night – I was on the second night – and I can remember the two women who were…just gobsmacked, because the first caller was a woman who had been abused as a child and of course, you know, we just didn't expect that…I mean, that wasn't on any radar at all. It was totally unexpected…she was the very first call and she was in contact with the centre for many years in different ways." [Siobhan Canavan]

> "Within the first week we had a woman…who rang us and said she'd been sexually abused as a child and we went 'Aargh! What do we do?' So we had to have another training thing about sexual abuse and I didn't know any more than anybody else. I just went and read some books and started the work that I still do, really, on sexual abuse, and everybody was horrified, and within the first six months, a third of our calls were from women who'd been sexually… abused as a child." [Liz Hall]

> "Our emphasis at the beginning was very much on rape and women coming to us having just been raped. And that's how we imagined it would be and those would be the bulk of our calls but, of course, they weren't… It was all about sexual abuse…
>
> My very first call was from a child who was at home and said her father was abusing her and she was on the phone for about an hour. But I didn't really feel I'd done very much for her cos I couldn't get her to involve someone in the situation. And I felt so helpless cos she didn't want to say who she was or where she was… I felt to some extent …talking through what had happened had perhaps helped, and I did certainly introduce her to the idea of trying to involve an adult in the situation. But she said she would phone the next week but she never did, so I suppose that was a bit, it made you feel a bit that you hadn't succeeded." [Maureen Porter]

> "It definitely wasn't what we were expecting…I remember going on some Reclaim The Night march… 'Whatever we wear, wherever we go, yes means yes and no means no'…there was the kind of feeling that…most feminists were fairly young and it was a kind of freedom for us to do what we want kind of thing and you didn't think you were going to be finding out about little kids…being terrorised or years…and suffering in adulthood – didn't expect it." [Morna Findlay]

> "I think what we were surprised about as a group was…from the very beginning …the proportion of calls that were in relation to incest…we'd discussed the issue prior to opening the centre, but I think that we had expected the majority of the calls to be from women who had been raped by strangers, but a substantial proportion were from incest survivors….and of course, that meant that…an awful lot of the calls were relating to things that had happened many many years ago, and in a lot of cases as is common, women had never ever spoken about it to anybody." [Isla Laing]

For the first time ever, women in Scotland who had been raped and abused as children felt able to begin to talk about what had happened, to be supported in dealing with the hugely complex issues raised by these experiences, to know that they were not alone, and above all, to be believed:

> "Women who were much much older by this time and hadn't spoken to anyone over all the years." [Moira Kane]

"I think sometimes women came forward…and they had been maybe carrying that secret for decades…where they'd had been as children or as, as young adults and it was maybe the first time, there was this feeling that you could actually speak and [be] believed. Even if it didn't go any further…I really believe that if you create the right sort of safe environment, the truth will come out." [Florence Germain]

"It was really…that early Rape Crisis movement that brought the childhood sexual abuse to the fore. Very much so. And forced people into accepting it just by the sheer numbers of women coming forward and saying 'This is what's happened to me.'" [Brenda Flaherty]

"A lot of women that phoned also were phoning not about a recent rape, but about maybe being abused as a child, and never having spoken to anybody about it and then finding out that yes it was ok to phone Rape Crisis and talk about that, that it wasn't just for women that had been raped like there and then." [Sheila Brodie]

The role played by Rape Crisis workers in these early days, when child sexual abuse was thought of as a rare occurrence, was crucial – not only in the support they offered to women, but also in raising public awareness of the issue, and the reality that there was every likelihood that it was happening within their own communities:

"People stopped saying 'Oh sexual abuse is something that happens in the working classes or in the Outer Hebrides' and began to understand well actually policemen did it, and lawyers did it and judges did it. It happened everywhere. So that was a change." [Aileen Christianson]

And child sexual abuse continues to be central to much of the work undertaken by all Rape Crisis centres:

"Still to this day, our child sexual abuse always outnumbers, quite significantly sometimes, rape." [Norma Benzie]

The publication of Sarah Nelson's book "Incest: Fact and Myth" (published by Stramullion) in 1982 made explicit the realities of child sexual abuse in Britain, many of which were already widely known – but never acted upon. In an article in The Glasgow Herald, she said:

"While researching this subject, I have heard from professional and lay people – often in confidence and always 'on the highest authority' – that incest is rife in the following areas: County Antrim, rural Aberdeenshire, the Outer Hebrides, a problem area of Portsmouth, an East Lothian mining village, Dublin, the Fens, Greenock, two different Edinburgh housing estates, several districts of Glasgow and parts of Wales.

The message is clear: incest is rife everywhere. It is supposed to be taboo. Yet as soon as you start asking about it, the wall of silence is broken by a flood of information. The moment you mention the subject to doctors, social workers, teachers or residential care staff the stories come pouring out…Only the other day a trendy young doctor remarked to me that when he worked as a GP in a rural area he encountered the problem on many occasions. When I asked him what he did about it, he replied with some surprise: 'Nothing, – it's a way of life.'" [*Time to remove taboos around incest* – The Glasgow Herald, April 28th, 1982]

Rape Crisis workers in the '70's and early '80's faced a very steep learning curve in order to learn more about child sexual abuse and how best to equip themselves to give women the support they needed:

"We were expecting women who'd been raped once, who needed help going to the police, who needed support in telling their story, cos that was what you did then, who needed whatever they needed at those times when we were on call. We didn't expect someone who'd been abused from day one, through their childhood till they're 18, perhaps being abused, perhaps never being raped but being molested in different ways, who were completely messed up, and some of whom were very strong women…and whose personality structure, everything, their ways of coping with things were quite beyond anything that anybody had ever seen. " [Liz Hall]

"Some of them… now I know…had what's called dissociative identity disorder, multiple personality disorder as it was, had the most extreme problems, you know? Should have been in psychiatric units. Some of them were, in and out…the woman who first spoke to us, became a client of mine, and she could sit and cry and not knowing that she was crying. She didn't know that… her shirt would get wet and she wouldn't even know. She was so switched off. She did some writing for us in the front of our book." [Liz Hall]

With a background as a mental health practitioner in the health service, Helen Mackinnon was shocked at the sudden realisation that the extent of the child sexual abuse revealed through her work with Rape Crisis was something that had been overlooked entirely – and denied by the health service for which she had worked for so long:

"We called it incestuous abuse at the time and then it was sexual abuse of girls… At that time there was still a lot of folk in denial, a lot of the health service in denial and that was one of the things that was very difficult for me thinking back, thinking gosh all these people that I've met in the Royal Edinburgh… by that time I had moved out…I had moved into education. The way nursing's set up…once you move into education…at that time you sort of almost left clinical contact. So in a sense, my Rape Crisis work was my face to face and immediate contact…which was great for me to have that because it did keep me very grounded. And I thought there was a dichotomy because I quite quickly realised there was a lot of women in the 70s that I had been looking after who had anorexia nervosa, young women and [with]… the breaking understanding about incestuous abuse I realised, I thought…I bet you half of these women had suffered sexual abuse as girls. And the women that we'd known had been depressed, there had been one or two in the Royal Edinburgh like that they'd disclosed…at case conferences, they've been sexually abused. And at that time there was still…the ends of Freudian theory, which was that maybe women were making it up for hysterical purposes… I don't think I ever subscribed to that because you would think well why? But, nevertheless, I think it was this whole business about people at that time didn't appreciate the scale…But then…beginning to meet women that it had happened to more and more, women I thought my God, this has been missed." [Helen Mackinnon]

Dorothy Degenhardt's work with the Rape Crisis centre in Dundee also offered a similar hindsight into what earlier work she had undertaken had probably signified:

"And then the surprise was that…it was rare for someone to phone up saying they'd been raped that week, which was what we were expecting…It was more that it was un-tapping sexual abuse from the past…And the majority of the referrals were from people's abuse from earlier…cause this was all at the point when all that was opening up …because I remember when I worked in social work in the '70's and I worked in the Royal Edinburgh Hospital…I mean I just think back with horror now…I realise of course about 60% of the women who come in have been probably been sexually abused, but at that point we didn't even have that lingo, it was called incest… And that was seen to be very rare. And when I look back about how the misdiagnoses by psychiatrists and certainly by ourselves as social workers…I did a lot of sort of like crisis intervention stuff out in the community. …And we just …didn't have the words, we didn't have the information or the knowledge or the words to talk about it. So it was a real eye-opener being involved with Rape Crisis and realising that so many people have been abused as children, and were talking about it for the first time. So the people that were phoning up, yes it was very much the first time …it might have been 10, 20 years ago." [Dorothy Degenhardt]

In Aberdeen too, Sue Hunt's professional life benefited from her work at the Rape Crisis centre and the awareness of child sexual abuse that she gained there:

"What I was able to take back into my work at the children's hospital was my growing awareness of the problem because at times, we did have children coming through child and family psychiatry, you know, who had sexual abuse histories. So, you know, in some ways, I was fortunate… I was able to keep it on the agenda." [Sue Hunt]

Efforts to gain support on this issue from other agencies in Aberdeen did not always meet with a positive response:

"When it came to the sexual abuse issue, I think something like a third of our calls in the first year were from women who'd been abused. And so what we did then was we set about asking agencies about this issue and about could people help us, could they support us, could they train us and we got really interesting and shocking replies. One was… 'That doesn't happen round here.' Or 'We're dealing with it – keep out.'… We got in touch with Social Work, with Education, with the Police, who were actually much more open. It was ironic, that was the last thing we expected. Psychology…doctors, actually the Fiscal's Office, mental health agencies…it was just like an organisational denial." [Siobhan Canavan]

Liz Hall and Siobhan Canavan wrote up what they had discovered as pioneers in working with women who had survived abuse in childhood. Liz describes with vivid clarity the moment the idea for the project came to them :

"Siobhan and I had been for a swim. Siobhan was extremely pregnant and wearing her Mothercare polka-dot swimming costume…and we were sitting in their kitchen…and we were chatting about some of the women we knew through Rape Crisis, and her husband came in and said 'I am sick of you two talking about this. Write it all down and then I'll never have to hear it again.' And Siobhan went… you know, 'I've got three weeks to go' and I had two small children by then and I was working full-time…and we kinda looked at each other and she said 'Well, have we got enough to say?' and on that afternoon…we covered sheets and sheets and sheets of paper with chapters and ideas that we'd put in this book, and then Siobhan went off and had her son." [Liz Hall]

Liz approached a woman who came to talk to the collective about working with abuse survivors:

"I approached her afterwards and said 'Do you know anybody who's wanting to publish a book? Cos we might have an idea for one', and she said 'Yeah.' And she got hold of this woman who was called Christine, at Taylor & Francis, and so I wrote to her and she wrote back and said 'Can we have some chapter headings?' and Siobhan and I went 'Aargh!' [laughs], so we did some chapter headings and we sent them off and she said 'Right, OK. Can I see a sample chapter?' and we went 'Aargh!' again [laughs], and I wrote the first bit and Siobhan looked at it, and I remember panicking after I'd given it to her cos I didn't know what she was gonna say, and we sort of took out each other's jargon and we sent this first chapter on the long-term effects, which I'd kind of got written for something I was doing at work, and I remember sending it to her on a Wednesday night and coming back into the office, and we worked in two little cottages on the park at that point, and the secretary handed me this letter at sort of five o'clock cos I'd only just come back in from doing something all day, and there was the acceptance from the publisher, within less than a week. So we then set to and started writing it, and I think we finished it about a year later and it was published in '89 and sold out within three months." [Liz Hall]

After the book came out, Siobhan and Liz travelled extensively, delivering five- and six-day training training on the subject to a huge variety of different groups and individuals:

> "Anybody. Volunteers, police, professionals, social workers. You name it, we did it for them… We did in-house training, locally, and that was when we had all these different professionals, and…we'd do a day on myths, we'd do a thing about what it is. In the front of our book…we said we had to write down what it was, and so we had just page after page after page of what an abuser can do to a child in detail, in just one-liners. And we used to get people to read it out in our training. Take it in turns round small groups… people had very different reactions. They were preparing themselves to read… they thought 'Well, it's my turn three down, so I'll get… won't get those three, but I'll get that one. Oh God, I've got that one to read! Oh no!' and people would be switching off and people would have all the sort of reactions, so it was incredibly powerful and we'd have a group of 18 students and there'd be three of us and we'd have six each, and we'd go round the group until this list was finished. You didn't have to read anything, but it was pages. Pages and pages and pages and pages. So…that was all about what it is and how you feel about it. Then there were sort of certain therapeutic things that you'd always have to do – boundary setting, there'd always be something about guilt and anger and loss, there'd be something about family of origin, the statistics of it all. So it'd be a fairly intensive five days, five or six days." [Liz Hall]

The discovery, among many other things, that perpetrators were usually very far from the monsters of their imaginations shocked many:

> "I just routinely say, well, of course, 80 percent of abused children are abused by people they know, and even now people go 'What?', you know? It's logical, isn't it? I mean, they're the people that children are around. I mean, my granddaughter gets up in the morning, sees her mum and dad and goes to school, sees her teacher and maybe some of the parents in the playground after school and goes home with her mum and dad. She doesn't see anybody else. Sometimes goes to the doctor or sometimes comes to see me or her other grandparents, and those are the people she knows." [Liz Hall]

Liz Hall was later involved, from 1990, in setting up the Grampian Survivor's Project, a multi-agency initiative, looking at resources for women survivors in the Grampian area.

In order to meet a growing need among service users, Highland Rape Crisis, like several of the other centres set up an Incest Survivors Group, which met at IVOG, Inverness Voluntary Organisation's building, which was run, owned and taken over eventually by the blind school in Inverness, and then ceased to be available to the group, who had to move elsewhere:

> "The Incest Survivors' Group was really hard. It was hard work, it was hard going. These were… women who had been…very badly traumatised by their experience, I think very badly…that was tough, and… we had more of those than we had rape calls. A lot more." [Gale Chrisman]

Incest survivors' groups were established in many of the centres, and were often quite distinct from the other services they offered:

> "It kind of developed as an offshoot and…it was definitely separate…the need…was obviously becoming apparent in terms of phone calls and stuff and women were raising the issue of child sexual abuse… But it was a wee bit like a wee secret kind of thing happening, do you know it was almost like a lack of connection really between… I think partly because child sexual abuse…even in the 80s I suppose it was kind of like a new issue really that was…becoming broached and coming out of that kind of taboo, we don't really want to talk about that because that's about family. It was easier to talk about rape and

sexual assault in terms of *a man* who is outwith your kind of family relationship who has abused you."
[Margaret McCutcheon]

"In 1980 I think it was the first Incest Survivors' campaign was set up by a group of women in London. And it was certainly something that we'd been aware of before that because by 1980, there was at least a couple of women who'd joined the centre because they'd been abused through incest. So through them, they were very aware of it and ...Rape Crisis certainly had leaflets on incest quite early on... naming it as a form of rape...So in 1980 when the incest survivors' campaign started, we were in touch with them quite a lot." [Jan Macleod]

"Those women who wanted...a service or wanted a self help group around it, wanted to really focus in on that as a really major issue for them in their lives. And there was something there about it being childhood issues that required a, I don't know, a separate kind of way of separating it off from your experiences as an adult woman. It was almost like you needed to deal with that first before you could deal with other things." [Margaret McCutcheon]

"When we first opened, the majority of our calls were from woman, adult women who had been abused as children, and so, I think it was about '82, we set up the Incest Survivors' Group, and that sort of became separate but was kinda linked in, obviously. And then, Esther Rantzen, when she took that up and set up Childline...that's what people think of as bringing that to people's attention. She did that on the basis of what Rape Crisis Centres all over Britain had been doing, and I think we were all the same – we all got a lot of calls, not somebody who'd been raped yesterday, but somebody who was raped twenty years ago by her father or her brother or her uncle..." [Aileen Christianson]

The Edinburgh Incest Survivor's Group led to the development of the Incest Survivors' phone line, which offered support to individual women. In Glasgow, a similar development had already taken place and led to Action Against Incest:

"It kind of emerged from Rape Crisis...my recollection of it...was that Frances Monaghan and a few other women had joined Rape Crisis and kind of realised earlier on...before kind of coming into the group that there was a need for a separate group and so Frances' interest in supporting people, women who had been abused as children really kind of grew out of coming along and doing the Rape Crisis training and then fairly quickly separating off....and that kind of brought in some volunteers as well for both organisations...some of the women who came along to the group then became volunteers. Some for Rape Crisis some for Action Against Incest. That was the one in Elmbank Street. But the links were just so close." [Heather Forrest]

Some of these groups were open, while others were closed:

"They tried different things...I think there was a closed group that ran in the place down in Hope Street, sort of up above a Chinese or Indian restaurant, something that went on fire one time we had to come down, out on a Sunday morning...And then I think the group in Elmbank Street was an open one. And I think everyone had their preference about what was best...in terms of...safety and security and how people felt about trust, letting new people coming in. I know that what I felt personally was that it was important to build up trust, so that people would really feel safe." [Heather Forrest]

The need for extreme sensitivity and an awareness of the best ways to offer support were very much what underpinned the way these groups operated:

"There was an incident once...I was in the other room, and the group was meeting, and someone had said something that really upset somebody. And the woman ended up ...running out of the room and locking herself in the toilets and being really upset. So I think people learned from that in terms of...

just the way to support people better so that people are… given more ground rules…so that…if you're talking about things you have to make it really clear that this is your own stuff, so instead of …saying something like you know I should have known…and saying things that would upset people…it puts people under pressure to kind of think, you know well because I kept on taking sweets or, …taking a new bike and getting a new Space Hopper and whatever…if someone says… I enjoyed that…that can upset people." [Heather Forrest]

Helen Mackinnon, Heather Low and Caroline Armit initiated the first incest survivors' group in Glasgow:

"We had to put our heads together. Caroline was in Social Work…I knew what it was like to have a therapy group and Heather was just coming fresh in a very grounded way…I think we just felt our way…people just took turns…the women were talking about what their issues were. And we tried to make it as supportive as possible. And to talk about their experience and to disclose with each other what that experience had been. And to try to then together be as helpful as possible about what they could do and refer them on.

There was successor groups to that…I remember the first one I think that was done through the Women's Support Project had an education focus…for women that had been sexually abused as girls…By that I don't mean anything didactic …just much more what you need to know, what are the facts and who you need to go to and what the issues are and if you feel like this, there's every good reason why and this is why, so it's very informal…it was done on…you know the power of information…

I think we were careful…I can't remember if it was six times or ten times or over a year we met…it wasn't…let's all sit for hours and hours exorcising somebody from…it wasn't like that…it was geared to women talking about what their issues were and trying to foster bonds between them…I think there was three of us and there was about four or five of them. And I think it was a closed group…we didn't have new additions…we started together and finished together… I think Heather went on to do another one." [Helen Mackinnon]

In a feature on incest that centred on the publication of two new books on the subject (Sarah Nelson's "Incest: Fact and Myth", and Jean Renvoize's "Incest: a Family Pattern"), the Glasgow Herald noted that the:

"Glasgow Incest Survivors Group can be contacted through the Strathclyde Rape Crisis Group, P.O. Box 53, Glasgow G2 17R or ring 041 221 8448, Mon, Wed, and Thurs between 7 p.m.-10 p.m." [The Glasgow Herald, April 28th, 1982]

Action Against Incest

"More and more, it became apparent, when people were phoning up, and phoning about instances of childhood sexual abuse, so people within the collective…decided to set up an incest survivors group, and I think it was probably the first of it's kind, actually. …So they set up an entirely separate collective, really, and to be honest, I don't know much about it because…It was a closed group." [Rona Clarke]

Action Against Incest emerged in the early 1980's in Glasgow from a group of women survivors who had been meeting to talk about the issues and their analysis of these:

"The Violence Against Women's movement certainly hadn't started talking about abuse of children and sexual abuse of children within their own families, or from people, from trusted adults or people that they knew. So we kind of got together, I have to say, on several boozy nights with lots of wine and lots of avoidance tactics, but eventually, talking about how we felt about these issues. And there was a woman there who was from Rape Crisis Centre, and she was saying that they'd noticed that there was more women contacting them and talking about their experiences of childhood sexual abuse." [Frances Monaghan]

There were initially seven women in the group, and they were quickly joined by several others. Conditions attached to funding arrangements for Strathclyde Rape Crisis meant that working with very young women who were experiencing sexual abuse posed real difficulties:

"Although it wasn't as restricted as it is now, in terms of what you're supposed to do and not do, they were very, very clear that it had to be adults, so they couldn't be dealing with any young women who were phoning, and women who were talking about their own experience of childhood sexual abuse, there was the whole issue that came up about, well what happens if the people who abused them still have contact with children?" [Frances Monaghan]

Getting Action Against Incest off the ground in Glasgow was a major challenge, at a time when agencies and individuals were only just beginning to confront the reality and scale of child sexual abuse:

"Twenty-five years ago, raising the issue of child sexual abuse was just not done. The feminist movement was just beginning to do it. Social Work Department certainly weren't dealing with it. Police, housing, health, nobody was dealing with that. They just weren't talking about it." [Frances Monaghan]

With the support of the Rape Crisis Centre however, the group were able to get underway, and start the support work:

"We tried to get some bits and pieces of funding, but we couldn't get it. But luckily, Rape Crisis…allowed us to use their telephone line room to have our meetings and run our own phone line from, so we got a new number set up and Rape Crisis Centre contributed towards that. They gave us some money… Action Against Incest probably wouldn't have been able to get set up and get the money and make the contacts with people that we made contact with if Rape Crisis Centre hadn't been involved in that level of support…I think we would have done it eventually, but we used the contacts that Rape Crisis had at that point. We used the women who had quite a lot of experience already, in funding applications and funding survivors lines." [Frances Monaghan]

With the assistance of Ruth Payne, a senior social worker who was involved with the Women's Counselling and Resource Service (which is now Breakthrough), Action Against Incest secured some council funding.

"It almost felt as if we were opening that door for a lot of people to come forward and start talking about it, but there was absolutely no resources and there was nobody there for support. So you almost kind of felt, oh God, what have we done? We've given women this hope and, you know, they can't get through to us, because we've no got any funding and we can only run the phone line three nights a week." [Frances Monaghan]

However, with support from Rape Crisis, AAI made swift progress:

"We relied very heavily on Rape Crisis Centre to say, oh, you know, that might not be a good idea, or what about actually doing training sessions? And so we joined up with them quite a lot when they were doing training, so that we could get access to their training, so that worked really, really well. I think a lot of us were just very raw and very passionate, but quite naïve in that we didn't really understand the impact that this was going to have." [Frances Monaghan]

The full extent of that impact quickly became clear:

"When it did start impacting on people like Social Work department and health services… individual women started picking up on that within these agencies, we started to get absolutely inundated with requests for information, for training, for support." [Frances Monaghan]

Action Against Incest became heavily involved in a number of multi-agency services that were set up:

"It was possibly the first multi-agency forum that was set up in Drumchapel. So we were there representing the voluntary sector, and we were there representing Action Against Incest, and we were there representing survivors, and at that point you thought you could represent survivors, which, of course, is extremely naïve because all survivors are different, you know? … But that was really quite innovative work, and all of a sudden, you started seeing the issue become much more public, in the same way that rape was becoming much more public in terms of naming it, identifying it, talking about the causes, talking about who does it, you know? Talking about patriarchy. Yeah, the whole bit. All of that was all happening at the same time, and it felt very, very powerful, but it also felt very, very scary." [Frances Monaghan]

One of the main obstacles AAI had to overcome were the prevalent myths they were confronted with in their dealings with workers in other agencies:

"Children can be very, very sexual, according to some of the agencies…children can be very provocative… there was very much an issue about how wee girls were dressing and how they were acting…In all honesty, when I was involved in the Drumchapel Forum, I have to say, most of the bad attitudes were coming from the police… some of the attitudes from the police were hideous, you know? Basically, they were taking all the bad attitudes they had about the rape and sexual assault of women…and assigning it to children…And female children, girls, you know?…And the issue came up about boys being abused and it was men, therefore the men must be gay, therefore it'll make the boys gay, you know? And we were kind of going, 'That's a lot of rubbish' but we weren't quite as polished in our arguments and our theories about it, so those times, although they were very, very good and very challenging and, they were also very difficult." [Frances Monaghan]

But there were allies too:

"The social workers, who were involved in Drumchapel…were possibly the main service where, you know, a flag would go up if there was any sort of child sexual abuse going on…the women who were involved in that were fantastic. A woman called Ouaine Bain, a woman called Maureen Sanders…Margaret Drummond, who's a doctor, paediatrician, a guy called John King, who was the senior social worker, a guy called Greg Gallagher who was also a senior social worker, and then there was the basic grade social workers who were involved in that. Every single one of them seemed to have a fantastic attitude, and I think that was pretty liberating, because I know that that was not the case in other multi-agency forums across the city." [Frances Monaghan]

As they progressed, Action Against Incest saw their activities mirrored in initiatives happening elsewhere in Scotland:

"We found that there was kind of satellite Action Against Incest being set up all over the place, in different parts of the country, which was great. There was Falkirk, there was Edinburgh, there was

Dundee...there was Aberdeen. I remember going to Aberdeen and I remember going to Inverness for meetings... So we ended up having a Scottish Action Against Incest group, which was really based in the Falkirk area, and Kate Arnot, and a woman called Josie were involved in setting that up." [Frances Monaghan]

The monumental effort and sacrifices required in order to sustain the service they had developed took its toll on the women running Action Against Incest and was typical of the commitment (and price paid) for these desperately-needed – but desperately under-resourced services:

"The women in Action Against Incest got burnt out very quickly...very quickly. We were all doing this work on top of our own jobs and dealing with our own issues... women slogging away for years and years and years, on no money, and using their own phones and paying bus fares and cycling...we would all kind of contribute out our own pockets...

And that's changed because, at the same time all this is happening, women are going 'We actually can't do this anymore. We need to get some sort of funding.'...When we were really burnt out, we focused on fundraising or we focused on lobbying councillors and lobbying MPs and we had Strathclyde Regional Council at that point, as well as Glasgow City Council, so lobbying the different council departments. So that's the sort of thing that, I think, when we got really tired and burnt out, we kind of went, 'Well I can't do direct support work...But I'll do that'. And never really stopped to say, 'Well we're exhausted and burnt out because we can't cope with the demand.'

So unfortunately, that kind of led towards some women having to back out of the whole process. But also, at that point, it was recognised that Rape Crisis Centre could now start to say, 'We are providing services for women who have been raped and sexually assaulted, whether that's childhood sexual abuse, or whether that's...an adult.' And they started to widen their definition, so it meant that, when we sat and met with them and says 'Look, we think we need to call it a day'...I think Action Against Incest probably lasted about six years... But, by that time, we felt as if we'd made a lot of foundations, and an impact on other services. So I think, when Rape Crisis did that, we just kind of heaved a sigh of relief and went 'That's good. We're not leaving women with nothing, you know? They can now contact Rape Crisis.'" [Frances Monaghan]

Efforts within the Highland Rape Crisis Centre in Inverness to undertake preventative work relating to childhood sexual abuse took off in a big way and resulted in the centre's first ever paid worker:

Safe, Strong and Free

"I got impatient a bit with always picking up pieces afterwards, particularly since we got more abuse calls than rape calls, and that we should go into helping young people, children protect themselves, and we moved into what's called up here the Safe, Strong, Free Project...Oh, that was fantastic. I thought that was such a success [laughs]. Well, I just learned that in America they were doing training for children, to protect them, to give them techniques to protect themselves against abuse, and that wasn't just sexual, it was also bullying, and it wasn't just strangers coming up to you in the school yard, it was also about your parents or family members, not necessarily parents. So it was a three-part, three-stage programme that had been developed remarkably impressively in the States, and I got hold of ... this big fat guide on how to do it, you know, everything to do, from scripts for dealing with very young children to letters you write to their parents, to how you approach nursery schools and kindergartens. So that was... enormous help from what had gone before, and we ...agreed that we needed a full-time paid worker. This could not run as a volunteer. So...we got funding for that... Enough funding to pay... I remember the amount was £17,000 – to pay a full-time person, and we interviewed people. This was us moving into a kind of different level altogether of working. We weren't a volunteer group any more – we were people who were, you know, employers of a worker." [Gale Chrisman]

"You need children to be informed, cos an informed child is a much safer child." [Liz Hall]

Just as women who survive rape and sexual have little prospect of obtaining justice for their ordeals, the likelihood of successful prosecutions being brought for cases of childhood sexual abuse were and remain very slender:

> "You think about the hoops that the child has gone through to get somebody into prison, you know? She's told somebody, they've believed her, they've helped her to go to a professional agency who have believed her, there's been enough corroborating evidence, …the…Procurator Fiscal in Scotland put it to court, the court have believed her… the barristers…whatever they've done …have represented her right. And then the jury convicts and…then, maybe, the judge sends him to prison, and most sexual offenders…are still out there, not even having gone to stage one of that, you know?" [Liz Hall]

> "I still think that it's assumed children aren't credible because they're young or they're suggestible or they're vulnerable. The single biggest problem if I might look at it in a kind of forensic way…the early stages of an investigation is [when] a great deal of potential evidence is lost because the police and social workers, where they're involved in the investigations, especially the children, they don't follow up what they don't see…as relevant evidence. And in that way, it's lost because people's memories get lost, potential witnesses get lost, forensic evidence gets washed away, whatever it might be." [Fiona Raitt]

Ritual abuse

In addition to childhood sexual abuse, centres encountered women who had experienced ritual abuse:

"Coincidentally, quite quickly one after the other we ended up with two women who'd both been ritually abused. And that was very difficult." [Brenda Flaherty]

"Ritual abuse was horrible, but it was beyond Rape Crisis. It wasn't what I did in Rape Crisis at all. I think the first woman I met who was ritually abused was '87. That was awful, just terrible." [Liz Hall]

Where work on CSA had been uncertain but progressing tentatively with confidence as workers learned more, there was a serious risk with ritual abuse survivors of doing more harm than good:

"At that time, the fashion, from Esther Rantzen, really, was if you just tell your story, you'll be fine, but of course what we know now is that …although people need to tell bits of their story…telling it in a oner makes people completely off the wall sometimes, especially with ritual abuse." [Liz Hall]

This was an area about which very little was known:

"I think there was very little awareness… I mean, you don't start off by saying 'I'm going to work in…' so it emerges in the course of your other work. Whether you choose to then go into that further, in whatever area you're working in…whether you're psychology or social work or whatever, and stay with it, or whether you refer on to another agency, I don't know. But certainly…I can't remember…for a long time now, hearing anything on the news or in the paper relating to… Satanic ritual abuse. Now it hasn't stopped, so at some level…I would think it's a combination of lack of knowledge and denial. Just not wanting to see it." [Sue Hunt]

And scepticism around ritual abuse was widespread:

"The False Memory Society had clamped down and everybody was saying 'Oh no, this doesn't happen, that doesn't happen' and I used to say 'And how it is that I have four clients?' – 'Oh, well, you must have influenced them.' No. How would I possibly dream up the most obscure, revolting…you know, what do you think I am, really? But I got blamed, really." [Liz Hall]

"We knew of people in high places who'd been involved in all sorts of things, literally from the highest to the lowest in the land, and locally we knew of people, we could name people. That was horrible. That was the worst bit about ritual abuse, was finding out the names of people…when people consistently mention the same names who have got no connection with each other…It's really difficult." [Liz Hall]

"When I left Aberdeen and moved to Tayside for work, I moved to a specialist post in sexual abuse, and that was the time of Orkney, Ayrshire, Cleveland…for a few years there'd been a kind of burgeoning of services for children and women, and then you had this complete shutdown and the backlash, and I think that also happened with Satanic abuse. Satanic abuse, in a sense, I think was just too much for people. It was so unbelievable that people's credibility was stretched to such a limit, and it was so awful that people had to go into denial and my sense is that's still around." [Sue Hunt]

"I don't think it's moved on at all…in fact I think it's worse because of things like Orkney and Nottingham…I mean it was starting to come out from under the carpet and now it's gone right back under…You know when you mention it, oh people think about it they just think it's people in cloaks doing dances round a fire you know and it's just a subject for derision and laughter. And it's just, just terrible really." [Brenda Flaherty]

"When I was involved in Rape Crisis, that's when the Orkney thing kicked off and the… Cleveland kicked off so there was a lot of sort of anti sort of feminist organisation feeling around …and I think…that's really coming back now because lots of people are coming out and saying you know it wasn't true, you know I wasn't actually abused…So I think there was a mix and I still think people don't want to believe it and they don't want to acknowledge that it happens." [Heather Forrest]

But faced with the reality that the support work forced them to confront, the scale and nature of this type of abuse was of another dimension altogether:

"She talked about standing on the floor, and I said to her 'Were there points on the floor?' And she said 'Yes.' And I said 'What kind of shape?' And she said 'A kind of star shape' which must have been a pentagram and it just clicked for me…she'd been born into a Satanic abusive family and been abused from the day she was born, abused siblings and…been involved in killings…they still knew where she was, and still pulling her back into it." [Sue Hunt]

Even within the Rape Crisis centres, there tended to be workers who felt able to work with RA survivors, and those who felt they could not:

"Liz Hall and I worked together. We worked jointly with a woman, and Brenda and I worked jointly with another woman. So I suppose, what emerged were those of us who either picked up the cases or felt able to, or more likely, just didn't know what we were getting ourselves into, because that would have been true for me. I had no idea, when I started, you know with the first woman, exactly what, and Liz was the same…we spent a lot of time…meeting and just trying to make sense of what was going on and researching…So we didn't really have any outside help, though Liz…have made other contacts with other people working in the area, but…I didn't." [Sue Hunt]

"It ended up being quite disruptive in the group…because not everybody was willing you know kind of able to take on the fact that it was happening. And there was a bit of a split I think in the group about women that were willing to accept that it happened and other women that thought no there must be… something else going on here and these are very disturbed women, but…you know this can't be true what they're saying…not scepticism… I think it was more they were scared. Scared to admit that that sort of thing would go on." [Brenda Flaherty]

The nature and extent of the support to which Sue, Liz, Brenda and other workers supporting two RA survivors committed themselves did in many ways set them apart from the rest of the collective, and communication on these matters with the rest of the collective was limited:

"It was very, very time consuming with both of those women, and one who was…thirteen …I've always felt with her, she chose the Rape Crisis group that was furthest away from where she lived to make it safe for herself, but as we built up a relationship, and she began to trust us, it developed into her coming and staying with us, and she had our home telephone numbers…because we got to the point where these two women were taking so much time off the line, that we had to address it…of course, once we did that, I suppose we were seen as kind of holding it separately." [Sue Hunt]

These workers were charting completely unknown territory, and the question of boundaries was not explored or discussed in the early days of their work with the women they supported:

"I have no recollection of that… I think we were just all learning on our feet… We just responded to what we felt was best, but we were very much learning as we went along… they were both multiple personalities, and…so often, we didn't get what we thought was the core personality, and we had to work out ways…to actually bring her back… she had an adult son…we never quite worked out how he fitted into it or, but we found, if we produced that photo, we could bring her back… I remember, at one point, we had to trawl the pubs down in the dockland area, where the prostitutes were, 'cause she would prostitute herself. I think she, and I think, gradually, we realised that, in some ways, she was quite unsafe. Unsafe in that she couldn't keep herself safe…whereas with the other one, I had no hesitation in giving her my address and my telephone number when I moved and left Aberdeen… those two women… were very, very significant for me during that time." [Sue Hunt]

"If I was presented with the situation now, I would think very carefully…my boundaries would probably be very different…it's always a dilemma…there were constant…crises and really horrific things going on that, confining them to sort of, you know, two hours, when the telephone line is open…wasn't going to work…we had to find another way of doing it." [Sue Hunt]

Sometimes unexpected details could make a big difference in terms of who was offering support:

"I know why Brenda and I continued with her – one very practical reason is that we both had English accents… and she was finding it difficult to understand, you know, the Scottish accents, the Aberdonian accents." [Sue Hunt]

Feminism

The roots from which Rape Crisis centres in Scotland grew were clearly, unequivocally, feminist. The backgrounds of the women who volunteered and shaped the development of the Rape Crisis movement were very diverse and their individual identities as feminists emerged from very different places, but when in came to the position of women in society and patriarchal oppression, they shared the same frustrations then (as now) and were able to identify sexual violence very clearly as a consequence of that:

> "The position of women is pretty appalling in so many, many countries and because on the whole…power is held by men…men will see the world in a particular kind of way, but the problem is I mean they want to impose that as being *the* way, and it's just one way of looking at things or indeed doing things…and it's wanting to hold on to that power by any means." [Florence Germain]

> "I suppose it's quite a difficult thing to …unravel really…I suppose there are roots of it in my family, cos my Granny always used to say if you've got a man you've got a master, you know? (laughs) That was always her saying…so there was a bit of that around in the family…some fairly strong women there… I ended up sharing a house with two women who were really active feminists, and it was round the time of Greenham, and all that kind of stuff, so they were a great inspiration and through student politics kinda got involved a bit with that …there were some just really active feminists around with interesting things to say…" [Linda Reid]

> "We certainly came from the view that rape and sexual abuse against women and children, was caused by the fact we live in a patriarchal society, so in that sense we would have called ourselves feminist – it was a feminist analysis… but whether everyone would've said they were a feminist…I'm not sure about." [Kate Arnot]

> "Everybody there was a feminist and was ok with saying 'I'm a feminist'…none of this nonsense, 'I'm not a feminist but…' – we were all feminists…Except we would tend…to say 'I'm a member of the Women's Movement' and occasionally we might say 'Women's Liberation Movement' but it took so bloody long!" [Aileen Christianson]

Which is not to say that identifying yourself as a feminist was an easy option:

> "I think that there's this myth that perhaps in the eighties it was kinda OK to be a feminist. It's never been OK to be a feminist, ever, and it has grown, I think…if we come up to this particular present moment in time, I think it is still very difficult to be a feminist and there's a lot of resistance…women who will say to me 'Yes, you know, but I'm not a feminist', and when you actually start to break that down, the media, et cetera, have done a very, very good job." [Margaret Brown]

> "I'd not put a name to it. I hadn't, I listened a lot to the company I was in, you know? Dundee working class men. 'Are you one o' they feminists, then, eh?' and it was used as an insult, and it was actually really good in Rape Crisis to begin to realise that yes, I am a feminist and I'm proud of that, and I'm wanting to stand up for equality, and to be able to reach that and give it a name was good, and to feel part of, you know, the Rape Crisis movement was absolutely fantastic, you know? And I certainly appreciate being able to have been part of it, you know, including the bad bits." [Laurie Matthew]

Jane Dorby's background in the Labour Party gave her some interesting and surprising insights into the way perceptions of feminism varied between different generations of women:

> "We really did get a lot of reaction from women in the Labour Party who were not feminist…they said, they felt that we were wasted in the Rape Crisis Centre, that women like us should be in the Labour

movement, fighting the good fight, and they didn't understand about feminist politics, and we challenged them and said you're in a male organisation, and you can only go so far…you're tied by the lack of radical edge that you have, whereas any movement which is separate has got a tremendous weapon because you don't have any boundaries except your own values…

I remember we went to one group in Kilmarnock in Ayrshire, and it was an evening thing, and Naomi and I were there, and there was a lot of trade union women and, there must have been forty or something, and we began talking about feminism and…the Labour Party and male organisations and how it's difficult to address things like rape because it's seen as a periphery issue…because there are bigger issues to tackle – economic class, you know, and all that. And a lot of the women didn't connect with feminist theories, but the older women in the groups did – ones at sixty, seventy and eighty were much more radical than the younger ones…because I think they had come from an era where that contradiction of gender…was very pronounced, and they knew exactly what we were talking about…

And the women who were in the same group, and who had gone, obviously, week on week to be with these women, didn't realise how radical these women were – and they were coming out with quite radical phrases, like they were saying 'Well it's more difficult to see the enemy now, because it's subsumed within culture', and it's, there's so many other problems that women always just get sort of slightly…sidelined, or drawn into the bigger picture, as if it's more important. So that was interesting." [Jane Dorby]

For other women working in Rape Crisis centres, their feminist views also reflected experiences, frustrations and difficulties they had faced personally as mothers, workers, socialists and students…

"It became a very big part of the…feminist movement that was going on in Aberdeen anyway at that time, and in Scotland generally, and people would go off on marches and people would, you know, shout about abuse against women and domestic violence was beginning to be talked about…I believed that women should go to work and should have the rights and they didn't have to just be child machines, and I got pretty cross with some of the men at work, at my work, who just sort of wandered into work, having done nothing… And all the childcare…I mean, it's tough now, but it was very much more tough then cos there wasn't the assumption that women would work in that kind of way, and I stopped work when I had my first child." [Liz Hall]

"In a way it kind of introduced me to a type of feminism that… I certainly hadn't thought of myself as, I might have thought of myself as a kind of socialist feminist, or socialism as first and foremost then I might have been into equality later. But it catapulted feminism right to the start …of everything yeah and it ended up framing my career … And it's what I've done ever since actually." [Fiona Raitt]

"I'd got involved in a women's group at college, so that was the first sense that there was where we talked about being feminists. And it was quite important because…at that point in time…Thatcherism was huge, you know. It was very much about, I had been or I was a single parent. So I was really in tune with in terms of like the welfare state, how single parents were…treated and just the whole issue of the world at work for me. Lack of childcare resources was huge when I applied to go to Moray House they talked about having a nursery. That actually transpired that there was no childcare facilities there, so very early on a few women, we got together to talk about and make complaints about the lack of childcare in Moray House…I think we managed to actually really get under their skin about it…So… one of my earliest kind of like on-site campaigns really was around childcare…Getting involved in Rape Crisis was very much more about an exciting aspect of that. This was something I could do with other women." [Margaret McCutcheon]

Collective working

Many of the groups of women who set up Rape Crisis centres in Scotland operated as collectives. This egalitarian approach was firmly rooted in their rejection of the patriarchal structures which had led to the gender inequalities and subordination of women in which sexual violence had its origins:

> "Our belief in working as a collective…had come from the politics of not having people who are in positions of power over us…who then potentially could misuse and abuse that power. So we wanted to share the power, share the control, share the decision making, as it was opposite to what was the normality. And also for women within the workplace. At that time, women in senior, in management positions in the workplace was still, you know, relatively unusual, women in positions of power. So seeing people forming alternative management methods wasn't normal…wasn't common…so there was a lot of compromise. I mean, the collective was working, and it's very much about reaching a negotiated compromise…But it also took a long time. And so our collective meetings would last, I think, two, two and a half hours. We usually ended up in the pub after them. We always ended up in the pub after them." [Elizabeth Shiach]

Collective working might have been a new way of working for many of the women now engaged in it, but they themselves determined what it meant:

> "We had state of the collective meetings…we learned about, you know, turn taking, silence, not talking, should people contribute, because it's, like in any situation, some people are good communicators…they like talking – other people are not so good or don't feel so confident…We wanted to make sure that everybody's contribution was heard in some way…so we tried to deal with that face on…we didn't want to say to people, 'You must have an opinion on this',…but essentially, if you didn't, you had to say, well I don't have an opinion on this at the moment, I need more time to think about it…rather than think, well somebody just sitting there silently because they're not confident enough to say something and it's actually not what they want…So I really enjoyed the experience of being in the collective, though I can see that…dependant on personalities, that could be a difficult issue but we were quite lucky at the time, with the people who were involved in the collective." [Rona Clarke]

> "I felt when you joined there was just really strong pressure, not in a bad way, but it was just like not the done thing for example, not to turn up for rota, we always had two people on for sort of safety issues. The collective meetings, people went weekly usually…if you got involved in it, you got caught up in it. So it wasn't so much that there are rules, just like a way of operating do you know what I mean? It wasn't all written down." [Jan Macleod]

For women who were used to working within a much more structured framework, the collective approach made a great impact:

> "There was this idea that nobody chaired meetings as such that there would be an understanding maybe that somebody…would facilitate it and that might rotate, but there was nobody in charge. And of course…in a way, it was…alien to me as a lawyer, because I had been used to this terribly structured meeting where you'd go to meetings with lawyers, you know it's… rigid to the point of militaristic and so…in a way it was lovely to have this freedom of, you can just pitch in when you want…and it wasn't a meeting that was dominated by men who would always be silencing whatever you might suggest. So that was a very new way of operating." [Fiona Raitt]

This positive perception was shared by many of the women who worked within the Rape Crisis collectives:

"I remember reading a book at the time…a short article that I've never forgotten and it was about magic mammas in collectives or in groups. And there was definitely a magic." [Margaret McCutcheon]

"It was just this sort of equality there which I really found quite fascinating… I mean I had never even heard of a collective, let alone been involved wi one. You know. So and there was I, in this collective making decisions about this organisation which I just found…really fascinating. " [Isabelle Kerr]

"I think if you've got a very cohesive, common focus, then the collective works very well. I liked it, because it's, it was about sharing, and it was accepting that you didn't have any particular right to, that your opinion was absolutely…valid…some people joined the group, I think, and left because it was too loose, as they would call it. But it developed an inner confidence in actually being your own person, and listening to somebody else's point of view, and then putting that aside, and still having that same common focus. And there was a lot of very divergent views in the group." [Jane Dorby]

"I think we ran really well as a collective when there were the eight of us, and because we'd all been through the same process together…from the beginning, and there was something very bonding about that…and we used to go away weekends together, you know, and kind of have Rape Crisis weekends and bring kids, some people would bring their kids or not or whatever. So it was very tight." [Siobhan Canavan]

"We established it sort of together, all of us doing different things. So you weren't coming in to a group where there was lots of sort of history in terms of cliques or divisions or something like that. People obviously had different views about how things should be done. But I mean my understanding of collective working is that it's sort of you're sharing skills and experiences and everybody's learning and there is an element of shared responsibility. But it doesn't mean to say that everybody has to decide everything. So…it seemed to be quite easy to make decisions, that's my memory anyway.

And there wasn't a lot of people sort of, you know…trying to win arguments, because it was almost like you could do anything you wanted… so long as you were prepared to put the effort in…we used to do things for like no money and with no money. God knows how we managed it actually. So, it was an incredible experience in terms of learning skills, fundraising, public speaking, the support work, just all sorts of things like that, working with the media, doing interviews." [Jan Macleod]

"I liked being part, well I certainly liked the theory of being part of the collective… probably if I'd been less conscious of the rules I might have said, look I do know something about this and I'm going to put it in…so I did think that the collective was interesting and I liked the way it gave everybody their space. And I think that…no matter where you were coming from…women were very quickly valued and I think probably …women who had been socially excluded or marginalised or…who had themselves been raped and then were into the collective…I think it was particularly welcoming of those women… It was a healthy mix. So that was good." [Helen Mackinnon]

"I have to say, Action Against Incest was, without a doubt, one of the most positive collective working experiences I've ever had… And I think it's because we were all so naïve (laughing)…Now looking back, I can say 'Aye, there was pockets of power.' Of course there was pockets of power. There was women who were much more confident than others. There were women who were much more educated than others. There were women who had access to money more than others. There was women who were really, really bolshy, and really, as I say, a bit rough, you know? But never, ever, ever at any point did you ever feel that anything you had to contribute wasn't purposeful, or useful. And I think, if anything, we all started off with the same focus, which was 'We need to do something about this.' And that was what kind of bonded us, and we did do an awful lot of work." [Frances Monaghan]

102

"As a collective, we were very, very strong, and every now and again, women were asked to join, or we would target women that we'd been to a conference and thought, oh she's really good, let's go and talk to her. So we did that quite a lot, and we were known for being quite cheeky, and quite bolshy. And none of us minded that reputation. I mean, some of us still carry that reputation, but none of us minded it, you know? Because, at the bottom of it, we were just passionate you know? Passionate, inexperienced, but bags of energy and I always think that's a good combination in lots of ways. So, you know, it was, the collective was just brilliant – it was just absolutely fantastic, and when we decided to disband and hand everything over to Rape Crisis Centre, oh we were all howling. We were all roarin' and greetin'" [Frances Monaghan]

"The collective was really quite a solid group …the kind of core…and then sort of around the edges people would come and go to some extent although you didn't encourage dipping in and dipping out – folk had to make a commitment as best they could." [Caroline Armit]

"I think it was all important…there was an awful lot of support within the group and I think the fact that we operated as a collective reinforced the support that was available, that…we all had equal responsibility." [Isla Laing]

"Collective working was never fashionable or popular, it was never easy…it was hard work, but there were huge gains to be made from it in terms of yourself, and what you learnt, your own confidence and I suppose that thing about growing consciousness as well – knowing that how you looked at the world, and that stays with me even though I can be an old cynic these days – that core never leaves you and I'll always be a feminist…that rock might have…started to form earlier but it definitely solidified during the time at the centre." [Linda Reid]

There were also other, less positive aspects to collective working:

"Difficulties blow up periodically over power (who has it, where is it), class (too many middle-class women, too many middle-class assumptions, some working class women have felt), sexuality (Lesbian women feeling excluded or undervalued by heterosexual women), different goals or emphases (pragmatic women who put support for women and work on campaigning first, and idealistic women who believe that discussion of issues is just as important as the day to day running of the centre). Sometimes the problems come from personality clashes hidden by opposing attitudes, sometimes from not listening to each other, and they're always painful to deal with or overcome." [Edinburgh Rape Crisis workers in Grit and Diamonds (Stramullion, 1990)]

"I think that collective working did become very, very problematic for the Rape Crisis movement and for other women's organisations as well and it's because a…type of working developed…I don't see it as collective working…it is just this idea that everybody has to do everything. That if you're in a collective, so long as you've got a clear vision about where you want to go, I think there needs to be an element of trust.

So say you've got a collective of twelve people or whatever, and four of them go away to look into a piece of work and learn all about it and meet with people and gather the information and come up with recommendations and bring it back to the big group…so often you hear, what happens is then people start discussing it and they totally dismiss the fact that these four people have been away working on this and come up with recommendations and may well decide to do something completely different without recourse to any of the discussion or information.

And I think that's completely demoralising for people and I think it's not effective, it's not efficient, it's not supportive, and it's a real distortion of collective working which is sort of interpreted as everybody's word's equal…whether you like it or not, that is not a realistic way of working when you're taking public money to provide a public service where you want to and you're expected to be consistent and effective and professional." [Jan Macleod]

Many different factors lay behind the negative aspects of collective working:

"For me, there is a natural movement towards collective working, because in theory…if that's your way of operating, then you have got an even playing field between the members of that collective. However, in practice that's not always what happens because you need to be sure that all members of that collective are working from the same premise, and that they are fully committed to that sense of fair play, justice and sisterhood… And I think that collective working has, over the years, ended up with a very bad name…partly because we have not ensured that at least those three things are part of what the individual is committed to when she is accepted into…an organisation that works collectively…and it is a very tall order." [Margaret Brown]

Factions

"There were factions and there were some people who came in and had some very odd ideas…When we had workers supervising workers, it was a group supervising the workers and they had this idea that it could all be secret…the rest of the collective shouldn't know. And that's not collective working, that's just somebody got the wrong idea…everything was confidential within the collective, it shouldn't have left, but not for one or two people… and that caused quite a lot of bad feeling." [Sheila Brodie]

Personalities & different perspectives

"It can be quite fair, but it can be dominated by people…a strong personality can dominate things." [Sheila Brodie]

"Every time there was a new influx, you know, you had all these new personalities to get used to, generally they didn't understand what you were doing, and there was always this reinventing the wheel. You know, 'Why don't we try it this way?' and somebody like me would say 'Well, we did try that, you know, and it didn't work' but because somebody had raised it, 'Well, I feel strongly, you know, maybe it didn't work', and you had to do it all again, you know?" [Laurie Matthew]

"It was Aileen's analysis about how there was always a difference in collectives between pragmatists and ideologists and people that just wanted to get on with it and people that had ideology around it and the language…I thought that was quite a helpful analysis because quite often folk did want to just sort of [say] 'Look, come on…let's just do something, let's not spend another four days talking and arguing. And so what if they want to call it counselling or so what if we're collecting flags…Let's just get on and do it, if we want the money let's get it.' So there was that whole dynamic the whole time." [Helen Mackinnon]

"One of the major problems in the collective could be when there were rows between those of us who were (and I say us because I was one of them) deeply pragmatic and were there to try and change things and to try and cover the phone lines, and those of us who were idealistic and there could be great stooshies between the two sides." [Aileen Christianson]

"I think it's got its positive and its negative I mean to begin with I really thought it was excellent because, well the theory is that everybody gets a chance to speak… you have different degrees of facility…some people are…a bit more shy than others. But often they are much more observant so you need to create…the quiet space in which…they can also…function. And if we cannot do that within the collective how on earth are we going to have it work…when you go…to see somebody?" [Florence Germain]

Decision-making was often a long and tortuous process:

"It's not a bad way of working, it's a difficult way of working in that it can be very slow and ponderous and difficult to make decisions." [Sheila Brodie]

"It's really hard to make decisions when it's a collective and everybody's got to agree…Fantastically supportive, very interesting and incredibly frustrating, you know? So there was such a lot of good will and such a lot of excitement, and then nothing would happen. Decisions wouldn't get made because so-and-so…wasn't there and was on holiday or couldn't, and that got really frustrating, cos although I think we ended up opening without a collective decision, almost, because we just had to go with it." [Liz Hall]

"I think collectives ideally are a great idea but I don't think they're always the most practical way of working – I think they're a bit time-consuming and sometimes it feels like…nobody's actually taking responsibility for decisions." [Moira Kane]

"It became quite difficult in that there would be this interminable…you would never get things agreed at a meeting and you would pend it to the next week, and then it would come up again, and you would pend it to the next week…" [Linda Reid]

"I personally found it very difficult, though I felt it was the only way to work. I can remember often going home on a Monday night and saying to my husband 'As usual we decided nothing'. Because the collective way seemed to be not to make decisions. Just to talk about them. So I think that that's probably my personality – I'm sort of the person who likes to get things done and decide it and onward. But… we couldn't run it as a committee. You know with sort of office bearers and quorums and all that sort of thing – it just wasn't, wouldn't have been our way." [Maureen Porter]

Class
"Class was big issue in the women's movement in the early 80s, and so consequently, it also became an issue in the Rape Crisis… It usually was the idealistic side getting pissed off with the pragmatic side, and class was a handy stick to beat them with. So it was very complicated, and it was not straightforwardly middle-class oppression." [Aileen Christianson]

"There were a lot of English women, there were a lot of Americans…and sometime there would be class stooshies where people, Scottish people, would assume that somebody from England was actually middle-class, where actually, all it was they had an English accent…so they would get pissed off (laughing) so they could be, there were issues over class. There were not particularly issues over racism, other than because we were all white until later on." [Aileen Christianson]

Power
"I find it actually quite inspiring, at times intensely frustrating… and then…like any group of human beings…the dynamic goes on and there is always, unfortunately, sort of power struggle…How do you see it? How do you share it? Do you want it? Is it good, is it bad? I remember a discussion about that." [Florence Germain]

"I still think the notion of collective working is wonderful, but it's very difficult to share the power like that…the more articulate and the more knowledgeable and the …people who are comfortable with their power tend to create more power in the group and…people who understood group dynamics more could manipulate it, not necessarily in a nasty way but in a positive way then have more power… I probably was one of those unwittingly because I had worked a lot in groups – before Albany Street Hostel I worked in Barony Hostel and I had supervision from what was institutional relations then. So we…had a lot of experience working in groups and stuff.

And…I suppose…there was another divide between those of us that were in professional jobs and sounded more knowledgeable, not necessarily were more knowledgeable but were used to working the systems and influencing people. Between those who were volunteers and maybe were unemployed or weren't in professional jobs…And that was hard to recognise that there were those sort of splits… I think it did create a bit of tension… And then… there was a bit of tension between how much we should be a support group to women…and how much we should be a campaign group and awareness training. And really speak out irrespective of the…consequences…That was certainly a big tension … some people left the group." [Dorothy Degenhardt]

"The whole thing about control, I mean that's what's in collectives isn't it about who really is in control…I think there was sometimes a kind of subtle competition for who could be …the most feminist…and the most motivated rota person, who would do the rota? And you saw people coming and working on the rota four or five days a week at their height, at their peak, you thought how can they…do that? And you knew that would all burn out. And then before you knew it they weren't back…Coming and going… fair enough, but quite often new volunteers out of a group of twelve six months later you might have two." [Helen Mackinnon]

"It was a great opportunity to hear other women's opinions, ideas, doubts, thoughts, you know visions. And that sense of being part of a group that was part of a movement was really exciting and that we were all unpaid made a difference I think. I've never worked in a collective where there was a paid and unpaid collective. So we were all unpaid so in that sense we were all equal. But as time moved on I realised that we may all have an equal status on paper, but people's involvement in the running of the collective provided them with different levels of information and power and resource…There were some women who had a bigger investment in the organisation in the sense of keeping it in a particular way…for me it was all…about the funding and finance of it. Because we had women who provided money on a monthly basis direct debits etc. And I didn't have the money for that kind of thing do you know what I mean?" [Margaret McCutcheon]

Disputes arose over all sorts of issues, sometimes quite unexpectedly:

"I remember it was all to do with smoking…it was the one cigarette at a time rule upset a couple of women who felt very nervous and they wanted to smoke when they wanted to smoke… I think what had happened was that everybody was smoking, or those who smoked, smoked…me being one of them… And of course remember in the 80s that was, smoking was the norm as opposed to not, being a non-smoker. And so when the non-smoking women said 'Oh you know this is getting far too smoky in here I can't stand it, my asthma' etc, etc. 'We're going to have to instigate a rule' and this was obviously women, older women, women who had been around in the collective for a long time… it was one of the earliest kind of feelings for me about where the power lay within groups. And also there was definitely a class issue going on for me as well…because the women who left were working class women who just almost did the you know…'If that's what it's gonna be like I'm off.' And they just left." [Margaret McCutcheon]

Discussions were key to the collective's cohesion and development and the means through which the women gained a deeper understanding of the issues around sexual violence – and how best they could communicate these more widely:

"One of things about having a…collective…was just the discussions that you had to be having cos a lot of this was very new to almost everybody, in a general sense…In any kind of professional field…even psychiatry, psychology, they were really still very confused about rape…they just were nowhere…then after the late 70's people were starting to write and the women's movement had really kicked in…we were screaming and shouting about stuff." [Caroline Armit]

"It was an important part of our growth as a collective, also to talk about ourselves. I mean that's obviously based back down, back to our consciousness-raising roots, so very much talking about ourselves, our own experiences." [Elizabeth Shiach]

"Things like…whether we should allow male children to come into the service because they were male…The consensus was that they should, and…I had thought that would be the right thing, but there was a couple of very radical…women in the group who joined us, and actually, having listened to them, I thought hmm, I probably yes, I could have changed my mind…But it wasn't that important to me, whether they were, 'cause they were still kids to me. But some people felt very strongly about it, so there was differences in that way." [Jane Dorby]

"They were generally about the boundaries of our involvement and, you know, under what circumstances we would have to make it clear to women that while confidentiality was in the main part guaranteed, that couldn't be the case if it came to things like child protection issues and safety." [Isla Laing]

"We talked about how we saw wurselves, what wur experience was, talked about wur confidence, wur upbringing, what we would like to be in the future, what were the barriers in our way – we talked about feminist people like Shulamith Firestone, about the stereotypes of feminists, wur bra burning and we talked about Germaine Greer and her book, The Female Eunuch, at the time… There was a lot of discussion around that, and a lot of people didn't like her views at the time, and I remember thinking that I really liked it because she was very much talking in the book about your independence is in your pocket, in many ways – it's in your finances, so get a grip of your finances because that's a lot about control of your life…And a lot of feminists in the group said no that's not what it's about, it's about your mindset and so on. So we had a lot of discussion about how d'you get a mindset – maybe that's, you can get a mindset because you do own certain things, you can walk out of that house, you're not trapped, you can change your lifestyle with money…I think that was quite radical at the time, because there was a lot of looseness about feminism at that point…whereas I felt, at that point, Germaine Greer was coming in with quite a harsh, good, meaty agenda for women. So there was a lot of discussion around that." [Jane Dorby]

"We had quite tense discussions because there were women in the group who were survivors of sexual violence, who didn't want to talk about it, who didn't want it on the table…who'd come along to be part of the Rape Crisis centre because they wanted to do something for other women, or they wanted to do something that was political, but where their own experience wasn't what they were really wanting to be talking about…And there were women in the group who were not identifying as survivors of male violence…there began to be a feeling of, where your view's more or less legitimate if you were a survivor or not a survivor. You know, it was a really difficult…and it didn't go on for long, but I remember it as feeling quite fraught and…also quite fundamental. And it was, in some ways it was a difference between women who had a kinda strategic view of what needed to change in the world to stop this happening, and women who were coming from a much more personal place, and were concerned about what needed to change in the world to make sure that women were properly supported." [Lily Greenan]

"I think we all went into it a bit naïve and thinking, well this is a good idea we're going to help other people, and then it brought up a whole load of emotional stuff for all of us, but also a lot of tension in the group…There were issues amongst us as to how best to tackle it…some of the discussions, sort of arguments we had…like, how long we should work with each individual if there was only a few of us and there was a demand for more people needing support…should we support them through the court system, if they're going to court – course very few of them did. And how long…that support should be, should we have a time limit, and then also how emotionally involved we would get…cause some of us got very involved with one or two that you know, now you look back and you think you know obviously tapped stuff in ourselves, but we couldn't even name it then." [Dorothy Degenhardt]

"It was like the personal to the political I remember and I remember how that really struck home to me about all of a sudden, my kind of personal life had a connection to other women. In that it was, you know that you could get angry about it and you could do something about it and you could make it external rather than just being an internal process." [Margaret McCutcheon]

The idealism which had led these pioneers of the Rape Crisis movement to embrace collective working practices was tempered over time by the realities of running the service, the accountability required by potential funders, the advent of paid workers, and by the difficulties in reconciling the different demands all of these factors presented. Although some centres still operate as collectives today, the majority do not, and work instead under a more hierarchical structure.

"We loved it at the beginning…we didn't have any problems about the way it worked – it just did. And I think that if…there was something going on in the very early days, people were quite willing-ish to bring it up, and – let's sort it – it was that kind of attitude…I think possibly it all began to maybe go a little bit more difficult when we got funded – when we got workers. That became…bit more complicated, and then as time went on, it got even more complicated!" [Norma Benzie]

"Collective working as a way to deliver services or to influence change at a more strategic level, no, I wouldn't see it as the way to go. I think it requires a huge level of maturity from the people who are involved in it. I think it can be done. I have very, very good memories of collective working in the early years I was involved with Edinburgh Rape Crisis centre and that's probably what kept me trying to make it happen and trying, you know, willing to keep working at it because I had the privilege of being involved in some fantastic collectives.

The golden winter – there was a six month period where there were eight of us, that was all that was left…It would have been round about 1985, maybe the winter of '85, '86. Margaret McCutcheon, who now works next door to me here, was part of that collective…and it wasn't perfect, but we were eight women who had, I think, a fairly equitable level of commitment and interest in what we were doing and it meant that we just got on with it. We were quite practical…able to be practical but able to hold on to what it was all about. Have a sense of where we were going. We ran the phone line, we dealt with the mail, we did talks, we responded to the media. We didn't have a political lobbying campaign going on that winter – that was the only thing we didn't have. We did everything else and it worked like a dream, it worked really, really well and so I know that it can. Maybe it's something that can happen for short periods of time, in crisis. Maybe it's something that is very dependant on the mix of people that you have in the room, you know, the kind of particular mix of personalities, but I do think, as well, that some of it is about maturity…You have to be able to do what you're doing for the good of the group, or the good of the organisation…and if it doesn't have that…it's like a wheel that gets a kink in it, you know, and it stops working." [Lily Greenan]

"Some of it was really, really powerful and uplifting and other parts of it was quite challenging and destructive. I think it's, it's a very difficult thing to negotiate your way through. I do still think that it is a wonderful ideal. But it needs some kind of structure that can stop…people from having, losing sight of what the real goal is." [Heather Forrest]

"Where you're dealing with matters and issues around power and control, then it seems a natural progression to be operating and organised in that way…However…there are now managers being appointed in local groups, and…as long as those managers have a feminist analysis of the world, then we will be OK, but if they don't…that's part of the threat that's on the horizon, because it will take us down a completely different road." [Margaret Brown]

"With the benefit of…being away from the place for a long time and looking back, there was still probably for me anyway more gains than losses in having that collective structure because of the opportunity that it did give people to grow…and to support one another, to learn from each other – really just that kind of inspiring thing that women can do this without having, you know, men in suits telling them what to do…That whole grassroots thing…can be very powerful…" [Linda Reid]

"Working in a collective is incredibly difficult, and it never ran perfectly. However…a supposedly non-hierarchical structure is a much more comfortable structure to be in, and particularly back then. I mean, it was all very radical and we were all very paranoid…but…it was very supportive, except when we were falling out with each other of course!" (laughing) [Aileen Christianson]

Investigation and prosecution of rape: the reality
Reporting, the judicial process & attitudes to women

Whatever sexual assault or abuse she had suffered was often only the beginning of a woman's ordeal. If she wanted and felt able to report what had happened, the subsequent chain of events could be very protracted and painful – with no guarantee of success. Rape Crisis workers became very familiar with the many attitudinal and procedural obstacles faced by women in their search for justice – very often presented by those whose job it was to aid that process. The first of these was the police, whose responses to women approaching them with complaints of rape or sexual abuse was often sceptical and far from sympathetic.

In a piece published in December 1980, which highlighted low levels of reporting, Jean Donald wrote in The Glasgow Herald:

> "The Glasgow Rape Crisis Centre experienced this earlier this year when three Glasgow University students turned up for help on separate occasions after being raped. They did not report their cases to the police. Perhaps that is not altogether surprising when in the same city a [?] year-old boy held in jail pending trial on two rapes charges, was let out on bail only to find a third victim the very next day. He was later jailed for four years." [The Glasgow Herald, December 15th, 1980]

Trying to help women who had to decide whether or not to report what had happened to the police was not easy:

> "The relationship with the police was quite different from what it is now. It's changed a huge amount… I think apart from occasional individual police officers, quite often women who phoned were very wary of going to the police because they wouldn't be believed basically. I mean it happened constantly. And the police quite often did behave quite badly…
>
> Quite often…women that were phoning would ask things like, you know, 'Should I go to the police?' And you'd just have to go through all the pros and cons … this might happen, that might happen, you know all the different sort of things around about that and then basically so it was up to them to make up their minds whether or not, or what they wanted to do." [Sheila Brodie]

> "We were asked by women what should they do…you know, all you could say was that it would not be easy, and expect it to be very hard, and, that, really, it was up to them, but it wasn't optimistic in terms of justice and a successful conviction against the man." [Kate Arnot]

> "The biggest source of problems with legal-type people would be CID…sometimes they have hurt women so much." [Norma Benzie]

Some insight into police attitudes at the time that the earliest Rape Crisis centres were being set up can be found in articles like this piece, which appeared in the Glasgow Herald in October 1978 and was composed largely of observations from Detective Constable Valerie Beaton of the Serious Crime Squad in Glasgow, who is described as "a chatty curly haired girl in her early 30s":

> "'I think a lot of young girls let a boy go too far, don't manage to control the situation when they mean to, and afterwards panic – even these days girls are terrified of pregnancy – and claim it was rape. It's difficult having to tell parents that despite their daughter's claims, there is no sign of rape.'"

The article continues:

> "But it's not always the youngsters who are silly.

'Not all that long ago a middle-aged Edinburgh woman accepted a lift home from two unknown young men, then claimed she'd been raped. Then we discovered that when she left the car, the two boys were standing quite happily beside it, hardly acting like criminals. And her husband was furious with her – calling her a liar.' She doesn't agree that women are pressurised by police questions after a rape. 'We have to be firm because of the mental condition of some of the women – some have been bashed about a bit, others are embarrassed and don't want to talk about it.'

Valerie was among the policewomen who had special training to deal with sex crimes and their victims.

'And I'm sure it helped. A lot of the younger women officers don't really understand the importance of getting the details of sex crimes. It's embarrassing but it will be expected in the courtroom anyway…'

Like most of her colleagues she thinks that women get over rape. 'It's a shock at the time but it gets less and less. The most damaging thing is the publicity. Neighbours somehow get to know what has happened and certainly when this happens a woman has a hard time coming to terms with what has happened.'"
[*Inquiries that are never easy* in The Glasgow Herald, October 16th, 1978]

The focus of police questioning was very often on the woman's behaviour, dress and demeanour rather than on what had happened or on the behaviour of the man who had assaulted her, with all sorts of prejudices and assumptions advancing the notion that there was a good chance that she had been in some way to blame for what had happened:

"But the most harrowing was going to the police…but that was part of the support that we did, and that, I suppose, fused, for me, feminism with the actual what was happening to women, because the police, at that time, were appalling in their treatment to women. They asked them if they were on contraceptives, did they have a boyfriend, how much they had to drink that night – they were just up for question, completely…I remember one particular harrowing thing, and she had her underwear, she'd had the examination, she was sitting with her bag, and she had her pants and everything, and the police sort of picked up her pants, and they were quite frilly, if you like, whatever, and he said 'This doesn't look like somebody's not asking for it, to me.' And it was quite intimidating, and her head just went down, and it was just an enormous sense of anger, you know? It really was harrowing. The most harrowing thing for me was dealing with the agencies, definitely, but particularly the police… the police were still very fixed on the fact that it was a sexual act…rather than a violent one." [Jane Dorby]

"Police attitudes were… silent…you know, the shutter comes down. You can see it in body language and facial expression and the expression in the eyes, the shutter comes down. However, having said that, they did set up a family room and they did listen to what we were saying about women officers. So there was a will there to try and…get it right, but that didn't happen overnight. I mean, that was a long haul, to get those kind of things changed and in place." [Margaret Brown]

"Generally they hadn't been dealing with it at all well. And still some of them don't. But there were a few that were trying to do it and there were a few that were trying to set up these separate units that were dealing with it well…my memory is that the police headquarters in Bell Street had opened up this room…I don't know whether they've still got it, but like a room where they interviewed…and showers and a bed…it would always be a woman police officer that'd interview them as well… Well that's what they said…but as I say not a lot of women come forward immediately afterwards. So they were working it round the facility of you know women that day coming forward having been raped and then how they would deal with it. But actually that was very few out of the number of women we were working with. And I think it took them a long time to grasp that." [Dorothy Degenhardt]

The forensic examination could be a very difficult experience for women who had been sexually assaulted, particularly as the vast majority of police surgeons were male:

> "One of the things that women talked to us about when they phoned was how it felt to be examined by a male police surgeon, and this was something, I'm sure, I think that we raised…you know, why there weren't female police surgeons…all of that." [Elizabeth Shiach]

An utterly callous response by the medical profession to the ordeal experienced by women who were raped was vividly highlighted in an article which appeared in the Glasgow Herald on 16th October 1978. Entitled "***The medical expert who sees no need for change***", the piece revealed the casual and dismissive attitude towards the impact of rape in the words of Dr William McLay. Dr McLay was at that point the Chief Medical Examiner for Strathclyde Police – which meant that he examined more survivors of rape than any other doctor in Scotland:

> "To be honest, I seldom get the impression that the girls I see are suffering from any deep psychological damage…Let's face it, chaps have been trying to loosen up girls with a drink or two for a long time. And when you hear of the situations these girls get themselves into missing buses home after a night on Carlsberg Specials, I think we are entitled to lose some sympathy for them."

He conceded, however, that

> "Being thrust into a totally unknown environment, like a police station, after an experience like that can hardly be pleasant",

but nevertheless concluded:

> "But at the same time, many of these girls live in a violent community and are not as shaken up by rape as is sometimes made out in the press. You know there are countries in Eastern Europe where rape is simply regarded as aggravated assault. Sometimes I think we get it a little out of perspective here." [The Glasgow Herald, 16th October, 1978]

However, Dr Elizabeth Wilson, who was director of Greater Glasgow Health Board's Family Planning Centre, made numerous efforts to persuade local police to include the centre's address on an information sheet they gave to survivors of rape and sexual assault. In a report which appeared in the Glasgow Herald on August 5th 1983, she stated:

> "Most woman victims who make a complaint do so at a local police station in Strathclyde. The facilities for such examinations can be truly awful. They are called medical examination rooms, but they are in reality little more than cells usually used for examining drunks. The rooms are unheated. The woman is asked to strip and it is only recently that they have been given gowns to wear. She is then asked to lie down on a bed with no covering until a police surgeon arrives. He is usually a GP with very little training in forensic examination. If the police surgeon does not find any evidence of injury that can be more or less the end of the story, because it is then often only the girl's word against the man's. She is then treated as though she were the criminal. Whatever the police say, there are certainly officers who call these women whores and tarts."

> Dr Wilson said that in cases where there is other injury present and prosecution possible, the assault or rape victim is often requested to return the following day to be examined by the chief police surgeon at Pitt Street police headquarters.

> "They then have to undergo a second time what is a painful and horrifying ordeal, often because the evidence of an inexperienced police surgeon is not thought good enough to be tested in court," she

stated. "It is very difficult to convey to men the real horror of what these women can go through in our police stations. The need is obvious – for examinations in hospital by women doctors, for privacy, and for a totally different and sympathetic approach." [The Glasgow Herald, August 5th, 1983]

In fact, in Edinburgh for many years, forensic examination of women who had been raped took place under the same roof as the police mortuary!

Understandably, a woman might not feel able to report the assault right away, and because of this, forensic evidence was often absent:

> "I suppose the other issue about going to the police and going through all that procedure was that a lot, women you know feel really dirty afterwards and the first thing you might want to do is go home and have a wash and then that's all the evidence kind of gone. So there was that issue as well. So what was the point if there was no evidence." [Sheila Brodie]

There were, however, small pockets of encouragement that changes in approach and attitude were possible. In an article published as early as October 1978, the Glasgow Herald reported on a "unique project" led by Dr Donald Rushton, a consultant in forensic medicine at Dundee University into evidence-gathering from women who had been raped:

> "It is regarded by many as the most enlightened programme for analyzing sexual assaults to be found in Britain. Dr Rushton says: 'We are interested in developing new ways of obtaining evidence from women who have been subjected to sexual assault. Basically, this involves the use of audio-visual equipment, automatic photography and video recordings.'
>
> He believes that women are not prone to making up false allegations about rape and that what is required is a more sympathetic handling of victims.
>
> 'Police expect far too much of a woman who has been raped,' he says.
>
> 'They judge her by a male yardstick. Women do not always do the kind of thing that men would expect them to do. For example, they do not always report the sexual assault straight away. They go home, clean themselves and wash their clothing and this creates disbelief in the eyes of the law. I understand that the police estimate that about half the rape cases are false allegations. I would challenge that figure.'" [*Is the soft line the answer?* In The Glasgow Herald, 16th October, 1978]

The 1983 publication of the Scottish Office Social Research Study "**Investigating Sexual Assault**", by Gerry Chambers and Ann Millar was key in highlighting many of these issues and owed a great deal to the persistence and commitment of Rape Crisis centres in bringing them to the fore. Rape Crisis centres also contributed to guidelines for police investigation of sexual assault which were published in 1985.

Chambers' and Millar's research also provided the context for later research carried out by Michele Burman and her colleagues Lynn Jamieson and Beverley Brown:

> "We were quite fortunate in Scotland because there had been some very good research that'd taken place – by Chambers and Millar …and that was a sort of two-staged research, one was about the police investigation and the prosecution construction of the case in the investigating phase of the project, and then they looked at the prosecution and the courtroom contexts of sexual offence trials, and had found and demonstrated the empirical evidence of sexual character and sexual history evidence being introduced, that didn't seem to be entirely relevant at all to the case in hand – that there was a very high level of distress among complainers. They documented very hostile, intimidatory questioning by the

defence, lots of allegations of a woman making false allegation, and something that the Law Commission were very concerned about, which was a technical matter of law about the potential that this kind of evidence has for throwing the jury off the main facts of the case, for being able to attack the credibility of the complainer by showing that she had a predisposition to consent." [Michele Burman]

Chambers and Millar were not alone in recognising the damage done by the introduction of such evidence to the chances of women complainers in rape trials:

"There'd also been a very influential report by...Sheriff MacPhail, who was a Scottish Sheriff who had looked at the law of rape...at the time, and put up a number of recommendations about restrictions to be placed on sexual history and sexual character evidence precisely because of...the ease with which one can conflate evidence of consent and evidence of character to show consent, evidence of credibility to show consent, evidence of consent to show a particular kind of sexual character and how all of these things were pulling the jury around, had the tendency to mislead. There was also, at the time, a concern about levels of underreporting – of women coming forward to report." [Michele Burman]

Fully aware of the judgemental reactions they might face, women often chose not to report what had happened, and reporting rates were very low:

"Very low, and I mean that's looking at the proportion of women who'd been raped or sexually assaulted who reported to the police...incest survivors...there'd been very little reporting." [Isla Laing]

"I think if somebody had been physically abused as well, then it was easier to go to the police...They didn't understand...it was almost like well, why didn't you fight? Why didn't you do this? But you know if you're in fear of your life, then you don't. You just wait till it's all gone, you know, and get away as quickly as you can. And also I think because the men who tend to know the women that they attack, it was almost like well, but you talked to that person, but you knew them, you know? ... And women of course felt really guilty because they felt that by just being friendly to somebody somehow... they'd encouraged something or...unbeknownst to themselves they'd given some kind of signal or whatever." [Sheila Brodie]

Central Scotland Rape Crisis workers were so appalled at the treatment they saw being meted out to women seeking justice for rape that they went to see the Procurator Fiscal:

"I remember it being an extremely difficult meeting, and him being, if not hostile maybe that's too strong, certainly not welcoming...

In Falkirk...we'd had two women that used our service that had been charged with wasting police time after stating they'd been raped, and then they withdrew that after police treatment. Both of them were always adamant that they'd never said...that they hadn't been raped – what they'd said was they didn't want to proceed with the charges...

At the meeting with the PF...his attitudes were, well basically, you know, 'good women aren't raped'. And of course we were also aware from Women's Aid that women were routinely being raped and other forms of sexual abuse, and I do remember us arguing with him that rape within marriage was a crime, and him refuting that...the Rape Crisis groups in Scotland...consistently argued that before it was accepted." [Kate Arnot]

For many women, in addition to the initial police investigation, the prospect of going to trial and reliving the experience in front of witnesses in court was a terrible prospect:

> "I think women found …the whole trajectory of going through court horrendous." [Helen Mackinnon]

And the prospect of what was usually a very protracted process was an additional disincentive to many women considering reporting:

> "For those where it was very recent, I think the kind of feeling it would be harrowing to go through the process, a fair number didn't want to go through that. It was…you want to close that quite quickly and … it was so slow. And there was no sort of fast track system so it, it would take such a long time." [Florence Germain]

Rape Crisis support for women could and sometimes did include support around the judicial process if the woman decided to report what had happened to her:

> "If somebody wanted to go and visit the court before their own trial, then we would try and do that…But what I remember is very few women went to court. Very few cases went to court." [Jan Macleod]

> "One of the things we were very clear about in Rape Crisis, that we weren't about forcing people to go to the police or going to court and things… It was very much supporting the woman in what she wanted to do and helping her…have the information and make the right choices for her." [Leslie Brown]

> "The line we were taking was … obviously it was a woman's decision whether she went to court but really indicating that it would be hard, she would be having a hard time and there was no guarantee that even if she felt as if she had quite a strong case that she would win the case. In fact I can't even remember any successful. I mean I remember there were a few women who went to court and…some of our collective going with them, but I can't actually remember anything positive coming from that." [Dorothy Degenhardt]

> "The woman would speak to Procurator Fiscal…she would ask them 'Can one of the counsellors come with me – be with me?' and generally speaking the answer was yes. And the…Clerk of the Court would take time out to explain to us 'You can only sit here, beside the woman.' She would be there, and we would sit beside her – there was no eye contact, no words spoken, nothing…it was just that she knew there was somebody there. And usually the judge would be fine with it…on one occasion, the judge made a kind of fuss about it, and he wanted to know what qualifications we had, and oh, it was a big lengthy lecture to the…worker who was supporting the survivors…" [Norma Benzie]

> "I remember one woman, a young woman, she was only 18 or 19 and it had been a neighbour had come to her…had realised she was on her own and forced his way into the house and raped her. It took a lot of courage for that woman to go forward. It cost her dearly in all different ways. But good for her, she managed to stick to it, and it got to court and she begged them to allow me to be in the public gallery, and I mean begged, you know? Eventually it was allowed and, it's the usual, you know? You're not allowed to smile, you're not allowed to make any gestures, you know, don't do anything at all that appears to be supportive…Might as we get us a fucking cardboard cut-out, you know? And you know, you've to sit there and watch somebody get tortured, you know? Just bloody awful. And she was made to hold up the nightie that she was wearing the night she was raped, and that poor woman was in fucking bits." [Laurie Matthew]

Supporting women through the court process could benefit the woman greatly, not only at the time, but in giving the worker the sort of background to her experience that could greatly enhance the support work undertaken afterwards:

"It was tremendously helpful, because we knew exactly what had happened, and if she was saying 'Well I felt really bad about this', we could say 'Oh yes that's what was going on then, but I can see why you felt' – so it was much easier to support her afterwards if you'd been in the courtroom." [Aileen Christianson]

Whether or not a worker was permitted to do this, however, was entirely at the discretion of the judge.

The advent of the Witness Service occasionally created an unfortunate and unnecessary sense of rivalry, which was not helpful to complainers:

"Then they introduced…Witness Support…that was very difficult because they were a bit hostile at first – it was as if they had been given this remit …On one or two occasions …hostile tactics were used to keep us away…I once sat for an hour thinking that the survivor hadn't shown up, and in the meantime she was sitting in another room where they'd taken her, thinking 'Oh, Norma hasn't come – what am I gonna do, what am I gonna do?' and they went into the court with her…and came back out and said 'Oh, I though you knew…'…It was so bad – it was so silly. It needn't have been that way." [Norma Benzie]

Another area of potential conflict or difficulty for Rape Crisis workers was the possibility of being called as a witness:

"I mean this is…another huge..controversial area, the extent to which workers within a Rape Crisis organisation or any kind of support workers would worry that they should and might be witnesses at some point…my view would be actually they can often be terribly important witnesses, in the sense that if they're the first point of contact…[if] this is the first time this woman's actually made a disclosure… there are complications over what might be seen as hearsay evidence, but the way that you perceived that woman's behaviourism and whether she's upset and distressed or…what she can recall out of the incidents, all of those things actually could be crucial evidence…and they tend to be glossed over by the police… But actually there can be some very important pieces of evidence tucked away in there. But I think there's always a bit of difficulty on the part of Rape Crisis workers about well, we're really only here to support the women, not to give evidence to another body." [Fiona Raitt]

"There was that whole concern about…if you did too much work with a woman, you know, before, during she was in court, would that damage her credibility…because she's too together?" [Leslie Brown]

Myths and preconceptions about who rapists were and what "real" rape was really all about emerged time and again as a major problem for rape complainers:

"I think it's…that the legal system is completely wedded to gathering evidence in a way that…makes absolutely no concession to the person who has been assaulted… especially sexually but also domestically. Assaulted you might say by somebody who's not a stranger in particular, but somebody who is in some sort of position of trust, some sort of position of familiarity, because …if the police just think oh it's definitely a stranger rape…it's a different setup. But …where it's some kind of acquaintance relationship, it may only be a few hours, maybe months, but there's some sort of connection and that seems, there's a sort of barrier of suspicion immediately descends…" [Fiona Raitt]

And this continues:

"I would assume that there are police around now who understand the arguments that it's not always a stranger leaping on you. On the other hand, being a police officer is always going to make you cynical and not all of the police are going to have the view that we want them to have… You see things in the papers now where you see people on trial for rape and you think…that person would never have been put on trial in the past, you know…the horse and cart would've been driven through that and the police would not have proceeded with that…but then they're not convicted, so I think there's maybe a gap between the professional view, and the average person's view – the jury member's view." [Morna Findlay]

"Everyone in the justice system goes through this terribly strict, 'I'm going to collect evidence in this way'…you know, the defendant has the right to a fair trial and innocent till proven guilty and…there's a deep suspicion about the kind of complaints … that women make, I still think there's an anthology around the number of, of false complaints that are made…and there's no account then taken of why … It might be days or…weeks, months before she makes a complaint…sexual assault cases cause problems for the system and the system hasn't been found a way to adapt to it, still after all these years. I know with the training that the police is given is so much better when there's input from Rape Crisis and Women's Aid but this, you are still battling against quite dominant myths." [Fiona Raitt]

There was a sense among some Rape Crisis workers that the minority of women whose cases did make it to court were those who were considered to be 'righteous' victims, who had attained a level of credibility that other women fell short of:

"We supported not that many women, because not that many women made it to court, and those that were getting as far as court, I think were more likely to be those that had been treated relatively sympathetically. They tended to be the women who were the righteous victims, you know?…They were the women who were easy for the police to see as victims, and to believe and they'd managed to attain that credibility. So they were more likely to be supported elsewhere, but we did get some women who came to us who'd made it as far as court, despite best efforts by the police…to not facilitate it happening and then the best efforts of the procurator fiscal services, 'cause it was by no means perfect either." [Lily Greenan]

Even when women themselves were prepared to leave no stone unturned in their attempts to obtain justice – to the extent even of taking civil action, prospects were not great:

"There was one woman … I remember who had been to court and her attacker had been found not proven…and she wanted to do something about it – she wanted to have some kind of civil action against him and that's why she phoned us to try and find out about what could be done. This is quite a while before… the Miss X case…and we went to see her. Her family were behind her, she'd been attacked by several men and they'd got off…been not proven…somebody contacted some lawyers and asked if anything could be done and it didn't look at that time that anything could be done so I was kind of surprised when the Miss X case came up a few years later." [Morna Findlay]

"Certainly two women I can remember quite clearly…it was bargained out …that is really devastating as well…" [Caroline Armit]

"Siobhan and I were both involved in supporting this one woman… I remember us both sitting in court when this woman was giving evidence… and in this particular case, the guy got found not guilty…it did feel that she was on trial, and she certainly felt that she was on trial all the way through the process. We supported her while she was talking to – while the pre-trial stuff was happening… We met a lot with her during that time, so she'd somewhere just to talk about how she felt about things. You know, that dangerous line of not to be influencing, guiding someone, but for someone to get support through that and particularly through the court process. It just felt…that there was no chance…It felt like the cards were stacked against her." [Elizabeth Shiach]

"In the first study, we'd found an acquittal rate of 78%…of all of the rape cases at the High Court level… and that's just looking at cases that are at court…there are very very big problems there about attrition." [Michele Burman]

The Glasgow Rape Case

One event in Scotland which provoked national outrage and placed rape firmly on the public agenda was a brutal rape that took place in Glasgow's East End in October 1980, and the legal decisions and other developments which emerged subsequently as attempts were made to bring three young men to justice. Although there was considerable evidence against them, the decision was taken to drop the case (thereby dropping the charges against the three accused for all time), as the young woman (Carol X) was deemed unfit to withstand the rigours of the trial. This led to a public outcry, the sacking of the then Lord Advocate Nicholas Fairbairn, and eventually, to an unprecedented private prosecution which led to one of the accused, Joseph Sweeney, being sent to prison for 12 years.

"I think..the Carol X case was the first time that I remember the national media…it was Nationwide… where there was a real focus on rape. And that led to changes in how they dealt with…the prosecution of rape, the Lord Advocate had to resign and after that, things could only be dropped if …the Lord Advocate had agreed it personally. And then after that the Woman and Child Units were set up and after that, the conviction rate plummeted if I remember rightly, because previously, basically I think what happened is that the Crown Office sort of sifted out the ones that they didn't think had much chance. And then when the Lord Advocate had to look at them all personally, a huge number got through that previously would just have been dropped. But because the juries weren't you know, up to speed, they weren't getting convictions." [Jan Macleod]

"It was all over the media. And the private prosecution that was taken…it was quite a turning point because it was in the media and it was…the first time I remembered seeing these arguments in print… not just in the sort of quality – in inverted commas – papers – it was all over…And I do remember people in my family reading it and friends…who I wouldn't necessarily define as feminists reading it and thinking gosh, this is important." [Helen Mackinnon]

Letters like this one, which appeared in The Glasgow Herald, were typical:

"Sir – The decision by the Crown to drop charges in the Glasgow rape case raises a very interesting point. It would appear that in order to avoid being charged all he accused requires to do is so disfigure the victim that it is considered unwise or unhealthy for her to appear in court or face her attacker.

This decision will no doubt bring great joy to all future rapists (or indeed to any criminal) who will undoubtedly endeavour to achieve, if indeed not surpass, the standard set by the case in question." [James Banford – letter to The Glasgow Herald, January 1982]

The case also had a major impact on the way rape cases were prosecuted, as Arnot McWhinnie (a journalist who covered the case and later co-wrote a book on the subject with Ross Harper, a lawyer who acted for Carol X throughout the private prosecution) recollects:

"It has had ramifications which still affect the running of rape cases. Now the Lord Advocate or Solicitor General has to make the decision whether to drop a prosecution in a rape or murder case, and that stems directly from the Glasgow Rape Case. Also, victims have got to be told if a case is being dropped, and kept informed about its progress all the way through. From that point of view it did a lot of good." [Arnot McWhinnie, quoted in The Firm, 14th February 2008 – http:// www.thefirmmagazine.com/features/360/Writing_wrongs.html]

Rape Crisis workers were also instrumental in highlighting serious problems faced by women going through the judicial process and broke new ground in fighting for the most basic changes – even in relation the geography and practical arrangements surrounding attendance at court:

> "I had tried to explain that she could not be in the Witness Room with the accused, so I had already set up at the courthouse that she would be with me in a separate room, so when we arrived at the court, I went and found a court officer. However, I can recall giving feedback and saying 'It needs to be a separate entrance for this as well' – she could have walked into the courthouse and come face-to-face with the accused… But prior to that, I mean, if you didn't request it – in fact I think it was the first time that it had ever happened… and me being allowed to remain in court, I think was the first time that that had ever happened." [Margaret Brown]

> "One woman that I did accompany, we never got as far as into the courtroom. First of all, when we got there – somebody I'd been supporting for quite a while…we'd got this all sorted out…how it was going to be…I met her outside and we got to the court…Only to find that they were expecting her to sit in the same room as the guy that was accused of rape. And we had to make a fuss about that… So they got her somewhere else to stay… and while we were waiting, the Procurator Fiscal came in and said 'I'm sorry, we've decided not to go ahead'… They didn't feel the evidence was strong enough… we'd been waiting for about half an hour…absolutely appalling…why wait till that? …And the guy got off with it. And she was, as you'd imagine, devastated by it…it was just like, how can you do that?" [Sheila Brodie]

Chambers and Millar published a second report in 1986 which exposed clearly the impact these realities had on the chances and experiences of women seeking justice for rape. However, while such publications and the efforts of the Rape Crisis movement did go some way to raising awareness, the fundamental change required in the attitudes and practices of those working within the legal system was not forthcoming. As Edinburgh Rape Crisis workers reflected in 1990:

> *"There has been no conclusion yet to this long-term campaign for improvement, and, until Lord Cameron ceased being Lord Advocate in January 1989, not much progress. He seemed not to understand that there was any particular problem and thought we had "fundamental misconceptions" about the law" [Edinburgh Rape Crisis workers in Grit and Diamonds (Stramullion, 1990)]*

Lord Cameron was not alone among a judiciary who failed to grasp the realities of rape, and routinely assigned blame to women. The attitudes that confronted a woman in court and the difficulties she faced there could often depend on the personalities (in particular of the judges) involved, and the extent to which they were in tune with the realities of the situation:

> "There were good judges and there were bad judges and it would depend entirely on what judge it was, how well the woman felt she had been treated, but quite often, she did feel that the judge had somehow been kind to her and that was a tremendous, that made it, even when the bloke got off with a not proven, or a not guilty which was much, much worse, she would feel somehow supported by that." [Aileen Christianson]

The comments made by judges in the course of rape trials frequently revealed deeply-held misogynistic attitudes:

> "Naomi and I collected cuttings, because we used them for our staff development exercise. So we had almost like a scrap book where we would sort of look at the Daily Record, Daily Mail, Herald, big

papers…things like judges sentencing was horrific. You know? And their comments were unbelievable. Things like, I can remember one particular one that Naomi and I cut out, and it was a judge, I think it was in, near London, and it was a particularly horrific case, and he said to the jury something like, I mean it's probably quite a well quoted one now…'You mustn't always listen to the views of small boys and women, because they're prone to lying.' And this was what he said to the jury before they delivered their verdict. And the guy was found not guilty. But it was awful – some of the judges' comments were unbelievable. They're worse than the police – the judges' comments were shocking. And very learned, they had all the cloak of respectability…We used to cut out a lot of quotes from judges, and details of cases that we could use." [Jane Dorby]

Under the heading "*'Negligence' and a fine for rape*", a letter from Patricia Bell on behalf of Strathclyde Rape Crisis appeared in the Glasgow Herald on January 14th 1982:

"Sir, __The Strathclyde Rape Crisis Centre protests strongly against the decision of Judge Bernard Richards to fine a man £2000 for the crime of rape. We were further horrified to read the Judge's comment that "the victim was guilty of a great deal of contributory negligence."

There are a number of points to be noted. The man pled guilty. There was no doubt that the rape occurred. By deciding to fine the accused, rather than give a custodial sentence, Judge Richards has diminished the gravity of this offence and the obvious adverse effects which it has on the woman.

We are convinced that his decision, and his comments, unless publicly repudiated by the legal profession, will lead to other women deciding not to report rapes, for fear that they will be similarly attacked in court. This will lead to the true incidence of rape being further concealed. We are equally convinced that this case will not act as a deterrent to men in the future.

The idea that the woman contributed to this rape is absolutely unforgivable. If these comments are allowed to stand it is horrific to imagine the extent to which women could be denied basic human rights by the allegation of contributory negligence. To say that she was "negligent" to hitchhike home is only a short step from saying that she deserved to be raped. Hitchhiking is not against the law, and it is difficult to see how hitchhiking is any more dangerous than walking or standing at a bus stop. If she had hailed a taxi and then been attacked by the driver, would that have been negligence? If she had been murdered, would the sentence have been reduced?

It is clear that judgements like these reinforce the idea that women are expected to live within certain limits, which are set by men, and that they will be punished if they step outside these limits.

The penalty for rape should match the gravity of the crime, Judges should not be allowed to let their views about the type of women likely to be raped, or the type of man likely to be a rapist, cloud their judgement. We had hoped that Judges were in a position to know the facts of rape and not be influenced by popular myths, but this is obviously not the case." Patricia Bell, Strathclyde Rape Crisis Centre

Later on the same year, Judge David Wild, in summing up another rape case, said:

"Women who say no do not always mean no. It is not just a question of saying no. It is a question of how she says it, how she shows and makes it clear. If she doesn't want it, she only has to keep her legs shut and she would not get it without force and there would be marks of force being used."

As Jimmy Reid commented in his column (where the judge was quoted)

"I suppose, according to this logic, the best evidence of rape is when the woman resists until she is battered near to death. It would certainly make it easier for the courts." [The Glasgow Herald, December 13th, 1982]

The double standards and attitudes prejudicial towards women evident in much judicial commentary also underpinned the decision-making processes of some juries:

"I remember them staring at her a lot…she seemed to be on trial basically…here's a woman who's saying she was raped, let's have a look at and see what she looks like and how she sounds and stuff. She's a working class woman as well and…there's certainly issues for me…my feminism was very much about… thinking about class issues as well. And I did think that, as a working class woman in the court…she had less standing." [Margaret McCutcheon]

"And juries…clearly often think well, I think he probably did force her to have sex, but I don't think it's really gonna ruin her life and he seems like quite a nice guy and that I think is something that society is not 100% behind – a notion that…rape's just the same… whether you've had loads of partners or whether you haven't. I think they clearly think no, what difference is it gonna make?" [Jan Macleod]

Very occasionally, it was possible to witness this first-hand:

"I think there still seems to be a punitive attitude amongst juries…a member of Edinburgh Rape Crisis… was a jury member on a rape trial once, it was very interesting, and she said that when it came to the jury deliberations, she expected people to say well, 'he said this' and 'she said that', and it seemed to come down to 'she was a bit of a slapper – he seemed alright'. And what was interesting – this was 20-odd years ago is…they'd been in a relationship these people which had ended – some of the jury members seemed to feel it wasn't worth sending him to jail for, and…neighbours had heard fighting – the woman had had rope burns round her neck, you know – there was physical evidence…Then people said 'Oh, yeah, right enough, she did fight him off then' – but people seemed quite keen to jump in straight away and say 'Do we like him or do we like her?' And I think partially through her intervention, the man was convicted." [Morna Findlay]

Another worker at the Edinburgh centre also served on a rape jury and had a more positive first-hand experience (although brief) of the judge in the trial, though her impression of the defence advocate was less positive:

"I can't remember which judge it was, but he was so angry…the Defence Advocate …often defends rapists, and he's an Edinburgh advocate. And…he had waited 'til the morning of the trial to ask for more time to get psychiatric reports, 'cause…the complainer and the accused…were educationally challenged…Anyway, the judge was so angry that [he] had waited until then to ask, thereby causing distress to the woman, he had everybody who was in for the jury that morning into the court, and then he tore a strip off of the advocate. He had to allow him the time, but, and then he dismissed us all…He was just spitting and I think he was one of the judges that we knew was actually sympathetic to what we did because you know, you could see the judgements."

In the course of rape trials, women were very often held responsible for what had happened to them:

"There was still very much this idea that women were partly responsible. That they had a part to play in what was happening because maybe they'd been drinking or the kind of clothes they were wearing or they put themselves in a position of danger by hitchhiking…the usual kind of excuses made for men… But at the same, which was kind of infuriating…there was definitely…a sort of willingness to alter and to have…police officers specifically trained to deal with women who were reporting … a sexual assault or rape and also to have special premises so, in that sense that was very encouraging. But …these two strands…have kept going actually over the years. Because there is still a large number of the population who believe women are responsible." [Florence Germain]

"I remember her being absolutely and utterly distressed…being cross-examined. I remember her reputation being talked about. And all of the things that would be normal in your life suddenly becoming skewed about who you had had a sexual relationship with, who you'd had a personal relationship with…with the defence lawyer really turning it into a woman-blaming position. And I remember specifically…he talked about a tattoo she had, because of course…women with tattoos in those days were deemed to be a bit mad… And she had a tattoo which gave an indication that she might have been involved in hallucinogenic drugs as well…She had mental health issues as well, which had pre-existed the rape and of course that again was used …against her…it was to do with, you know, drugs and alcohol being a factor and…the tattoo being a symbol of this woman who's not really an upstanding citizen." [Margaret McCutcheon]

As a lawyer, Fiona Raitt found that her legal training had not prepared her for the reality that faced women who had survived rape and sexual abuse:

"The pitch that I'd been given and which was very much the straight view of this is the law of rape, this is what happens in court, this is what the police do, this is what the police surgeon does, this is how we gather evidence, this is the outcome. Oh and by the way not many people are convicted. But there was no explanation of why not many people were convicted or why women make a complaint and then perhaps don't want to follow it through. That instead of being seen as that's a false complaint, it might be because actually the system makes it very uncomfortable for them to continue." [Fiona Raitt]

Involvement with Dundee Rape Crisis changed this for good:

"It made a huge difference to me as a person but also to thinking, I've got to change the whole way I do my practice…and to start making it almost more… the term now would be client-centred, but just really trying to make sure you listen to what people are saying and not assume that because they say this has happened to me that things have happened the way…they ought to have as opposed to how they really have… And so stories about how badly people might have been treated by the police…that will be exactly how it was…it was a real shock.

It allowed me… in a small way, to start telling other lawyers about do you really know how this goes on? And of course, even at that time and I suspect it's still true now…most people in dealing with law as a rape or…in sexual offences…they were defending the offender, they weren't actually thinking about… the women and if you talk to Procurator Fiscal or people who are…prosecuting, they certainly don't now even, certainly didn't then, have any sense that they were responsible for acting for or taking care of this woman who was … the complainer." [Fiona Raitt]

The myth that false accusations were common persisted, as it still does today:

"And it was just quite clear that they had been given the message that rape was a crime that is often false and that you don't need to sort of prosecute it with a great deal of vigour. I mean they wouldn't have said that officially obviously but it filtered through. It changed quite quickly though, I mean that was before 1984." [Jan Macleod]

"The way in which cases are initially recorded by the police can have, obviously, a major effect in terms of prosecutorial decision-making – the stereotype of the woman making a false allegation out of malice, spite, trying to get out of a difficult situation…there is still…a very pervasive belief in the woman as making false allegations…Other research in this area has found that, in relation to false allegations, women who allege rape are no more likely or less likely to make false allegations than other victims of other kinds of violent crime…so there's nothing remarkable about cases where women are alleging rape or whether they have a higher level of false allegation, but there still seems to be a very pervasive myth about that." [Michele Burman]

An article in The Glasgow Herald in October 1978 stated that:

"False accusations of rape have made the police very wary and cautious. We believe that these accusations are on the increase."

An officer was quoted in the same piece as saying:

"In my opinion they are more prevalent now than they were say, 10 or 20 years ago, and I attribute it to present-day attitudes among young people who are far more promiscuous than previous generations." ["*Sex evidence that can prolong the woman's ordeal*" in The Glasgow Herald, October 16th, 1978]

Rape Crisis workers, however, were always well aware of the realities underlying these myths:

"There's…I suppose an issue about 'frivolous'…prosecutions…saying in the papers, this is happening all the time when in fact it's not. And to actually go through all that and then not to be able to complete the thing is not a frivolous prosecution, it's actually just somebody not being able to cope…and the fact that a case is proven not guilty or is not proven… it doesn't mean it didn't actually happen." [Sheila Brodie]

Aileen Christianson (on behalf of Edinburgh Rape Crisis) took issue with Glasgow Herald journalist Bruce McCain's remarks on this subject in a piece he wrote about the Glasgow Rape Case:

"Sir – Bruce McCain, in an otherwise helpful article on the legal facts surrounding the current Crown Office controversy over rape still betrays an uninformed attitude to so-called "false reporting" of rape.

He, apparently at random, chooses to worry about "an alleged rape victim…not telling the truth" as a possible reason for Crown Counsel doubts about a case. The Edinburgh Rape Crisis Centre cannot emphasise strongly enough that this is a thoughtless use of an inaccurate and dangerous prejudice. There is no evidence to support the view that women "often" make false reports of rape. A New York study found that the percentage of false report of rape was about 2%, roughly the same as for any other crime.

Yet somehow the belief that women make false reports of rape is still repeated as a justification for harsh questioning by police, procurators fiscal and defence Counsel of women who have been raped.

The various events of the past few weeks must have made it clear that no woman voluntarily puts herself through the ordeal of legal procedures in rape trials if she has not actually suffered the worse trauma of rape. That there is not always sufficient corroborative evidence to lead to a conviction in no way means that she has made a false report.

And the sooner all involved recognise this consciously, the sooner writers like Bruce McCain, plucking this misleading example from their subconscious, will stop reinforcing this myth of "false report." [The Glasgow Herald, January 1982]

This sort of dismissive attitude and the reduction of rape and sexual assault to something that was, in the scale of things, not such a big deal anyway, was something Moira Kane, in her capacity as a social worker, was already familiar with:

"When I was working…one particular family that I worked with, the father was a hell of an abuser, it was just awful…but he also had other kinds of convictions, and the police constantly did deals with him – if you plead guilty to those burglaries…we'll let you off with that…that had to be the conclusion I came to – that wasn't as important…it was his sister that told me some of this – she had been abused by him…by this time the man was in his 50's, it had been going on a long long time. His daughter was my client and she'd been seriously abused by him and the police knew…they must have known, and yet they did these deals with him…the sister had approached the police and was happy to give evidence. The daughter was a bit more disturbed, I don't know how well she would have done in that sense." [Moira Kane]

Ignorance of the impact of child sexual abuse was widespread:

"Sometimes it was taken seriously. But I think overall, it's still a long way to go – I think it very much depends on the judge you get, if there's a judge involved who's had someone in his or her family who's experienced rape or sexual assault they know the impact…" [Heather Forrest]

"I do reports for the Court now and I still get barristers saying 'You're really telling me this would have harmed this child?' 'Yeah, this would have harmed this child.' 'How would this have harmed this child?' 'Well, actually it would have affected their brain development in this way and that way and the other way'…so the new research has been really helpful…the new research on the brain and how the brain reacts to trauma." [Liz Hall]

As a woman complainer in a rape trial was (and still is) technically a witness to the crime, and the Crown's role is not to represent her interests but the "interests of justice", women can feel extremely isolated and vulnerable. The accused has a lawyer acting on his behalf (with whom he is familiar by the time of the trial), keeping him informed and representing him throughout; a woman has no one acting in this capacity for her:

"There's a very strong public service element which at one level is very commendable, but it means that …there is no one there to explain to the woman why this has happened and she is left feeling, well there's nobody acting for me. And I certainly feel as somebody…who used to spend a lot of time trying to support women, just by giving advice and information, if I'd been able to be in court doing that and been able to watch out for the questions that were inappropriate and jump up and object, which I bet somebody else does, but they don't bother to do it…if my brief was to object to those questions, there'd be a whole different…set of checks and balances…I don't know if it'd make a difference…but I certainly think we should give it a try." [Fiona Raitt]

This sense of no one being there to represent her, to limit the extent and nature of her questioning – or even communicate the most basic court procedures to her was often in evidence, and had a terrible impact on rape complainers:

"I thought that the length of time that she was questioned was appalling. I thought the information that was given about her was appalling, and it wasn't properly explained to her…when the public were going to come back in that she could actually exit the court…Which meant that when the public came back in, both her and I were sitting in the court. Now, it would only be the first two or three people… into the public benches that would know, 'Oh, they're already here, so it's one of them.' but it wasn't explained to her properly, because I tried to say to her quietly 'Do you want to remain here or do you want to leave?' And she was so…shaken up that she couldn't really take in what I was saying to her, and I felt that somebody should have taken responsibility…it would be the Judge, cos it was the High Court…to say 'Now, this is what you can do, you've got choices here' and taken his time to explain that to her." [Margaret Brown]

As the accused is under no obligation to take the stand, there is no opportunity to examine directly his account of events, or to scrutinise his behaviour, motivation or demeanour (although every opportunity can be taken to scrutinise the woman he is alleged to have assaulted):

> "Colleagues in England tell me that the fact that…when juries see the man in the witness box and then have a comparison between the two sets of behaviours, it does often make a difference…all those things become, is that really plausible? He said, 'Well yeah she didn't want this and she didn't want that but … at the end of the day she consented'. And I think the jury would think 'Oh yeah…', but…they don't have to get into any of that if he just sits quietly and all they've got is a police statement which might be very bald, where he's simply said 'I'm saying nothing except that she consented'. What are you gonna do with that?" [Fiona Raitt]

The adversarial nature of the Scottish legal system can present real difficulties to prosecutors attempting to mount effective prosecutions for rape:

> "Our legal system is basically…adversarial, it's…confrontational – it's about who argues the best case. I mean…when you look at the Tommy Sheridan trial…if you put up a really good show, that can sway a jury…" [Rona Clarke]

> "The prosecution service are very, very under resourced…and they often have to recruit people who… if they have experience of the criminal courts, they'll be as defence lawyers, so …they know what the tactic is but they won't have worked out…how do I counter it? … And…not necessarily intentionally… there'll be a deep empathy with the defence because …that's the position they've been trained in for many years, that's how they've gained their experience. It'd be different if they started off in the fiscal's service and been trained all the way through… then again, their disadvantage is they don't know how the defence are thinking…and of course then this makes it sound like a game and in some respects it is…you're duelling with the person on the other side and it's…like chess, who's going to make the next move. And it simply shouldn't be like that…that's all very well if you're arguing about a contract to build a house, where there's an inanimate object that you're dealing with. If you're dealing with a woman and women's bodies and injuries, or a man or a boy or a girl, where it's a person, then you can't reduce it to… these very stark terms it's quite, it's quite wrong." [Fiona Raitt]

Gender-based misconceptions were also (and continue to be) used to undermine women complainers in other ways:

> "I know quite a lot of women lawyers now, who are at the bar, who do nothing but defend men…they do a lot of defence work, for men who are accused of rape. And I believe that…men often choose women because…there's maybe a belief that if they've got a female lawyer, the jury will think 'Oh well, if she's thinks…', and of course they're making the wrong connections because lawyers don't necessarily believe their client, they're there to represent their view and they don't have to like what their client did or didn't do." [Fiona Raitt]

Sometimes it seemed that juries would rather believe almost anything than convict a man, or give credence to a woman's account of an assault, however well supported by evidence:

> "Juries were horrific…they seemed to listen to any old guff, yeah I remember one woman that she got a lift home with somebody that she knew from a social situation and he broke her nose on the door frame he just whammed her head off the door frame and pushed her into the house and raped her and she was quite sure that he would get convicted cos her nose was broken. And he just said, 'Oh it was rough sex'. And the jury went for it, you know, and she was just could not believe it. You know I mean

it was totally dismissed. I remember the Fiscal didn't even bother asking about it or anything, so you got a general impression, and it is a general impression cos there were exceptions, that the Fiscals did not prosecute it very actively." [Jan Macleod]

If a rape trial did result in a conviction, the kinds of sentences that were handed down were rarely long ones, and did little to convince women that the crime was taken seriously. Jan Macleod recalls one conviction following the case of a woman she supported:

"He got a big sentence, he was an American soldier, and also he's black, which probably got him a bigger sentence I have to say if I'm being honest. And he'd seen her from the airport or something like that and raped her, but she also miscarried her baby so you would have expected him to get quite a big sentence…so she was one of a few people that I remember getting a conviction. I think then he only got six or eight years, it wasn't a huge sentence. I really can't honestly remember many other women who got a conviction." [Jan Macleod]

And very often, if a conviction was obtained, it was for a lesser offence, with little or no consultation with the woman as to how she felt about this:

"It's important to say to the woman look, this man's willing to say, willing to plead guilty to a particular kind of a sexual assault but not to what you say has happened. Now women really get no choice in this because if the Crown think well I'd rather get a conviction out of this and actually maybe there's not enough to prove …whether he assaulted her with something that…wasn't just sexual intercourse but there was a weapon that he assaulted [her with] or whatever, and then you think, I'm not going to prove that, so do we want to lose everything and he walks away, or do we try to prove, he's gonna plead to something so do we, do we accept that? Now I don't know how Crown prosecutors do it, but I suspect they don't even discuss it with the woman, she just finds out afterwards this is what. Now…part of what I would want to do would be to say to her look…it's Hobson's choice, you're not gonna like whatever way we go. But do you have a view about it?" [Fiona Raitt]

Many women lived in fear of their attacker's release date:

"We'd get a lot of calls from women who, where there had been a conviction they thought 'He's due to get out now' but they wouldn't be told when he was due for release…just living in that fear all over again…it was usually always, if there was any sentence, a pretty short sentence…even trying to get an interdict was just so difficult for people as well…" [Linda Reid]

A woman's demeanour or interpretations that were imputed to her appearance or situation were deemed relevant not only to the guilt or otherwise of her alleged attacker, but also to decision-making around what an appropriate sentence might be:

"One of the things I remember, one of the cases I remember being very live at the time that I was involved in Rape Crisis, was that, the Ealing Vicarage rape case… and it was a horrendous rape… she was a fabulous woman, but one of the things that seemed to be a feature of the court decision was that she didn't appear to be badly traumatised, so the guy got some sort of reduced sentence. You just think 'Oh my God!', you know?" [Leslie Brown]

Heather Forrest recalls her experience of supporting one woman in particular during a trial:

"She did really, really well and she talked about what had happened to her…she had been raped, semi-recently. She was one of the few women who had and…went forward and reported it, and she'd actually become pregnant as a result and had a son. And by the time the court, actually came to court her son was…a year old practically. But because she'd kept her son, I don't know if this played against her, but she'd kept the son and she loved him dearly and she'd separated… the baby from the rape. But…a lot of what…I felt happened there was because she'd accepted the baby and because this man had a good career and he came from a nice middle class family and he was a member of some posh tennis club…and because she didn't fight, she didn't struggle that much, she wasn't cut, she wasn't bruised…He was given sort of like 18 months suspended sentence, something pathetic like that…" [Heather Forrest]

And although legal arguments may have been modified slightly to accommodate more recent social changes and scientific developments, underlying attitudes seem to be very much the same as they were 30 years ago:

"In fact I think…what's happened very, very quickly is that in that period I was talking about when they stopped dropping so many rapes and putting up ones that weren't having a good chance of success, a lot of these are what they call date rape, acquaintance rape or whatever. And what the defence lawyers just did straight away was invent, you know instead of saying 'I wisnae there – it wisnae me', now that they've got forensics and that it just became 'Yeah well we had sex.' Do you know what I mean?

Even to the extent that you've got footballers and that going, 'Ah but we just had sex with her' and there's like five of them in their 20s and the girl's sixteen and yet, that is seen as acceptable, do you know? So the whole thing's just slightly twisted…but maintains the same thing which is to say well, if you were raped, which you might have been, you shouldn't have. You should have been more careful … it probably wasn't very nice, but you're young and you have been having sex since you were 14 so is it really worth locking this guy up for five years?" [Jan Macleod]

"We did see some legislative progress over that period, but the ability of defenders and their advisors to sort of wriggle out of that…was probably greater than we had anticipated." [Sheila Gilmore]

"A lot of those attitudes were around initially, and then they kind of pulled back a bit, and then because of the change in the way younger people have their social life now, apparently, I think they've probably crept back in again…So I think that is a new and different problem, and just the sheer amount of drink that the girls assert their right to be as pissed as boys, and I think then, probably, attitudes come in on them or they don't report or because they don't remember or something. So that's a change back, which is horrible." [Aileen Christianson]

It's hard to predict the extent to which new generations of Scottish lawyers might adopt alternative approaches that could redress the balance for rape complainers:

"I find I can have quite useful debates with students especially the older students who, when they understand a bit more about how law might construct women's stories in a particular way, and they understand more about how the justice system works…you can push them a bit, to say why is it happening like that and why do you think this is going on …they've got information but they also understand that they've come to accept certain beliefs about things that actually, come to think of it, might not be right. So in that sense, I feel you can, you can push ideas towards them and…some of them are quite receptive. But I also know that, and I come across them as young practising lawyers, five or six years later, that they've often reverted to the old type. Yes, yes they've trained with somebody who's very melodramatic about cross examination or something and they've kind of followed that pattern and that troubles me." [Fiona Raitt]

The deeply conservative nature of the legal profession creates serious problems for those attempting to effect the fundamental changes required to change this:

127

"The difficulty too is if you strike out as a bit of a person who's different, you are ostracised, and then you'll change nothing, so you are always left with this dilemma." [Fiona Raitt]

"The system has not changed ...really at all ...you could say we've tinkered at the edges with different things but for me it's pretty much the same as it always was." [Fiona Raitt]

Michele Burman describes the background to research she undertook in the late 1980's with colleagues at Edinburgh University into the impact of sexual history evidence legislation:

"I was doing an MSC in criminology...and then I went on to work at Edinburgh University immediately afterwards, and the research project that I went to work on was with Lynn Jamieson and Beverley Brown who were the grant-holders on a project which later became the sexual history evidence research project...I was employed as a researcher on the project, and this was a piece of research that'd been commissioned by The Scottish Office at the time and it was to evaluate a new piece of legislation that was introduced in 1986... The aim of the legislation was to restrict – limit the use of sexual history and sexual character evidence relating to complainers in sexual offence trials in Scotland. It was the first time that...so-called shield legislation had been introduced in Scotland, although...similar pieces of legislation with similar...legislative intent had been introduced in other jurisdictions around the world, and this had followed on from some recommendations from the Scottish Law Commission, and a great deal of debate... about the need for such legislation – how it was going to work... ...and that's how...I started specifically in relation to rape." [Michele Burman]

Michele had previously had contact with Edinburgh Rape Crisis when she attended some of their meetings with a view to becoming a volunteer, and now (in 1987) re-established the connection:

"This is where I came back into contact with Lily and the Rape Crisis centre...we went to Rape Crisis centre...to see if we could gain any assistance through Rape Crisis centre of women that would be able to be briefed and trained as researchers on the project, and as a result of that...Aileen Christianson was terribly helpful, and there are a number of women who basically signed up in the project...

We had some training days and discussion days and there were a group of women in Glasgow and a group of women in Edinburgh and a couple of women in other parts of the country that we got to know through the Rape Crisis network that could have some availability to attend trials...

We'd got advance permission from the Lord Justice Clerk and from the Lord Advocate to actually attend trials and we had identification so we would go in to the trials and sit through the entire... proceedings and take notes of the evidence – these were in the days before laptops and we weren't allowed to tape record for obvious reasons, but we took verbatim notes – there were a lot of women that did that so that was hugely helpful for the research because it meant that we had really good coverage than otherwise between the three of us, physically wouldn't have been able to do this – we would've probably been very much restricted to the central belt, and so we were able to do that." [Michele Burman]

So in addition to the support in court they already offered to women, Edinburgh Rape Crisis workers gained extensive further experience of the workings of the judicial process in rape and sexual assault cases in Scotland through their involvement in this research into the use of sexual history and character evidence in rape trials:

"We were approached in 1987 by Lynn and Beverley Brown and Michele Burman who came and talked to us as a collective about what they were doing, and said that the ideal would be that they would have access to full transcripts of the trials but that there were two difficulties with that – one was it was way too expensive and the Scottish Office wouldn't fund that...you had to pay for transcripts if you were a researcher…you have to pay for a transcript even if you were a person who was directly involved in the trial. So they couldn't afford it, but also, they felt that they could read transcripts and they would get what was said, but they would miss some of the nuances, and what they were partly interested in was how far the nuances had an impact.

And so they were asking for people who would be interested in doing…some field work with them… So there were about four of us, I think – it was myself and Bernie Kelly and Sue Hammersley. And somebody else – can't remember who the other person was. And we did a very basic training session, and then, what our job was, was to sit in court and transcribe. Write down everything we could get down about what was happening, and to try and note gesture, nuance, tone of voice, etc and really, really try to get it down as accurately as possible. Mostly, initially did Sheriff Court stuff in Edinburgh, and then they expanded it out and they wanted to cover the circuit, so I did some of the Stirling cases, High Court…1987 was when we started it, and I think it ran through to…near the end of 1988 or even into early 1989." [Lily Greenan]

"So a very important element of the research was called observation, and another very important element was interviews with legal practitioners about their views on the legislation – about the necessity of the legislation and about the value of the legislation and their interpretation of the legislation, and their views about sexual history and sexual character evidence. And a third aspect of it was we monitored every single sexual offence trial…we couldn't possible have covered them all [*Explanatory note: without assistance from the Rape Crisis workers*], but we monitored every single one at High Court and Sheriff Court level for three and a half years …" [Michele Burman]

What the women who were involved in this piece of research witnessed and recorded, even as seasoned Rape Crisis workers, was shocking:

"It was wearing and it was appalling at times, but it was also fascinating…how much of a game it is, that it's theatre to many of the people who are the key players in it, and the witnesses and victims are… brought in and they play a bit part. They're central to the action but they're not players. And the players were the…person sitting on the bench, whether a Judge or a Sheriff and the Advocate Depute and the defence QC…and their equivalents in Sheriff Court cases, and the jury are the audience…they're the ones who are there to observe and make up their mind about things, but they don't actually play a part – you know that they're the target for it – they're the focus of the activity and the action. They're the people that everyone else is playing to, but they don't really understand…at an academic level it was a fascinating process to watch. And the protocols…what was allowed and what was not allowed…the defence could…imply just about anything about the woman or any other witness, but there was a point at which they had to stop… They were very polite with each other, in some ways, whilst attempting to rip each other's work to shreds." [Lily Greenan]

And what that work appeared to comprise, to a large extent, was institutionalised misogyny:

"It got clearer that it's inbuilt, it's in the system itself to be anti-woman. It's not just about the people in it, there's something about the structure of the law and the way that it has developed and the way that it's played. It doesn't matter what the laws say, it's the way… that it was embedded in it, that it was profoundly woman-hating and you could almost feel it coming out the walls. It wasn't a place for women, it wasn't a place for women in any role. You could see it in the way that the women who were …the lawyers who were doing the prosecuting and the defending, you could see it just in the way that they had to conduct themselves. They behaved like men, they behaved like their male colleagues…They were part of the club. They dressed like them. I mean at one level, the robe and the wig are supposed to be about making everybody the same, but they're not, they're based on a white, male vision of what is authority and that really came across. I never saw a black or Asian face on the bench or sitting round the lawyer's table, and there were a couple of women that would be in there, just a couple." [Lily Greenan]

The so-called "rape shield" legislation was not, it emerged, providing very much, if any protection for women complainers:

> "We found that despite the existence of the legislation, the prohibited evidence was still being introduced…and we found…three key problems – one was simply the legislation was being ignored, and the defence would ask the questions anyway, and no one would prevent or object…so…there was straightforward breaches of the legislation, in that case. The other problem with the legislation is we found that even where an application was made to introduce sexual history evidence…often the judge would place parameters around the questions, so well you can ask that but not that, and don't stray into that area and keep it to this – certain events or this particular date or this particular encounter or this particular relationship…so the legislation would be introduced, and… the questioning would be allowed, or at least some aspect of the questioning would be allowed, but the defence would stray beyond the parameters…or introduce entirely new evidence that hadn't been the subject of the application." [Michele Burman]

A further problem related to the introduction and impact of straightforward character evidence:

> "The use of evidence such as lifestyle for example…what she dresses, where she goes, how much she has to drink…is evidence which is actually nothing to do with sex, or sexual history, or sexual behaviour, but if you introduce that kind of evidence over the course of a trial, cumulatively, it can grow a picture of a woman who is likely to consent. This is a kind of woman who goes out at night into dives of low character wearing this, that and the other, on her own, and has too much to drink, gets into conversation with a man…if that kind of evidence can be introduced over the course of the trial, and elicited not only from the complainer…but from a range of other witnesses, the person next door, her friend, defence witnesses, about the kind of girl that she is, the kind of woman that she is, that that can be equally as damaging, equally as pernicious as straightforward sexual history evidence about how many men she's slept with in the past." [Michele Burman]

There was everywhere a sense of collusion and a system so entrenched in a "shared presumption of relevance" that these created an almost insuperable opposition to any attempts to end prejudicial questioning of women seeking justice for rape:

> "It's partly to do with the adversarial system…it may be that the evidence has been agreed in advance… with the defence and the prosecution…that this evidence is acceptable or is relevant…they may share a presumption of relevance that this is actually indeed relevant and admissible evidence…" [Michele Burman]

Everywhere Rape Crisis workers attended court to support women, similar experiences brought home the horrifying reality of the ordeal faced by survivors seeking justice:

> "The thing that sticks in my mind – what I think is a terrible thing to have exposed in court – in any kind of situation, actually – was that the defence solicitor spoke about …it was the part where they were talking about injuries…And the police doctor had said in the report that it looked as if there was some swelling around her vagina. However, he deemed it to be that she was…fleshier than most women in that area, and that it wasn't swelling at all…He was found not guilty." [Margaret Brown]

The consequences of this for the women seeking justice could be devastating:

> "There was a woman who was working as a prostitute in Leith, that he'd raped, and the defence shredded her, I mean absolutely totalled her…put her on the stand, everything about her – her

reputation, her character, I mean I'd never seen any person treat any other person like that. And the phrase 'wilting violet' sticks in my head, because what he opened with, he opened the attack by saying 'Well it's not like you're some wilting violet, you know, kind of character, is it?' And she didn't know what he meant and so he started by attacking her intelligence, and then he went on to attack what she was doing to earn money, and he left her nameless…and she was in bits but she kept saying what had happened…

She stuck with this is what he did, and there was something specific about the way this guy operated and the kind of conversation he would have with people …it was consistent with what other witnesses, there were three women that gave evidence – two of them that he'd raped and one attempted rape…I think what that woman did was she gave the evidence that was able to convict him…but there was no-one who could give evidence to support what she was saying, it was almost like she…set the scene, she was the first one up, and the next woman up was a churchgoer, a nice woman who was…out for a walk and he'd attacked her, and it was a very different kind of attack…But there was something that he said to both of them and I can't remember what it was…They had some evidence linking him to the murders – there was a lot of forensic stuff and he was done, in the end, he was found guilty. He was found guilty of everything except raping the prostitute." [Lily Greenan]

Criminal injuries compensation

Women who had been assaulted were entitled to claim Criminal Injuries Compensation. This could offer some small measure of recognition and recompense for what they'd been through, although it was dependent on reporting to the police. Sometimes it was only in discussions around their compensation claims that women managed to find out about the progress of their cases. Fiona Raitt recalled:

"I did a lot of cases involving Criminal Injuries Compensation. And I found even if people didn't want to go through that process because it did mean that…they would have had to at least reported it to the police, and to have been seen by a doctor at some stage, because it didn't matter that the complaint hadn't …proceeded and been not been successful in court – if you'd made the complaint and the police thought it was sufficient or the Crown thought it was sufficient to prosecute, you could often get compensation…All that meant was it hadn't been proven beyond reasonable doubt whereas, for criminal injuries compensation, if you had been injured, you really only had to show that in a balance of probabilities…

More and more it struck me that the women who were coming…to talk about the claim… suddenly realised…how little they were being told …if they'd been referred to Rape Crisis or had called, they knew a bit more, but sometimes they hadn't and they'd just gone with their sister or a friend or somebody … they certainly didn't know, they said oh yes, I gave a statement but I've never heard anything and it's months later." [Fiona Raitt]

Spreading the word: talks & training

Communicating the realities of sexual violence became a key part of the work of many Rape Crisis centres, even in the earliest days when resources were very minimal:

> *"We've given talks to anyone who asked us (including, since 1982, Lothian and Borders Police) and we've had stalls at annual fundraising events like the Charities Hypermarket or the Meadows Festival, in the belief that our visibility would spread the word to women that we exist and that talking about our experiences and beliefs will eventually leads to changing attitudes" [Still a long fight ahead, by ERCC workers in Grit and Diamonds – Stramullion, 1990]*

> "I began to tackle the agencies... And the politics of it, because that's where my anger was." [Jane Dorby]

> "In the 1980's the Rape Crisis Centre was really quite influential I think in child protection and there was a period when the Social Work department...took a feminist approach to incest and child sexual abuse and we...input quite a lot of training there...Some of that was done though the project, some of it was done through Rape Crisis Centre, sometimes it was joint." [Jan Macleod]

> "There were some women in the collective who would do the talks to women's groups, and there were others who would be quite comfortable doing church groups and people like the Guides, and the Scouts...I remember we did a session with 65 Venture Scouts once." [Lily Greenan]

> "I remember doing a joint thing with Social Work and some police. The police sat there in their suits, all bolt upright, and the social workers lounged on the floor in their sandals and their long beads (laughs) I mean, it was absolutely stereotypical." [Liz Hall]

Records kept by Highland Rape Crisis reveal that in 1983 the group gave many talks to a very diverse range of agencies:

> "We did five talks to the students at Inverness Tech, Nairn Academy three, nurses, first year nurses at Raigmore three, National Childbirth Trust...Soroptimists, postgraduate paediatric group...Women's Aid in Dingwall, Highland Association for Counselling...the Labour Party." [Sue Owen]

> "19 talks, and Sue was the main talker" [Gale Chrisman]

> "We'd talk about the work of the Centre, we'd talk about how we got started, what we were there for, what we thought the needs were, a bit about how we worked, always with an eye to maybe getting some volunteers out there...and then there would be questions and that would always get into a general discussion about the politics of rape...everywhere, at some point 'Yes, but some women ask for it.'... And young men... not so able to articulate but clearly going somewhere down the road of biological determinism, you know? 'We can't help it, really, you know? ...we have all these urges...which we can't control...'" [Sue Owen]

Rape Crisis workers often faced difficult challenges in trying to raise awareness:

> "Rape Crisis struggled to get heard. They did get heard, but ...There was so much that we had to fight against, and you know, people would go and do a talk and they'd come back in and they'd be defeated... Because of the response, because of the kind of really crass things that people said to them and, you know, they were just blaming women, really, and 'You know, what do you know about it?' kind of thing." [Liz Hall]

> "I think actually the more difficult people were the mental health professionals. Psychiatrists, psychologists. Because they have a particular power position, and they were very loathe to hear our

point of view…wouldn't be very keen on us doing training, would…sort of say…you know…' We're dealing with this' or 'There isn't a lot of this around' or, you know, 'Hands off' sorta thing." [Siobhan Canavan]

All sorts of organisations, groups and professions were targeted by Rape Crisis centres in their efforts to communicate the realities of gender-based violence, and sexual violence in particular:

"We'd try and go round social work colleges sometimes and went to Leverndale Hospital psychiatric nurses a few times…things like that…Women's Aid would often be doing that kind of thing as well… the one we were often called for would be…the Police Federation's Wives…" [Caroline Armit]

Glasgow Rape Crisis workers even contributed to training given to inmates at Dungavel prison as part of a pre-release training programme:

"I remember Jan and I did…Dungavel prison… an open prison…for men…the Governor was a woman… it was really serious – we were out for a few weeks…I remember the first one we did…we tried to… do sexism… a wee bit of gender raising awareness, so…we got baby cards…so you had the pink… girl cards, and your blue boy cards, and of course the reciprocal wording…a few things to stimulate discussion…a group of maybe four or five of them and a couple of warders…

It went alright – to be honest I think one of the things …I remember thinking about was one of the warders was equally as frightening as any of the men…" [Caroline Armit]

Police training

The police were always high on the list of agencies targeted by Rape Crisis centres in their efforts to spread the word about the realities of rape and sexual assault. Rape Crisis workers knew, not only from what women had told them of their own experiences, but also from attitudes expressed by many of police they came into contact with while developing the service, how much work needed to be done to change attitudes and police practice:

"When we requested that a police woman…come and speak to us, she came in uniform, and she told us about women who told lies…about rape…that was awful. She said that often they would find that they would go through a complaint with a woman to find that it was a lie. And then she told us this story about a young girl, just in recent times…who had been out late and she was going to get into trouble at going home late so she thought she would create a drama by reporting that she'd been raped and that would get her off the hook with her parents…One of the volunteers…Tanya, she was a real little fighter…she was 'Wow…I'm really gonna challenge you' – so we all had to kinda hold back, and calm it down a bit – it really was horrible…I can remember her kind of smiling in a not very pleasant kind of a way…you kind of got from her that she kind of felt sorry for us, being so naïve." [Norma Benzie]

In October 1978, the Glasgow Herald ran two pieces which described the minimal training given to police officers on rape and sexual assault:

"Ironically the Sex Discrimination Act diminished what scant opportunity existed in Scotland for trainee policewomen to attend specialist lectures on sexual assault at the Scottish Police Training College, at Tulliallan. Such facilities were deemed sexist by the Act" ["*Assaults that women do not report – time for changed police attitudes?*" by Anne Simpson, Jean Donald, Ann Shaw and Doug Gillon in The Glasgow Herald, October 16th, 1978]

In a second item entitled "A low priority in the crime fight", The Glasgow Herald reported in October 1978 that:

"Trainee policewomen in Scotland used to attend special lectures on rape or child molestation cases, but when the Sex Discrimination Act came into force this was stopped.

According to Superintendent Peter McNab, director of junior training at the Police Training College, Tulliallan, this has meant the loss of a lot of expertise. Instruction in dealing with this type of crime now takes up a mere one-and-a-half hours of the nine week training course.

'Now rape is simply included in the teaching of Common Law, then we have a practical role-playing session where the part of the victim and assailant are played out,' says Superintendent McNab. 'It's a great pity that we don't do more. In the past, we had lectures by experts. Now all we can really do is emphasise the importance of treating these women with special consideration'" [**Glasgow Herald**, October 16th, 1978]

Developing and delivering police training was a major challenge for Rape Crisis workers. Persuading the police to include the issue of violence against women within their training programmes was no easy matter, as Women's Aid workers had already discovered:

"Women's Aid had been running in Central Scotland since '74…in terms of domestic abuse, the police were only just beginning to be willing to have training, and to discuss with us, and the relationship was often quite fraught, even at a very senior level." [Kate Arnot]

The talks themselves were never an easy prospect, although they paid dividends in developing skills within the collective:

"Jan was very good at the links with the police…she went over to Tulliallan…that was…a huge issue and difficult, even though I considered her a superbly competent/confident woman, I don't think that it was easy…it was just all the attitudes at the time were hellish…" [Kathy Litteljohn]

"I really value that experience for what it taught me about how to construct an argument, how to avoid defensiveness with a group…and how not to show fear (laughing) you know, it was really important with those early police talks, not to show them that you were scared. You had to be able to go in and be super-confident, without pissing them off because you were too smart…it was fine tuning, it was learning where the line was." [Lily Greenan]

"We asked for interviews with Chief Inspectors and things like that, and they were polite and they realised, there was some quite enlightened views there, definitely, and there was a particular Chief Inspector, I don't, he was quite an elderly man at the time, and he said, well we have a staff development programme, perhaps we could give you an hour. And we went, and we did say some shocking things, because we prepared quite well for it, and we got quite a reaction… We had been to talks and things, and we got a big sympathy vote, 'cause nobody wants to be unsympathetic to rape but when you get into the politics of it, and the gender of it, and the feminism of it, that's when you really connect with people." [Jane Dorby]

"Certainly when Caroline and I went to talk to these CID officers they were all grown men…they were older than us, and she was only in her early 20's at the time, I was 18…so these looked like a bunch of Dads to us – that's how I remember them. I don't think we were the first in the group to visit them and there were subsequent groups – I think someone in the police must have been quite interested in having us visit…this would be '79, maybe 1980, and my memory of them was that they…felt freely able to say 9 out of 10 women who report rape are lying. A woman comes in and reports her story and we'll drive a horse and cart through it. Somebody might have come home late, and rather than get into trouble with her parents…she'll tell them that she's been raped cos that's easier than getting a row…for being half an hour late. This is what they believed… It's maybe juries that have these attitudes now…less so … the police…so I do remember us sitting there in a lecture theatre with this big bank of people from The Sweeney, and…I'm kind of impressed that we took them on…" [Morna Findlay]

"And we began to talk about the psychology of how you regard women and how do you come to dehumanise a woman at that stage…what makes men so dehumanising and so apart from women that they can regard them so violently? And we started talking about gender roles, about young women and how we're brought up… and they started to poo poo it…we had quite a reaction from the audience. We had a question and answer session, and it was quite aggressive…but it actually showed, I think, the police, who were organising the staff development, that this was quite useful – because I think they were quite taken aback…. So they invited us back, and they gave us a morning and an afternoon, so we had groups and things like that going. And that was good, that was very good. It was slightly harassing (laughing) but it was good." [Jane Dorby]

"Initially, of course, they just thought we were interfering, stupid women and I can remember quite early on…I started doing radio stuff, news programmes, and I can remember somebody from the Police Federation being really stupid and idiotic, and I basically was arguing with them on air. They had some terrible attitudes, but…we began to do training talks with them …down in Stockbridge, and we did them along with Women's Aid…At the police, I always felt that if you could get them comfortable with some of your ideas, they were gonna be open to more of them." [Aileen Christianson]

The publication of the Scottish Office Social Research Study "**Investigating Sexual Assault**" by Gerry Chambers and Ann Millar, which laid bare for the first time extensive problems in police practice and procedures in dealing with cases of rape and sexual assault, led to Rape Crisis centres becoming more involved in police training, as the messages they had been struggling to communicate for years began finally to start trickling through:

"There was a meeting with the Assistant Chief Constable in Lothian and Borders police to talk about what we were doing and what we were about…there were three women from the centre who went, and they met with the Assistant Chief, I think…and they talked about…what would be helpful as a response. It…came after the publication of the Investigating Sexual Assault report…That was the trigger…so out of that came an agreement that we would do an input…to police probationers and subsequently, we got involved in doing inputs to the sergeants' refresher courses, as they were called, which were a nightmare…And later we did them to inspectors, and they were forty minute – they were talks, they weren't training, they were forty minute inputs as part of…training… weeks, usually or days that Fettes were putting together for their officers." [Lily Greenan]

"We did a number of sessions with different police officers…and some outside Aberdeen as well…" [Isla Laing]

"I remember being involved with training with the police…which was quite interesting, I mean some of the language…and some of the views that the police had…we shouldn't have been surprised…so we developed some training materials…you know, do you think this is true or false?…

Some of the questions were like… 'Women often falsely accuse men of rape…' We had the police into small groups to discuss…and it was quite amazing the discussions they used to have amongst themselves, with some people maybe quite strongly thinking yes women frequently falsely accuse men of rape, and other people saying of course not…" [Isla Laing]

"We would kind of use little vignettes to get people to think, and…we'd look at myths and stuff. We'd look at Sarah Nelson's book and, you know, take ideas from that. I mean, we just had to really devise it all ourselves…that was very experiential and it was, it always had a commitment to having the survivor's voice in it, always, so we would use a lot of things that people had written and stuff and things that people we knew had given us that…we could use for training purposes." [Siobhan Canavan]

"In those days, there was no way they would have invited us to talk to them or anything, oh no. We once invited the Detective Inspector …to a training day, and it was one of our very first – it was inter-agency. I don't know why it was so ambitious – it was terrible! …we did it well, but I remember it being absolutely nerve-racking. And we asked him to be a mother – in the mother-child-daughter, and he kept losing it – he kept forgetting that he was a mother! And he would say 'It's ok – the problem's sorted – I've killed him!'…so that was a good experience! That seemed to be the start of – they must have been sort of looking around and saying well, you know, got to start taking this seriously, and it all got better after that." [Norma Benzie]

The reception to the input to police training undertaken by Rape Crisis centres was variable:

"It was hit or miss with the probationers, although it depended on who you had in the group. They were polite, because they were trained to be polite to visitors, but they were told that they could argue with us, and that we welcomed challenge, so they argued with us and they challenged us…

The sergeant refresher courses were literally like going into the lion's den. You knew you were gonna come out mauled, and you had to be up for it. I mean…you could come out knowing that you had reached one person…once, I came out and I had turned the whole group round and I was amazed… like they had actually kind of grudgingly accepted that maybe there was something in what I was saying.

All we were trying to promote was…your job could be easier if you were to consider other ways to work with women who are making allegations of sexual assault. We quoted evidence that suggested that aggressive questioning of women was not helpful, and we did that every single time. We did it from 1982 until 1992. We did that in every single police session. We said the evidence that we have seen, heard and read tells, us that you will get more out of women as witnesses of a crime if you are not aggressive in your questioning of them. And they just kept saying 'We have to test them to make sure…' And they did that for ten years, and then they began to move…

We had some really kind of quite specific examples that we used to use, and one was about a woman who had been questioned using a fairly gentle layering technique, who suddenly remembered she could smell yeast when the guy was attacking her, she could smell yeast, and he turned out to be a baker. You know?… So we used stuff like that, you know… but what we got a lot was, '98% of allegations are false' and…all that kind of stuff." [Lily Greenan]

"Mostly, they were relatively hostile or polite, and whatever they thought – who knew, initially…maybe five years into that, you could see a substantial change in their attitudes. Not all of them, obviously, but some of them quite clearly thought what we were saying was useful…there was one terrific afternoon where I said something and somebody attacked me, and one of the other police then defended me, and they had a big row, and I just sat back and watched – it was fantastic, and that would never have happened when we began, 'cause they were suspicious of us…what we always felt was it didn't matter what they thought of us. If one of them subsequently treated a woman better…that was worth it." [Aileen Christianson]

"There were still some incredibly strange attitudes…I remember going to see the police and saying, you know, 'If a woman doesn't seem upset, remember this is a big trauma and they shut that down.' I remember saying that to them…Some went 'aha!' and the light bulb went on and others went 'Yeah, yeah, yeah'." [Liz Hall]

"Some of it felt quite scary sometimes and intimidating in a way – we'd had this arrangement where we would go and speak to…newly qualified police officers…Sandra Hood was the person that we spoke to…And it did kind of feel a bit intimidating but when we went and we were speaking to sort of like 50 police officers…we thought they'd be like quite aggressive and stuff, but they weren't – I mean they were really, really good. It was quite amazing that they were really supportive and understanding… they wouldn't be judging… saying it doesn't matter how much woman's been drinking, yes obviously that doesn't help sometimes, but it's still not a woman's responsibility. So it really was impressive. Not right across the board but it was." [Heather Forrest]

"There was a lot of resistance… from well, it was mainly male police officers…I don't know if we were talking about having more, maybe women police officers and I remember one higher ranking chap, it was about, you know, women, 'But then they go off you know and have babies'. Big deal, I mean if men had babies, the work situation would have taken that into account." [Florence Germain]

Progress was slow, but it was made. In 1984, sexual offences support units such as the Woman and Child Units (WACU) in Edinburgh and the Female and Child Units in Glasgow were set up and the input of Rape Crisis centres was a major contributory fact in that development:

"At that point, there was kind of a switch because…the high heid yins realised there was a real problem, and it was kind of top down… they did begin to think yes well maybe there should be units…'cause they had abolished the Women and Children's Unit, which always had been policed by women police officers when the Sex Discrimination Act came in, because they assumed that they would be against the Sex Discrimination Act. They never bothered to check it out, just abolished them. So they began to reintroduce those units, and they were quite proud of themselves for that…I reckon by '84, there was substantial changes in the way the police approached it. Not to say that all women got a fantastic response, but they got a much better response than they could have got five or six years before." [Aileen Christianson]

"The other achievement, which we weren't directly responsible for, but I think Rape Crisis, more generally was, was beginning to have designated places in police stations where women and children who'd experienced violence could be interviewed… I don't think the police would ever have done that on their own, and I think it was campaigning…I really, really believe that the historic line of that was through Women's Aid and Rape Crisis. I have no doubt about it. It just wouldn't have happened unless women had said 'No – no more. We want something different.'" [Siobhan Canavan]

"[The] Female and Child Unit…was introduced, and they had…dedicated suites and such like. And things very quickly got better after that although at first, they still – I don't know what they get now – they were still only getting like a week's training…to work with the Female and Child Unit…they were kinda told that that's where they would be working. They didn't get the option to apply to work in that unit, so, I believe that has changed now…" [Norma Benzie]

In Glasgow, the Rape Crisis Centre fed into development of the new units, working with Sandra Hood, who became the first woman police inspector in Scotland (she became Assistant Chief Inspector in 1999):

"She was really very, very keen on trying to ensure that conditions for women were improved…I mean she wasn't like this feminist in disguise or anything – it wasn't like that, but she had…a sort of framework of values for what women could expect from the police, which was really good… she was quite…a strong woman. So that's when…there was a move away from women being examined in the police station and agreements being built around women being examined in health facilities. And that was groundbreaking at the time and then women getting information from the police and information and trying to get the police to give…our contact number and phone number." [Helen Mackinnon]

In February 1988, Patricia Bell's observations from her experience of the Female and Child Unit in Glasgow indicated that on some occasions police perceptions of the advantages that the new units and their fresh approach offered, were rather different from those intended:

> "At first the units were out of uniform but I'm sure are now back in them. On the face of it it seemed great being less formal but then I heard a policewoman speaking about how plain clothes were an advantage because she got so much information from one woman who thought she was a social worker." **[Letter from Patricia Bell to Aileen Christianson dated 19th February 1988]**

The success of the units was also hampered by internal attitudes among the police:

> "Also there does seem to be quite a lot of hostility from policemen who resent the units being women only and getting extra training and attention – so it will be a long time before the raised awareness of the women in the units is reflected in police attitudes in general…
>
> Certainly the publicity around the establishment of the units initially caused more women to have more confidence in the police ~ but my impression is that the service women receive is still patchy." **[Letter from Patricia Bell to Aileen Christianson dated 19th February 1988]**
>
> "I think when they set up the female and child units that the, mainstream police were… looked down on them a bit, it was seen as like women's work sort of thing and you did hear police officers making sort of unsavoury jokes about them. But that soon changed and I mean they're a very, very valuable and important unit now and they deal with major crimes." [Jan Macleod]

As part of the Domestic Abuse Forum in Dundee for several years, Fiona Raitt's experiences of police attitudes was among the more positive:

> "They were fantastic actually – they were completely on board…they were also in part of the child and family unit so they did deal with sexual offence cases as well. Gradually they brought along their… senior people, who were men, but…if they weren't pretty much signed up, they were making a good job of pretending they were and that actually was quite heartening …somebody would be reporting on an incident they were dealing with and they would say 'Oh that's completely unacceptable' and, 'I'm really sorry about all that', that was it was usually the bobby on the beat who didn't have much experience and 'We'll make sure these things don't happen again'…and often they did follow it through. And the current Chief Constable has certainly made an issue of promoting the need to protect women" [Fiona Raitt]

The first guidelines to the police Chief Constables on how to treat victims of sexual crimes were issued by the Home and Health Department at the Scottish Office in 1985. A combination of this guidance, and other initiatives such as the development of sexual offences support had a very significant impact:

> "That was the beginning of me understanding that the police are so command and control driven that actually, if the boss at the top says this is what you're gonna do, it will reach everybody at the bottom. And they might take a while to do it willingly, but they will do it. By the time I left Edinburgh Rape Crisis in 1999, I would say that Lothian and Borders Police had achieved a complete culture shift." [Lily Greenan]

Several other developments around the same time, such as Roger Graef's 1982 "Fly on the Wall" documentary which exposed callous and disbelieving behaviour on the part of Thames Valley Police towards a rape complainer, also made a big impact on public awareness of the way in which women in this situation were often treated by the police:

> "It was a real situation…and it was just absolutely horrendous. And it was miles away from what happens now, we are led to believe…it was really abusive and violent and she was questioned about her behaviour, what she was wearing, what she was drinking, she wasn't believed, they called her a liar, I mean she was cut and bruised, she was a nervous wreck – she could barely speak a lot of the time and she was being doubly abused by these officers and it was really awful…And from that kind of that led on to the talks and things we had with the Procurator Fiscals and it seemed to change." [Heather Forrest]

This programme excited a national outcry, some of which was expressed in letters to the papers, such as this one from an Airdrie man to the Glasgow Herald:

> "Sir, On television I witnessed an extreme form of bullying whereby three men, using all their male arrogance and aggressiveness, took advantage of their superior physical and mental strength to humiliate and degrade a woman who was totally unable to deal with such an onslaught and was without anyone to assist her.
>
> This was not, however, a rape I was seeing: it was the brutal and offensive questioning of a rape victim by three police officers shown on BBC's "Police."
>
> As I watched this disgusting performance, including the cruel, sneering and foul, abusive language of the supposed defenders of the weak, I felt ashamed of my sex.
>
> Women can complain all they like about the way in which rape victims and their cases are dealt with; but they have little chance of making significant progress until all decent-minded males express their outrage at such events as those broadcast and demand a change in procedure which will enable rape victims to be treated sensitively and with respect, so that they will come forward to make their complaints without fear of being made to feel degraded, gulty, and in some way dirty." [Peter V. Towndrow, in The Glasgow Herald, 25th January, 1982]

The publication of Chambers & Millar's "Investigating rape and sexual assault" had also contributed to this shift:

> "Chambers and Millars' Report on police treatment of women complainers…was tremendous, because once we had that, we could use that to say 'This is what you don't do…here is the evidence of what we've been saying to you'". [Aileen Christianson]
>
> "And then of course, there was always the favourite thing of, 'Oh what about all the false complaints?' and we were able to say, quoting a police officer – two percent, about the same as any other crime… Same as in false reporting of stolen cars – actually no, false reporting of stolen cars (and we got this from a police officer) was much higher (laughing) obviously…" [Aileen Christianson]

Siobhan Canavan and Michele Burman carried out a research project over a 2 year period looking at specialist police units which had been set up to support women and children:

> "It was a sort of a small, basic step, you know…and now, the movement towards always having a female forensic examiner – it surely…doesn't require very much to be able to provide that, but…we're talking about a time when none of that was available when there were no facilities like the ones developed by…

the specialist units, where…women would be sitting in police cells and in police offices, sitting…in a paper bag with their clothes being taken away, for hours on end, being questioned by two, you know chain-smoking male detectives sitting under a light bulb as if she was the accused." [Michele Burman]

"Our specific remit was to look at these units which had been set up within a five-year period up to that point and to see how they worked, what sort of work they got, what was the experience of working in them, and…what was social workers' experience of working alongside police? What was police experience of working alongside social work, and what did other agencies think of them?" [Siobhan Canavan]

The results of this were not encouraging:

"We found that they…operated very, very differently in different parts of Scotland, and that …they certainly were getting a volume of work, that…some of them only worked with children, some of them only worked with adults…they had all different kinda categories, and… they didn't record who used them in the same way.

We discovered some pretty bad practice in relation to how, internally in the police, they were viewed… they didn't have their own cars for example, they didn't have their own resources…They had to borrow from other bits of the police, and of course, other bits of the police wouldn't really lend them. Men didn't want to go and work in them, because it wasn't seen as high status. I mean, it was probably very good that it was women to begin with, but…I mean, there was one bit in report which was about some of the names they were called. 'The Nappy Squad', 'The Women and Weans'…there were three or four different kinda names they were called.

Sometimes the room, which was lovely when you got inside it, maybe, was sited…there was one famous one at the end of a long corridor with the pool room for the guys who were off-duty, playing pool there, and then right across the corridor was this interview room… it wasn't private. But you know, I think that's all come a long way as well, and you know, who knows? Maybe our report did something." [Siobhan Canavan]

Campaigning

Campaigning was a fundamental part of what Rape Crisis centres were all about right from the very beginning. As their awareness of the range of inequalities and injustices experienced by women who had suffered sexual violence grew, so did the determination of the women supporting them to fight these on every available front.

Writing to the papers was one way Rape Crisis workers tried often to raise awareness and challenge attitudes, and journalists sometimes became real allies in the fight against sexual violence:

> "If there was stuff in the newspapers we would write and complain, if there was stuff on the telly, we might write and complain – I mean there were single issues connected in. We would do newspaper writings. I mean, I was forever writing to the bloody Scotsman…the Scotsman was a really good newspaper then… it had some very good journalists, many of whom we got to know… I mean, Robbie Dunwoodie…I remember him – he would come up and dig me out of the National Library and get unofficial briefings from me…when the Chambers and Millar Report didn't come out, because they were trying to get changes on it…So people, journalists like that were generally very sympathetic and would give us big spreads…yes, lots of newspaper writing." [Aileen Christianson]

Sometimes however, it was the papers themselves that the workers were obliged to take on:

> "The Daily Record had a terrible habit, which, of course, they still do, of putting violence against women stories on the same page as the Page 3 girls and so we had meetings with the editor of the Daily Record around this… we got to listen to him.. talking about the way the paper works and the decisions they make about where they put things and of course…Oh, it was hilarious because…he was saying 'We genuinely didn't notice we did this, you know? I'm so glad you pointed it out.' … which was a load of nonsense. He was a really oily character… a typical tabloid journalist – 'cause everything you said, he'd an anecdote about it, you know, and it was always a personal anecdote…all of which you knew was just – I don't believe you. But that was quite interesting…and I know it had an effect in the short term…they did change the practice. But I'm sure that just lasted for a couple of years" [Rona Clarke]

> "We've complained about different things to the local press…local press using sensational language: 'beasts' 'pervert' and in …a story of, say five paragraphs, the victim involved in the story was able to identify ten mistakes…things like that." [Norma Benzie]

The sex shop in Aberdeen

The Rape Crisis Centre in Aberdeen waged a 10-month campaign during 1983-4 to get rid of a sex shop in Chattan Place which had recently applied for a continuation of its license. The many tortuous developments in this successful campaign (the license was ultimately rejected by the Licensing Committee of Aberdeen District Council) are fully documented in a chapter Siobhan Canavan wrote on the subject in Grit and Diamonds (Stramullion & the Cauldron Collective, 1990)

> "I would say that one of our great achievements was that we… were involved in the sex shop campaign (laughs), when I look at it now in Aberdeen…it was huge…a sex shop had opened and it was in a residential area and they were applying for a license and we got wind of it. Somebody rang us or wrote to us or something, and in fact, I think one of the people who rang us was one of these right-wing church groups, and they said they were opposing it and they wondered what we thought about it, and we took it on as a…campaign… The thing was that…there was a piece of local government legislation which could designate how many sex shops could be in a particular area, and we wanted Aberdeen to say 'none.' This was inspired. And so we went to Council meetings, we leafleted, we joined up with

this, you know, right-wing group…it was something very different about the alliance in that… It was great. And…that was really an achievement. " [Siobhan Canavan]

"Siobhan was very, very much at the forefront of that one…they were gonna be opening a sex shop and she was there and I think Elizabeth and do you know I've got a funny feeling that woman Bernadette was involved as well… they were really the ones that kept the momentum on that one going. And she went to the licensing meeting… it was just a real success. And of course…you had…sort of strange bedfellows where you had…church groups and…horrified housewives…along with Rape Crisis and we were all against it for a whole range of different reasons…I'm sure a lot of these other groups really didnae see…pornography as violence against women. What they saw was…your kind of Mary Whitehouse type filth…we were coming at it from the direction of…this is violence against women and we don't want it to be here in Aberdeen. But that was a real success and…a huge amount of work." [Isabelle Kerr]

"We put in an objection, and I think the only objections came from us and an extreme Wee Free Church (laughing) and so we were kind of interesting companions. And I remember going along to when it was heard, and they threw it out. They threw it out, which was wonderful… I think I actually spoke at the meeting. 'Cause I also remember, with Maureen, sort of talking at a meeting – she and I were invited to do a presentation at Sunnyside…which is the psychiatric hospital in Montrose, and a huge board room… big table, you know? And I think we really socked it to them, actually." [Sue Hunt]

"I remember driving out to a bar somewhere on the South Deeside Road which was advertising in the paper wet t-shirt competitions and handing this letter, us objecting to treating women that way…that was about the same time as we were getting upset about the sex shop." [Maureen Porter]

"It came about because we felt that there really wasn't another women's group in the city to spearhead a protest…I think it did make a difference…" [Isla Laing]

Rape Crisis workers in Glasgow were also determined to make a difference:

"Any of the CND stuff…any of the marches that there was a sort of focus around Rape Crisis because of the links we saw between women, race, class, violence and different forms of violence." [Helen Mackinnon]

They took a very direct (and courageous) approach in their efforts to raise public awareness of rape and sexual violence, simply by addressing them from a soapbox and inviting people to engage with them directly to discuss the issues in Buchanan Street on a busy Saturday afternoon. Jane Dorby recalls:

"We were giving out stickers and things like that, so there's a lot of organisation in it, but we were the ones who were doing the shouting and Lorraine was really a driver of it, because we decided that there was just far too much – she was a person who didn't like complacency and she could sniff complacency out very quickly – and she would just say 'There's just so much complacency' and 'There's just so much silence about it'.

I said, well, you know, what could we do to make…she said, 'Well let's just, let's get on wur soap box'. And I said 'Yeah, that sounds like good fun', so we set out wur table with all the literature, and some of the literature was quite shocking, you know? We had good photographs and things like that…We'd gathered from magazine cuttings and things like that, and we made it up, and it was to shock.

It was to shock, and there was a lot of passers-by who lifted the leaflets and were, you know, 'Oh good grief', and sort of 'Shut it' or whatever, and there was a wee crowd gathered round us and we decided to do the bit about the leaflets – and we'd literally be saying, you know, 'What do you think of this?' and 'Do you think this is a good image?' And so a lot of people stopped, and a lot of women were saying 'This is terrible', you know? …

But then there was a lot of guys who gathered round, and there was quite a, not threatening, but aggression, quite aggressive – verbally aggressive, but you know, 'You need a good…That's what you need', that kind of thing. And the women who were there from the street began to be quite, to take them on a bit, so it was quite a kind of dynamic…The women who were there were quite annoyed. And the silence was almost certainly broken, because I don't think a lot of women hear that hatred. It was hatred. It really was hatred." [Jane Dorby]

The power of such a fresh and direct way of communicating their message did not go unnoticed and was brought home to Jane in the days that followed:

"But it was funny because I was studying at Glasgow University at the time, under a guy called Nigel Grant…I was doing a Master of Education. And it was Nigel Grant who passed away about two years ago, but he was an international educationalist, comparative person and…my tutor…he was a very, very dynamic teacher – very oral teacher. And he was shopping in Buchanan Street at the time, and I didn't know, and there was lots and lots of people there, and he stood for twenty minutes and I didn't recognise, 'cause it was such a harassing, kind of dynamic conversation, all the time, answering questions and… the next week I went back and I was doing an essay, and he looked at me and he said 'Do you know, I saw you quite recently on Buchanan Street.' I said 'Did you?' He said 'Yeah.' I said 'What, in Frasers, in shopping?' and he said 'No, on your soap box.' And he said 'I have never seen such a good educational exercise', 'cause he was very interested in learning and how people learn, and I was just so embarrassed, because I think in many ways, we didn't know, we didn't care whether it was a success – it was whether we just attracted a crowd.

I don't think I could do that now…I mean, at the time I think that was the sense of confidence that we had, that it didn't really matter what other people thought… we were quite determined to be, to noise people up. And it also, it generated a lot of enjoyment, because Scottish people really like when there's a banter and there was a lot of banter. It wasn't all dark…There was a lot of 'Eh, what would you know about it?' or this kind of thing. 'What do you mean? Don't tell me, I can tell you a thing or two…'

It lasted about three hours and we were utterly exhausted by it…I don't think we ever repeated it again… But it was, it was good…We definitely got a lot of phone calls following it, saying 'I was in Buchanan Street last week and I was horrified to hear what was…I would like to join your organisation to do something.' So that's when it got really quite big." [Jane Dorby]

Flag days also provided opportunities to engage with the public, and try to tackle what were very prevalent attitudes:

"I remember having a flag day one time and going out rattling cans on Union Street in Aberdeen. And we actually got quite a lot of money but we also got quite a lot of abuse. I was quite shocked actually by some of the abuse that we got… mainly people just completely denying that rape and abuse happened… People just said 'Oh that, it's just an absolute load of rubbish that. That just doesn't happen', and being really quite aggressive with it." [Brenda Flaherty]

Other campaigns centred on cinemas, where films featuring the rape, abuse and murder of women in the name of entertainment were not hard to find:

"There was a film called 'Dressed to Kill'…I think the director was Brian de Palma …we would picket it and distribute leaflets…it was a cinema in Renfield Street – I think used to mostly show porn films and that's the one I remember picketing in particular…" [Morna Findlay]

This sort of campaigning made women realise the impact that relentless mainstream marketing of violence against women as entertainment had had on their own lives:

"I remember after I got involved in Rape Crisis thinking about another film I'd seen called 'The Eyes of Laura Mars'…about a woman photographer who – her fashion shoots involve women in positions that look as if they've been raped and murdered…she's actually got a telepathic connection with the murderer and this is how she gets the inspiration for her photoshoots though she doesn't realise it…In the end…she meets up with the murderer…it's a thriller…

But I remember at the time just thinking this was a good thriller, and it was later on when I was explaining the plot to someone who was in Rape Crisis and I saw the look on her face…and I thought to myself oh…maybe I shouldn't be recommending this film. I did begin to think this is actually pervading a lot of my life…relationships that I'm having with people…its not like I'm going to Rape Crisis along the road on a Thursday night and that's it." [Morna Findlay]

Legal campaigning

As several members of the Edinburgh collective, including Sheila Gilmore and Eileen Scott, had legal backgrounds, it is perhaps not surprising that the campaigning pursued most actively by Edinburgh Rape Crisis at that time was centred on the law:

"Our campaigning tended to be focused on Parliament, Edinburgh…We tended to focus it very much on responding to Bills in progress, or lobbying for Bills. We lobbied around rape in marriage years before it happened…that had been there as a thing, right from the start, from 1978 they had been letter-writing about that one." [Lily Greenan]

"We were obsessive about being accurate about the law. We were completely anal about it because we got fed up at being accused by lawyers of not understanding it." [Aileen Christianson]

The issue of rape in marriage, and the challenge of confronting the widely held notion that in signing a marriage certificate a woman gave up her right to say no, was one of many legal issues around which Rape Crisis centres in Scotland campaigned:

"There was a campaign – it was maybe a little bit later…to try and have rape recognised within marriage…I do remember us writing to MPs…there was anonymity for rape victims as well." [Morna Findlay]

"I remember being out flyposting with Patricia Bell and we had…all these posters, fly posting them in the churches: 'Rape in marriage – make it a crime'…It must have been 1982…And the posters were really, I mean they'd all just been drawn up very quickly you know…wedding dresses and the…married couple and then 'Rape in marriage – make it a crime', I remember that. And…having to jump over the walls and fences of all of the churches and sellotaping it to the front doors of the churches…on their own notice boards… I remember that being on, like, a Sunday, you know at night, one or two nights." [Helen Mackinnon]

Edinburgh Rape Crisis lobbied relentlessly to have rape in marriage recognised as a crime. In the account of their first 11 years that appeared in **Grit and Diamonds** (Stramullion, 1990), Edinburgh Rape Crisis workers recalled:

> *"The first prosecution was brought against a man for the rape of his wife in 1982. We feel sure that our additional pressure for the recognition of rape in marriage as a crime had some influence on the Crown Office finally bringing a prosecution. After all, Gerald Gordon, a legal authority, had been saying it was possible since 1967, and yet no prosecution was brought until 1982. That and subsequent prosecutions firmly established the principle that for spouses not living together but not legally separated rape did exist as a crime. It took until March 1989 for a case to be brought against a husband for the rape of his wife while they were still living together. The defence argued that it could not be a crime as the wife, having said yes on marriage, had no right subsequently to withdraw that consent as long as she was living with the husband. However, on the grounds that attitudes to women were different from 200 years ago when that belief <u>was</u> prevalent, the judge insisted that rape was an aggravated assault and, as such, it was a crime with which the husband could be charged. His judgement was then upheld by the Appeal Court, fully establishing the right of women within as well as outwith marriage to say no." [Edinburgh Rape Crisis workers in Grit and Diamonds (Stramullion, 1990)]*

The situation in Scotland was very different to that in England and Wales, where the law on this subject was based in statute, and it was not possible for men there to be charged with raping their wives. In Scotland, there had been a presumption for many years this was the case within Scottish marriages also. However, Scots law was based on common law and not on statute:

> "In the 19th century, nobody had said 'Oh yes, of course you can rape her, she's your wife' because they assumed that he could, and there was a legal expert…Gerald Gordon in as early as the '60s… saying there is no reason why rape in marriage isn't as much of a crime as hitting your wife… And then Eric Clive, who was a professor here, and then was in the Law Commission, he took it up so there were two legal experts who were saying this…so we ran a campaign on this and in 1982 or 3, there was the first case where a man, who was separated from his wife…had raped her, and the advocate tried to argue that it wasn't a crime, and the judge said nonsense, of course it's a crime. And he got off – he raped her in the snow outside, and the jury…let him off, because…they were lagging behind, obviously…and then again, seven years later in '89, a man still living with his wife raped her, and again the advocate tried to argue that because they were still living together this wasn't a crime, and the judge said nonsense, of course it's a crime and he got off as well. But that was enough to establish, in Scotland, that this was a crime…
>
> That rape in marriage thing was a huge change, and the legal authority had been there before we existed, and it wasn't until we existed…that the Procurator Fiscal…thought let's just take a punt on this because there's so much evidence – the woman in the snow case – and I don't think they would have done that without a Rape Crisis Centre going on and on about [it]…When cases began to get brought, even when the woman had been drinking, that was a change because we were saying, you know, 'No means no.'" [Aileen Christianson]

Lily Greenan describes other legal issues on which the Edinburgh centre campaigned, sometimes creating an enormous impact:

> "Evidence, a lot of work on the Scottish Law Commission did a very big report on the laws of evidence in rape and sexual assault cases in about 1983, I think, and there was a similar report done around child witnesses, evidence from children…we did a lot of commenting on that, and we also did a lot of lobbying of MPs around that area.

Criminal Injuries Compensation was another one. We did good press on the Criminal Injuries Compensation stuff...We did a press conference to launch an annual report...it was just an annual report, but one of the things that I'd written about in the annual report was...Michael Howard's saying...he set up a tariff scheme for Criminal Injuries Compensation without taking it to parliament, and at the time, the TUC was having a go at him about it. They were taking him to court, because it had implications for their members who were in hazardous professions, and I had just written a piece that said that a man would get more for losing a testicle than a woman would get for being raped, or losing the ... ability to have a child, 'cause there was actually nothing in the original tariff that talked about damage to reproductive ability.

So a woman who was raped and seriously physically assaulted, and had to have a hysterectomy, say, as a result, would be not compensated at all for that. She'd be compensated for the rape, but that would be it and I mean it was ludicrous. There was that, so I quoted a couple of examples, but one of them was that a man would get more for losing one testicle than a woman would get for losing a baby, I think that was how I put it, and the press had a field day with it.

We hit every front page in the country. I mean it was nuts, because it was an annual report launching, as a courtesy we'd said could we have it at the Regional Chambers...it must have been 1994 or 5, could the Chair of the Women's Committee maybe come along and say a few words, and the Women's Officer was Carol Forfar and I think she had just relayed it to the Chair of the committee as...you know, it's Rape Crisis, it's their annual report, you'll only need five minutes sort of thing. They were late. By the time they got there, we had two television networks, three radio stations and ten newspapers in the room and they were just, you know that sort of thing (laughing) where you kinda sit there and go (sighs) that was one to us. So it was very funny, and so we did a bit of, just fortuitous being able to drop things in at the right time. That wasn't news. That was an old story. I had just rehashed it and I think it was that when it came out, it came out at a time of year where it didn't get a lot of coverage in Scotland and, for some reason, the TUC hadn't been putting it to the press and so then we got lots of coverage in the press, and then the TUC campaign heated up and there was more coverage of that. So it felt like it was a wee minor victory, so it did." [Lily Greenan]

Edinburgh Rape Crisis workers also campaigned for many years against the use of sexual history evidence in rape trials:

"'The onus of proof is on the woman. She has got to convince the police that she has been raped', says a legal expert and spokeswoman for the Edinburgh Rape Crisis Group.

'The best evidence is medical. If a woman does not go to the police soon after the assault, she is less likely to be believed. Unfortunately this does not take into account the fact that the woman may be far too upset to go through a medical examination shortly after being subjected to rape.'

The Edinburgh Rape Crisis Group, a voluntary feminist organisation offering counselling facilities to women who have been sexually assaulted, was formed a few months ago. So far it has had very little direct dealings with the police because nearly all its cases involve women who were subjected to rape months or even years ago. They simply want to talk about it for the first time ever to a sympathetic outsider.

The group is highly critical of the Scottish court system and questions by the procurator fiscal on a woman's sexual history. It has discussed the matter with the procurator fiscal in Edinburgh, who defended his questioning on the grounds that if he did not ask the questions then they would be brought up in court anyway.

'We were told that a woman would only have to go through it all when the case came to court, so she might as well get used to it now,' the spokeswoman says.

'The real change needs to be done in the Scottish courts. We would like them to adopt a similar system to the one already used in America and England; a woman's sexual history is only admissible evidence at the discretion of the judge.'" [*Sex evidence that can prolong the woman's ordeal* in The Glasgow Herald, October 16th, 1978]

Pornography was another topic which led to some very active campaigning – on occasion direct action really did mean a direct (if not entirely legal) attempt to dispose of some of its sources:

"I remember doing stuff outside Menzies…we would join in on the campaigns where there was the shelf clearing things going on so that you were there to give women back-up if the police were called etc, so it was much about a kind of, a sisterly support thing going on…Some of the campaigns were connected up anyway… a couple of women going in and just, you know trashing the top shelf and going in and just like clearing all the magazines…Picking them up and then dumping them." [Margaret McCutcheon]

Other, more formal efforts were also undertaken:

"We did the Williams Pornography Report – put in a report to Willie Whitelaw about that." [Aileen Christianson]

The findings of the report were disappointing however:

"When the Williams committee reported in 1979, it unanimously found that "given the amount of explicit sexual material in circulation and the allegations often made about its effects, it is striking that one can find case after case of sex crimes and murder without any hint at all that pornography was present in the background". It concluded that "the role of pornography in influencing society is not very important…to think anything else is to get the problem of pornography out of proportion with the many other problems that face our society today". So long as children were protected, it suggested, adults should be free to decide for themselves. The Williams report was, in fact, shelved by Mrs Thatcher's government, but its in-depth study of the matter and constant preoccupation with the freedom of the individual ultimately provided the basis for many of the guidelines in force today."

(Extract from obituary of Professor Sir Bernard Williams from The Telegraph, 13th June, 2003 – see: http://www.telegraph. co.uk/news/main.jhtml?xml=/news/2003/06/14/db1401.xml&sSheet=/portal/2003/06/14/ixportal.html

Reclaim The Night

Reclaim The Night marches, which protested the right of all women to have the freedom to go where they wanted without having to restrict their movements to accommodate the threat of sexual violence made a frequent appearance on the feminist calendar, and were enjoyed and often organised by many of the women who were part of the Rape Crisis movement.

Although they did not call it a Reclaim The Night march, the Edinburgh Women's Liberation Movement (in which the Edinburgh Rape Crisis centre had its roots) organised a show of feminist defiance on the night of 31st October 1978. This was reported in that day's Glasgow Herald as follows, under the headline "Women band together to scare off rapists":

"A group of vigilante women will roam the twilight zone of Edinburgh's Meadows tonight in search of would-be rapists. They will be in the park in the centre of the city where many local people are afraid to go after dark on Hallowe'en in an effort to scare off men who have been attacking women.

'We want to make Hallowe'en at least one night of the year that is safe for women', said a spokeswoman of the organisers, the Edinburgh Women's Liberation movement. The park patrol marks the start of a week of action by the movement to show how they intend to fight back together against rape.

The spokeswoman added: 'Rape is a threat which any woman, old or young, faces at any time. In Edinburgh between 400 and 800 rapes and sexual assaults occur every year, but only a small number are reported to the police. The Meadows area has been the scene of a number of attacks recently. We will take over the Meadows tonight to assert our right to walk freely without harassment at any time, anywhere, and especially at night.'

During the week of action, thousands of leaflets and stickers will be distributed throughout the city. The movement has set up the Edinburgh Rape Crisis Group, a women's collective involved in running a centre for women who have been raped or sexually assaulted. The centre offers a comprehensive service giving confidential support and advice on medical and legal steps that should be taken after an attack.

Edinburgh police said last night that so far this year there have been 31 assaults of an indecent nature reported against women in the south side of the city, which includes the area known as The Meadows. This was an unacceptable figure but was no worse that any other part of the city." [Ernest McIntyre in The Glasgow Herald, October 31st, 1978]

The Inverness Women's Group, to which all of the Highland Rape Crisis Centre workers belonged, organised several Reclaim the Night marches throughout the 1980's:

"Well, we read 'Spare Rib', we knew what was going on in the rest of the world [laughs]. We knew what was going on, so we… just followed the template and said 'We will do this' and 'We will reclaim the streets of Inverness'…We had wonderful attendance, particularly the first one. I think they dwindled, and that's why we didn't do any more than three. We did three." [Gale Chrisman]

"Torches, though, big proper… the real thing." [Frances Hunter]

"Oh yeah, torches. Oh yes. We were very serious." [Gale Chrisman]

Some of the press coverage these marches received could best be described as lukewarm – the following, penned by one Colin Campbell and bearing the headline "After Dark Protest Shows Men In The Wrong Light", appeared in *The Highland News* in March 1985:

"A number of women – it could be reasonable to describe them as "feminists" – intend to hold a torchlight march through Inverness on Saturday night, at the conclusion of an "International Women's Day Festival.""

This march, under the theme of 'Women Reclaim the Night,' is intended by the organisers – "to demonstrate our determination to change the situation as it now exists where women face the threat of male harrassment, intimidation and violence when they are on their own."

Well, good luck to them I suppose. But I can't help thinking that this march will be something of an irrelevance when set against the central question – How do we reduce the risk of street assault faced by everyone, male as well as female?

Reclaim The Night March in Inverness

Saturday's display of torchlit symbolism is unlikely to give any practical assistance in finding an answer to that question. I would also point out that 95 per cent of men (ALL of whom are apparently considered as a threat by feminists) would forcibly and unhesitantly intervene on any woman's behalf if she was seen to be harassed or attacked on the street. This has nothing to do with chivalry or gallantry, but instinct.

The fiery parade on Saturday may imply and exude a measure of hostility to the male population in general. But when it comes to actively trying to combat violence in the streets, we're all in it together."

HRCC wasted no time in responding:

"Sir – Since Colin Campbell has frequently expressed support for the efforts of ordinary people to improve the quality of their lives, I am sorry that, in his Vision feature of March 7, he could not find it in his heart, or anywhere among his instincts, to support our "Reclaim the Night March" through Inverness.

After dismissing our efforts as "irrelevant" Mr Campbell asks how we can reduce the risks of street assault faced by everyone. Are women not to be included among "everyone"?

In answer to his question I would suggest that he acknowledge that sexual violence (on the streets or off them) is widespread. Further, that is most commonly takes the form of attacks by men on females.

It's an uncomfortable truth for men who view themselves as kindly, but it is the reality. Such men should then try to understand the extent to which women fear sexual violence and the degree to which our lives are circumscribed by this fear.

To suggest, as Mr Campbell does, that women can rely on some men's protectiveness to defend them from other men's '(instinctive?)' attacks, is unhelpful.

First of all, attacks usually take place when other people are not around. Secondly, this suggestion does not deal with the heart of the problem, which is an attitude held by very many men that they have the right to do with women what they want.

We now know that wife-battering, child abuse and sexual assault are far more commonplace than previously supposed and that these acts are not carried out by a few perverted men, but by ordinary men.

Women must deal constantly with manifestations of male hatred, as it is expressed overtly in physical attacks, more subtly in sexist jokes, or denigration of their campaigning efforts.

Finally, I would like to define "feminist" for your readers who may have been misled by crass stereotypes found in the gutter press. Feminists are people opposed to sex-based social injustices from which ALL women suffer. There are other social injustices, based on race, age and class, of course (feminists don't deny this).

Feminists don't want to be discriminated against, exploited or abused because of their sex. We organise ourselves collectively to fight sexist practices. Marches are one tactic to draw attention to a serious problem. That is why, last Saturday, we marched." Gale Chrisman, Secretary, Highland Rape Crisis and Counselling Centre [In The Highland News, March, 1985]

These took place in other cities too, including Glasgow, Dundee and Aberdeen:

"The ones I remember…from the beginning about women say no, Reclaim The Night stuff, there was one or two, that…came a bit later…when they had the women's drumming group…and we had a couple of Reclaim The Night sessions which were fantastic… and…there was after a couple of afternoon sessions where you could go along and play the drums and…Liz, who was in the law firm she did actually take up drumming, so did Florence. But…on the marches…we just did it round the city square and [the] district council were very supportive…I think even they did civic receptions occasionally." [Fiona Raitt]

"We had a couple of Reclaim the Night marches… I suspect they probably were during the preparation time… they were tremendous fun – really exciting thing to do, you know, down Union Street, flaming torches, none of these candles…real, proper, flaming torches, you know? So a good support from women in the town, and just puzzlement I think, from folk, you know, because we had them at night, that's when you have these things…I would say folk just really not sure what the whole thing was about." [Elizabeth Shiach]

"There used to be a cinema in George Street, which showed blue movies and we all marched passed that." [Maureen Porter]

"I remember going to this National Union of Students conference in…Leeds or Bradford…it was before the Yorkshire Ripper had been caught and somebody decided we would organise a Reclaim The Night march and this conference full of women rampaged through town and people were bursting into pubs, and shouting at men in pubs and shouting 'Are you the Ripper? Where's the Ripper?' and there was rumours that people were dropping tampon bombs in men's beer…and really shouting at the police with hatred 'Why haven't you caught the Ripper?…that must've been about 1979…1980, maybe.'" [Morna Findlay]

"I do remember certainly at least one Reclaim The Night march in Glasgow. I couldn't tell you when it was though, except it would be after '79." [Morna Findlay]

Other protest marches also took place, including one against pornography:

"I think there was one we did in daylight, I know it was daylight, cos I've got the pictures. It's not that long since I looked at it, but we're all dressed in red robes that, looking at them now, they looked a bit like burqas. And when I think about it, it was a bit prescient because it was years before Margaret Atwood had written…'The Handmaid's Tale'…and they all wear red burqa-type things. And we carried a coffin around town…Anyway, it was an anti-pornography thing and we all dressed bizarrely in this red stuff and we carried a coffin around, and people again thought… [laughs] What are these women doing? It was so funny…We did have big banners, I think, saying 'Women Against Pornography', I've got the pictures." [Sue Owen]

And another on abortion:

"We…had characters, my daughter played a schoolgirl and I played a little old lady and… people played various roles, and we wrote a script…and what I most remember was at the end of the thing, we had made a circle and then this little girl, who was played by my daughter, was kinda pushed around from one to another. I mean, it was a very graphic representation of being pushed around by people." [Gale Chrisman]

Greenham Common

Many women from Rape Crisis collectives went to join others in the peace camp at Greenham Common. Rona Clarke went there in 1985:

"Oh that was a most empowering experience. I didn't go the first year. I went the second year – it was fantastic. There was a lot of us went. Two, four, six, eight, ten – I think there was probably about twelve of us went the second time and, you know, it was an excuse to take a great big picnic and things like this… And going down by bus…singing in the bus – that was great. And then as you went further down Britain, it was incredible – all the motorway service stations we stopped at, because of course, a bunch of women, we all needed the toilet all the time. There was all these buses full of women. It was just fantastic to see.

Greenham Common

Oh, it was wonderful. And then, when we got there, it was really well organised in a non-shouty, men marching up and down, telling you what to do, sort of thing because the women were doing it all by walkie-talkies. The Greenham women, but, and you know, the sort of direct action they were doing which was cutting the perimeter fence…that was great. And that was all done, I mean, it was being done on various points on the perimeter fence…there was whispered information about which person was gonna do it and there would be a distraction arranged, you know, so we'd all be doing this distraction, so this poor soul would be, with bolt cutters, opening it up – and it, I mean, it was a token gesture, but

Greenham Common

it was a gesture nonetheless. And it was really, really interesting because… Greenham Common was considered to be a bit of America, behind the perimeter fence were all these American soldiers with guns trained on us, 'cause, well that was it, it was America, really. I mean, of course, on the other side of the perimeter fence there was all these cops, British cops, you know? They really overreacted to it…

Just the presence. A huge amount of cops and you think, I mean, without wishing to belittle my sex, you think, for a bunch of women who have, you know, a commitment to non-violent action… I mean, what on earth is this all about? Police horses walking in amongst us as we sort of did various sort of sit-downs and things like this. I remember a lot of singing, and there was a lot of good humour, generally, and it was really interesting to meet up with women from other parts of the country, and we did sort of silences, your two minute silences for people who died as a result of nuclear wars, etc, etc.

… so we went down, overnight on the Saturday/Sunday, got there at five in the morning, or something, demonstrated the whole day, left at six o'clock, back into work on Monday in the same clothes, you know? (Laughs). To applause, I remember. Everybody at work was extremely supportive… I think, in Britain, at the time, people were really supportive of the whole idea of Greenham Common and…people really admired the skill of the organisation, in a fairly sort of unobtrusive way – very, very cleverly done… And just a different kind of mass protest, you know, from the mass protests that generally end with men shouting at other men, and chucking things at each other." [Rona Clarke]

"We were all going down to Greenham Common…it was the overnight buses and …it was really, for me, you know being a kind of legal observer…I was always a sort of a scaredy custard…but…I did try to be conscientious at the roles that I did take on…and I remember the Quakers, the Quaker women… at Greenham and…sharing tents with people…I wouldn't have brought a tent and they would say look there's room in mine…all the things that folk said about there being a good atmosphere and women being really good to each other…for all it was kind of like deathly in terms of overnight in the winter and freezing cold, I think we went down three or four times in these overnight buses and it was really, really good…it was the perimeter fence work and doing all that and that was very motivating." [Helen Mackinnon]

"We had…Strathclyde Rape Crisis centre banners at that…it wasn't just Rape Crisis people because…we had all got different pals on the bus…women from the islands that we dragged down, but…the banners were there from Strathclyde Rape Crisis centre. Irene Audain…got down and she's one of the women I remember from Rape Crisis…she brought that banner along." [Helen Mackinnon]

Closer to home, Faslane & the Holy Loch became a similar focus for peaceful protest:

"I remember us all piling into the famous university mini bus…heading …off to Faslane. That was for …the women's day. Which was always in December again. And it was always wet and cold. And that was the women's sort of protest day so we all piled doon to Faslane and …they ran a crèche for all the kids so you just piled all your kids and went off doon to the base to do your bit of sort of protesting and singing and pinning daffodils or whatever it was you had at the time …onto the fence…Pictures of your loved ones and things like that." [Isabelle Kerr]

Holy Loch protest

"Went down to Faslane down to a few demonstrations down there… They were a bit different…we were just part of a broad movement, organised, I think, by the CND, and I do remember there was a bit more of an aggressive, hostile atmosphere. And then, at Dunoon, at the Holy Loch, and that was quite good – again, that was non-violent, direct action, so women were lying down on the road and the police were dragging them away." [Rona Clarke]

Other, less obvious struggles also continued, for example, around aspects of language and in particular, the terminology used to describe survivors of sexual violence:

"The one battle we totally lost was the use of the word 'victim'. We fought from the beginnings, women are not victims. Yes, they have been a victim of that particular event at that particular time, they are not victims overall – they are survivors and they are complainers in terms of the legal process and that, that battle has been completely lost …we thought the complainer aspect of it was really important, because it meant that she was not a victim. She was someone against whom this horrendous crime had been committed, that

did not make her a victim. And newspapers or television will still talk about somebody still suffering years later – well yes, she may, but she may also have another life in which she has actually learnt to cope with it. So we always felt unhappy and we failed, we failed that miserably." [Aileen Christianson]

"We said in the introduction of the first edition that we wouldn't use the word 'incest' cos we didn't like it, except when we talked about incest survivors. So on every page there's the word 'incest' cos we talk about incest survivors…when I looked at it, I thought what planet were we on? You know, saying we're not gonna talk about incest but we'll use this term 'incest survivor' on every page, just about… so the second time we actually took out the word 'incest' completely, because people would dismiss it, because it wasn't incest. If you didn't have sex with your daughter but you touched her up every week or every night or whenever, then it wasn't as bad, but the kind of things that we were seeing was yes, that was bad, but this is also extraordinarily damaging…" [Liz Hall]

"I think women calling themselves 'survivors' rather than 'victims', that was just enormous, and it was so obvious." [Siobhan Canavan]

"Use of the word 'survivor' rather than a 'victim', was a way of moving people on, maybe them thinking, you know – you can survive this, you can get past it." [Sheila Brodie]

Conferences

Conferences were invaluable in the early years of the Rape Crisis movement in providing an opportunity for women to learn more about the issues, share their experience and develop skills and awareness in a field where they were the pioneers:

"In 1982, we went to the first UK conference on sexual abuse of girls…I've still got the papers from that conference… So we went to that conference, and then was it the next year we had the first Scottish conference? In the Dolphin Arts Centre was it? And then there was a conference in Stirling. A sexual abuse conference." [Jan Macleod]

Glasgow Rape Crisis held a conference in October 1982. A notice appeared in the briefing section in the Glasgow Herald on September 29th under the heading "Women only conference":

"A two day conference on the "Sexual Abuse of Girls" will take place in Glasgow from October 9 to 10. The first day will concentrate on child pornography, Scottish law on child abuse and professional responses to incest. The following day will deal with the practical aspects of working with incest victims.

It will be held in the Dolphin Arts Centre, James Street, Glasgow from 10.30 a.m. - 6p.m. each day and there will be crèche facilities. This is a women only conference organised by members of the Glasgow Rape Crisis Group. For further information write c/o P.O. Box 53, Glasgow." [The Glasgow Herald, September 29th, 1982]

Frances Monaghan recalls the impact that Action Against Incest had on the Stirling conference:

"There was a number of professionals there. There was people from criminal justice…a lot of the PFs were there, social workers, doctors, mental health officers, psychiatrists, psychologists – we were completely out our depth. Completely out our depth, but I have to say, we held these people in the palm of our hand, because once you got over that patronising, 'Oh, they're all survivors, therefore they've got a bit of a chip on their shoulder' – once they realised that we actually had really, really strong things to say, they listened." [Frances Monaghan]

One incident in particular was very revealing, and indicative of the ignorance and preconceptions that surrounded child sexual abuse:

"There was a number of major boobs during the day…[a survivor]…was facilitating that group, and one of the guys was saying to her 'I know, but you were fifteen when you were abused, and you should have told somebody. You could have told somebody.' And she was going 'No, I couldn't.' And he was like that 'You could have went to the police'…I think he actually might have been a police officer…and he kept going on, you know, 'You could have. You were fifteen, it's not as if you were a wee small child'… And he wasn't getting it. And [she] just kept saying 'I couldn't. I couldn't. I couldn't. I couldn't.' And he says 'I mean, give me one good reason why you couldn't have spoke out.' And she says 'My father was the Procurator Fiscal.' And everybody in the workshop just went 'Oh.' Like that. She says 'You tell me who I could have went to. You tell me who would have believed me.' …And this was also, like, about twenty years or something, thirty years ago that it had happened…and Procurator Fiscals do have a lot of status, but he had a lot of power in his community. She couldn't have told anybody. So stuff like that was really powerful and really, a lot of people went away, agreeing to take it to their services, and do something about it, and I think that it did, it did do that. I think, from there, the statutory organisations started looking at their role in it all. And, I suppose, when you look back you think, well that started from a group of women in a pub, one night, talking and somebody from Rape Crisis Centre bringing up the issue that they were dealing with a lot of child sexual abuse calls." [Frances Monaghan]

Isabelle Kerr recalls an early conference in Manchester and the hospitality she met with there:

"A conference had come up, it was a conference doon in Manchester… and I thought oh I would so love to go to that conference… it was an Incest Survivors' Conference, but it was, it wasnae just for survivors, and I thought oh I'd really love to go to that conference it sounds so interesting, but thought well, no in a million years is this gonna happen because you know…people like me don't go to things like that… And then it kind of went round the table and it was like who would like to go and…I can remember actually saying 'Well, if like nobody else is interested, you know I wouldnae mind' and I remember Jan went, 'Oh right well Isabelle wants to go'…and you know I thought 'Oh my goodness, am I going to this conference?' and I thought, 'Wait a minute I've got two children, I canny go' and it was 'Oh yeah just, just bring them' and so there was this minibus and we all met up at Hillhead Underground and everybody got piled into the minibus and off we went." [Isabelle Kerr]

"And people just put us up which again I found completely fascinating… Because at this time in my life of course, I would need to have the hotel room and the ensuite and would settle for no less. But at that

156

time I thought it was just astonishing that these strange women would just put you up you know – and your children. You know and say, and they would go off and just say 'Well help yourself, just what's in the cupboard' and I just found that astonishing…I felt so awful about staying with this woman, and basically kind of intruding on her, that…I said 'Oh can I contribute in some way?' and she was like 'Oh no, no, no don't be silly you know…we're really happy to have you,' and I thought 'My kids have ate her bread and drank her milk and I've drank her tea and all that and just offered nothing back'. And there was a kind of, event – a party, on the first night of the conference. And I didnae go because of the kids, because they were really, really tired. So I went back to her house and I had put them doon and I was sitting reading a book or something and the door went and it was the milkman and he said…'Milk money' and he told me how much it was and it was something like five quid…and I paid for it and I never ever told her… cos I felt so bad. God she's gonna come back in the morning and there'll hardly be any bread you know. So I paid her milk bill. I never told anybody that before. " [Isabelle Kerr]

Strathclyde Rape Crisis organised a major conference on violence against women and girls in Cardonald in 1987:

"That Violence Against Women and Girls conference that we had in Cardonald was in 1987. I think… that was like the first conference, big conference like that in Scotland that we had…It was huge and I mean I remember afterwards like interviewing people for the Women's Support Project or you know when…I was on the management committee and people would actually put it in their CVs…that they were at that, never even mind part of the organising committee, they would actually say they were at it… I remember Dorothy Kemp, she ran the childcare for that which was huge…I mean that was done really, really well…she applied for funding and got it so it was really like a big deal." [Helen Mackinnon]

"We also we did a conference as well…That was the one at Cardonald… it was really hectic and I spent all of my time…going to meetings, organising things, photocopying things…It was all different areas of violence against women and children…there was people there who did self defence as well. There was also a conference on self defence for disabled women at one point. Lots of things…tied in with a lot of the work…that the Women's Support Project did and they were really quite heavily involved as well… that was fantastic…" [Heather Forrest]

Some women travelled huge distances to attend it:

"People came from all around the world…from Africa, there was somebody from Japan who actually stayed in sort of me and Irene's house. There was a woman from Wiltshire as well who stayed with us…there was women from…all over the Highlands and things and it was quite amazing…the woman who came from Africa… it took her about ten or twelve hours to get from Africa to Glasgow, and the woman that came from Orkney, it took her about sixteen hours, just because of the different kinds of transport she had to get. So it was really quite bizarre." [Heather Forrest]

"A number of us, if not the whole collective, a number of us went down to Glasgow to a big conference. I think Scottish Action against Incest was formed at that conference…and I think as a result of that conference…one of the things that was identified at that conference, I think, was the need for a national initiative on sexual abuse, incestuous abuse." [Elizabeth Shiach]

"Probably before the centre actually opened, there was a conference in Glasgow, and I think it was around incest survivors…all the members of the Aberdeen group came to that and stayed in Glasgow overnight because I think the conference went on quite late, and members of the Glasgow collective managed to fit us all in somehow…some of the women who had originally started up the group had been in touch with the other centres…prior to that…" [Isla Laing]

Other conferences also made an impression on women who attended them:

157

"I remember one in the Pleasance which was a feminist conference in the Pleasance and I can't remember what it was called now…It was early 80s possibly about '83 or '84. Loads of different workshops, women coming from all over the place." [Margaret McCutcheon]

"Great big thing down in…Leeds or Bradford, I can't remember…sleeping on other people's cold Northern floors…a great big conference with lots and lots of workshops and…quite a lot of lesbian groups there discussing separatism…" [Morna Findlay]

Jo Richardson (who was Shadow Minister for Women) and Clare Short, both MPs at the House of Commons, tabled an Early Day Motion ('Prevention of Rape') in 1987 and convened a conference entitled Action on Rape, which took place in the Grand Committee Room at Westminster Hall in July of that year.

The motion, which was also supported by Renee Short, Margaret Beckett, Harriet Harman, Betty Boothroyd, Ann Clwyd, Joan Maynard, Oonagh McDonald and Dame Judith Hart declared:

"That this House believes that calls for higher sentences for the small number of rapists who are charged and convicted is a wholly inadequate response to the massive concern amongst women about rape; notes that women are vulnerable to rape by men of all classes and backgrounds and face a high risk of being raped in their own homes or by men whom they know; believes that the recent remarks of the judge in the Ealing rape trial are typical of the attitude of the judiciary and others in positions of authority who view rape as being more trivial than crimes against property and are part of the explanation of the massive under-reporting of rape because women fear the treatment they will receive from the police, the courts and the media; and calls for rape in marriage to be made a criminal offence, compulsory training of all judges before they try rape cases, the appointment of more women judges, a review of police procedures and facilities throughout the country, a review of the questioning to which women are subjected in the course of rape trials, improved support for Rape Crisis centres, women's refuges and advice lines, the removal of pornography from mass circulation newspapers and the exploitation of women's bodies in advertising, and the establishment of a commission composed entirely of women to make further suggestions on how women can be better protected, so that the incidence of this vile crime is reduced and women feel enough confidence in the system to report rape, and consequently more rapists face trial and conviction."

A total of 120 people, including representation from the Edinburgh Rape Crisis Centre, attended the conference, and a series of 6 workshops were held to address various aspects of the motion, including rape, domestic violence, sexual harassment at work, public safety, and women and the media.

The impact of such conferences were far-reaching, both in terms of the work of Rape Crisis centres, and also for the personal development of their workers:

"The thing that I think as a group, as a centre, that affected us, was… the need first of all to develop… from the Rape Crisis counselling we moved into incest, abuse, and that was the result of the conference in Glasgow which was so impressive. And so we began to advertise that we were prepared to do that, we would take calls that dealt with abuse as well as rape, and from that we set up an abuse…survivors', incest survivors' group." [Gale Chrisman]

"[A] significant number of our calls…were from women who'd been abused as children. Enough for us to want to go to that conference, enough for us to come back and also take on board to try and raise issues about child sexual abuse within agencies, and we did do that. We met with senior officials in the social work department, and my memory of that was that they told us that it wasn't a problem up here. And we also contacted nurseries. We wrote to nurseries. Just raising the issues, and talking about some of the signs and saying that we would, I'm sure we invited, the invite said that we would be happy to come and talk to them because what, we all left that conference, whenever that conference was, with a mandate – or we felt mandated." [Elizabeth Shiach]

"It was a fascinating time…for me – I found it fascinating meeting all these women who had a lot of similar views to me and…I hadn't met women up until that point that really felt the same." [Moira Kane]

"You did really blossom by meeting these other people. I remember for example being in a bookshop and looking at a copy of The Female Eunuch by Germaine Greer, which I'd heard of and I wanted to buy it but I was embarrassed to buy it because it had a kind of naked female torso on the cover…and I did buy it, but honestly the sweat was kind of pouring off me…I thought it was wonderful as well… then maybe…a year later I'm speaking to CID and saying well, you're wrong…it was a very transitional time." [Morna Findlay]

In September 1989, Sue Hunt and Liz Hall helped organise a one-day conference on ritual abuse, which took place at Dundee University. This was a remarkable undertaking, at a time when even less was known about this subject than it is now:

"Amazingly…I just don't think it could happen now, but we actually got a conference set up… we heard about an American woman and an American policeman… there was a conference down near Reading, 'cause there was a woman down near Reading, I think she brought them over, and we heard about this, and they were willing to come up, which was amazing. And we got money from the Scottish Society for the Prevention of Cruelty to Children, and also, the Social Work Department…my then boss, my line manager, became quite involved in the arrangements, and it just seems incredible, now…we limited the numbers, I think, to about forty, because we didn't want it huge, and I think it just blew everybody's minds away. I mean… Liz and I were familiar with the material, and Brenda, because we were working with it, but…it was completely new." [Sue Hunt]

Speakers included Pamela Klein, a psychologist from Chicago with long experience of working with children who had been sexually abused, who had also helped children and adults who had experienced ritual abuse, and Gerry Simandl, an investigator working with the Gang Crimes Commission whose focus was on the difficulties associated with presenting forensic evidence on ritual abuse for prosecution. The police were also involved:

"There was a woman in… a Women and Children's unit through the police in Grampian… I know Liz was liaising with her about one of her clients because this woman was coming into contact with the police, and so we also had a sort of link…with the police as well, and they attended…The woman, and I can't remember her name – she was very professional, and I think she was very careful… she remained very much in a professional role, but she would listen, and you got a sense that she believed and gave us credibility…anything that we took to her…which is quite interesting… And we got some press coverage as well." [Sue Hunt]

"We got quite a good reception because the people that were there were all interested… they were coming with open minds. And a lot of them…were there because somewhere along the line they had come across it as part of their work. Or things that sounded very like it, you know so it wasn't a sceptical audience as I recall. But I think the unfortunate thing was that we didn't really ever go anywhere else with it…had that one conference and then that was it. And of course there was so much like Nottingham and Orkney and that that just really dented the credibility of anything that could have been done." [Brenda Flaherty]

How Rape Crisis was perceived

Public perceptions of Rape Crisis centres and the workers who developed them tended to be variations on long-established feminist stereotypes. This, coupled with a reluctance to acknowledge the reality and prevalence of sexual violence, posed many challenges in getting their work taken seriously, if not avoiding outright hostility:

"I think the centre's name was that, women who were doing good work, helping out people who were victims to the others that we were barking mad, and we were, you know, rampant feminists." [Jane Dorby]

"Oh not particularly positive…whether we were or not that we were all a bunch of man-haters…and all the rest of it, there was a lot of that nonsense…and coming from women as well. Which was a little bit disheartening at times. But looking back I suppose we were so challenging, that's not a surprise." [Florence Germain]

"I think probably locally it was much the same as Women's Aid in the early days, that, you know, we were well-meaning, but really we weren't that clued up with the real world, and…I think again very similar to Women's Aid…there was a kind of sympathy for the woman that was very obviously…raped…in the mythical view of rape…again, even for women in that position, it very quickly turned into woman-blaming…So I think probably, I mean the same nonsense is around Women's Aid, you know – on the surface a kind of sympathy – a worthwhile organisation set up to help, but on the other hand, very very quickly going into woman-blaming…" [Kate Arnot]

"I don't think it was taken very seriously…I felt…when I was doing that social work course at the same time as I was…doing Rape Crisis…we got a bit of input about rape – incest was one of the things…I think we got something like one two-hour input for the course on these and it was very much…this happens in some families…I suppose at that time…I wasn't terribly confident…I probably tried to say a few things but I wouldn't have been confident enough to…take them on." [Moira Kane]

"I think they thought we were a bunch of weirdos, really. We were all slightly odd women. In fact, you know, most of us were women with children and lives and just doing ordinary things." [Liz Hall]

"They [*the police*] didn't like us. We didn't work well together, and some of that was their fault and some of that was our fault… I mean, I get a strong opinion about things sometimes, but I felt that when we knew things were happening, we should share it. My best example of that is there was reports in the press that women were being attacked and raped in a particular park in Dundee. At that point we had known about that for over a year, because we had been working with about six different women, all of whom were telling us exactly the same story, describing the same person, and my feeling on it at the time was that OK, we keep confidential with the women, of course we do, because they don't want anybody to know, but we should be telling the police that there's an issue." [Laurie Matthew]

"And of course you would get a lot of flak from people as well…you know, people would say 'Oh, you're just nothing but a crowd of lesbians' and big deal…or…you know, 'Women ask for it' or just would resolutely not look. That was mostly what you got." [Siobhan Canavan]

"I think mainly it was, you know just a bit hostile and that people didn't really think it happened and women were asking for it and very much campaigning along the lines of …just because you're wearing a mini skirt doesn't mean that you're asking for it type of stuff we were really down at that level still…I think we're still at that level…people still say you're asking for it if you walk home alone or if you go home with somebody for a coffee or whatever." [Brenda Flaherty]

"It was interesting just to see people's reactions…often we were outside Central Station…rattling cans… Folk would be a wee bit kind of looking you up and down…Rape Crisis, mmm, not too sure …it was never the kind of cute and cuddly cause for support, you know…Guys had an interesting response to it as well…to this day I very rarely tell people I was involved in Rape Crisis, but when I do there's usually quite a reaction…men in particular feel very uncomfortable, quite often you're written off right away… people have all kinds of preconceptions about what Rape Crisis is about…It often was about those kind of man-haters…that were all burning their bra, and down at Greenham, you know?…We used to laugh…there was a bit of us used to take pride in that, in some ways…I remember one woman coming in to do the training and she said she wasn't going to continue cos we were just a bit too radical for her liking, so we got these t-shirts printed with 'Too radical for her liking'…one woman had left who'd been with us for years, she always used to use that phrase so we got her a t-shirt printed…we liked the fact that we were radical and we were different and all that…but there was a price to pay for that …it wasn't popular at all…people would marginalise you for it, certainly, and it did make relationships with men quite difficult as well…they weren't quite sure where you were coming from…you know, it was probably best to keep Mum, and all that stuff…" [Linda Reid]

"I think it was mixed…because we started off in Women's Aid I think some people saw it linked to Women's Aid. Some people obviously thought it was a good thing because it was another support. My memory is that linking with the Police…cause it was the time when the Police were having to look a bit at domestic violence and Rape Crisis…on the surface they were always quite supportive…and worked with us as much as they could – well some of them, that were interested. But I think some people also… thought of it as 'those feminists doing that and they're doing it for their own ends and…you know, what's it all about?'… Cause it was all still quite new wasn't it?… And…of course people don't want to acknowledge there was rape going on…and certainly…people didn't want to acknowledge there was child abuse going on, sexual abuse going on. I mean…not just men that didn't want to acknowledge they were raping people but also a lot of women, a lot of families didn't want to acknowledge that was going on." [Dorothy Degenhardt]

"People don't want to believe it and they don't want to acknowledge that it happens… because quite often in most cases of abuse, the person being abused is vulnerable in some way. And not as confident and I think abusers are very clever in what they do. …they're not gonna kind of march out into broad daylight and…challenge somebody … who's like a tower of strength and really physically strong…they wouldn't do that because…that would be difficult. So what they're more likely to do is, they'll find somebody…not as confident not able to look the world in the eye and not as physically strong and if women don't feel like that, they don't recognise that other women can." [Heather Forrest]

This was sometimes particularly evident during fundraising efforts when workers came face to face with public attitudes towards the subject of rape. People's reactions when they did become aware of the nature of the charity were sometimes a mixture of deep discomfort and avoidance, and sometimes horrifically inappropriate:

"I can remember standing outside Mothercare when I was pregnant with one of my children shaking this can and people giving me funny looks… I think the rape word is a bit of an anathema to some people. I remember once, I always try and give people money and this woman held it out and I said 'Oh what's it for?' and she said 'SPUC' and I went 'Oh', quickly withdrew my pound and I think people sort of feel like about Rape Crisis as well." [Maureen Porter]

"We learned very early on that people aren't comfortable having tins saying 'rape' on them put in front of their noses…We would go to things like the Holy Fair…a day in a park in Ayr where all the Ayrshire charities have a stall and Ayrshire would supply entertainment in the form of…people from different countries dancing…bands playing…whatever…it was June or July or something like that, so it was always a great day out…would do a bottle stall…everybody would do something to bring money to the stall, but if you went round with the tin into the crowds, they would kind of: 'Oh. What is it for?' It was horrible sometimes…One of the times we had a stall next to us – I think it was to do with hearts…heart attack type situations, and one of the men at the stall said 'Oh, that would give you a heart attack – being next to that!'…We were really outraged! …

They were surprised…that we were making it so public, and sometimes women could be quite disappointing as well…I remember one woman saying 'Rape – oh, I should be so lucky!' while she was putting a pound in the tin!…It was so kind of uncomfortable, doing those kind of events…so we stuck mainly to foundations and trusts and things like that…" [Norma Benzie]

But there were positive responses too, and some awareness that this was an area where work really did need to be done:

"I think we had quite a favourable climate in which to operate, in some ways…possibly even more so than…the very beginnings of things like Women's Aid in that…it was quite a big issue of public debate and there was a fair amount of interest in getting legislation on things like rules of evidence…Looking back, the problem is that a lot of that doesn't seem to have achieved what we thought it would achieve, so maybe the depth of the kind of change…might not have been as great as we thought it was, just because you were getting a reasonably positive kind of hearing." [Sheila Gilmore]

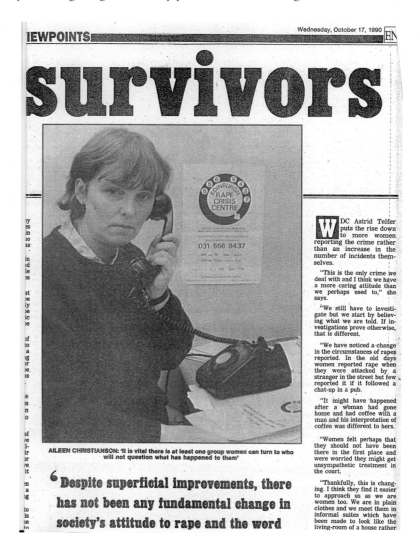

IEWPOINTS

Wednesday, October 17, 1990

survivors

AILEEN CHRISTIANSON: 'It is vital there is at least one group women can turn to who will not question what has happened to them'

❛Despite superficial improvements, there has not been any fundamental change in society's attitude to rape and the word

WDC Astrid Telfer puts the rise down to more women reporting the crime rather than an increase in the number of incidents themselves.

"This is the only crime we deal with and I think we have a more caring attitude than we perhaps used to," she says.

"We still have to investigate but we start by believing what we are told. If investigations prove otherwise, that is different.

"We have noticed a change in the circumstances of rapes reported. In the old days women reported rape when they were attacked by a stranger in the street but few reported it if it followed a chat-up in a pub.

"It might have happened after a woman had gone home and had coffee with a man and his interpretation of coffee was different to hers.

"Women felt perhaps that they should not have been there in the first place and were worried they might get unsympathetic treatment in the court.

"Thankfully, this is changing. I think they find it easier to approach us as we are women too. We are in plain clothes and we meet them in informal suites which have been made to look like the living-room of a house rather

And the work carried on by Rape Crisis workers added hugely to what was known about the prevalence and reality of rape in Scotland, and led in turn to a growing appreciation, in some quarters at least, of the service they were providing and their expertise:

> "The longer we existed, the more we could give figures and say 'Of the women who contacted us last year, this percentage were rape, women who had been recently raped, and this percentage were women who had been incestuously abused as children' and so on. So the longer we existed, and the more we asserted a public presence at the police or social work talks or women's groups or whatever, on the radio or on the telly – the more we were accepted, whatever they thought about us behind our backs, we were accepted as experts in this particular field." [Aileen Christianson]

> "I think in terms of Social Work and perhaps police, there was… I wouldn't say there was any kind of direct support for it, but in theory there was support for it. And the police at one point did take cognisance of what I had been saying about they needed to get a family room set up in the police station, and it needed to be a separate entrance, and I remember going to see the flat…I remember it being like somebody's living room. And I remember thinking at the time – but pushed it away out of my mind, because at least it was a step in the right direction – But when it's somebody's living room, if I were a woman who were coming into that room and it was a police officer interviewing me, be it male or female, because it looked like a living room, I would automatically see it as their space." [Margaret Brown]

Others, however, resisted engagement, feeling alienated by extremist associations they attributed to the centres' feminist stance, or their own fear of discussing sexual violence:

> "But there were some agencies didn't quite get the feminist part of it…that would be definitely a negativity for them, you know well why does it have to be?… and just the whole anti-feminist stuff that was going on then anyway, you know like 'mad lesbians' was always the…Although there were many lesbians involved…yeah there was a sense that you were men hating." [Margaret McCutcheon]

> "And I remember in terms of my personal life as well talking to my mother about being involved and…I remember her saying to me, what do you want to be doing that for? …and then the panic in her eyes was because like 'Have you been raped and that I don't know about?'" [Margaret McCutcheon]

> "There was a, a tendency to see all those women's groups as just biased, only presenting women's point of view…standing up to this slogan 'all men are rapists' and… there was a kind of extremist thing painted around you and it's so much nonsense…but just to give you an example of…how much it perpetuates itself, I had to appear on a radio programme with Douglas Mill who…calls himself the Chief Executive of the Law Society of Scotland …We were there to argue the issue about gender equality in legal affairs and how that affects women's position in law…of which rape is an example. And just suffice to say that we had something of an argument on the radio.

> This would have been…about 2000 actually, 2000/2001 and suffice to say that the very next time I was down at a Law Society meeting, he introduced me to the then President of the Law Society as 'that radical feminist from Dundee'. Now I don't mind that, but I just think, you know your language hasn't really changed for thirty years Douglas, it's really sad…and all I was doing was saying…we could talk about gender and equality for women in the profession. That was…how radical it was and that was presented as radical feminism… it also lets you know you can never lose a label, once they've got you down there. They've got you…and they do use it to dismiss every argument you put forward." [Fiona Raitt]

The role of the media

Media reporting and portrayals of sexual violence played a very significant role in shaping the public's view of sexual violence, in both positive and negative ways. Rape Crisis workers often engaged with the media in an effort to raise awareness on the issues and challenge common misconceptions:

"The media, a lot of it was focused on responding to horrific rape attacks so you had like the Carol X one that was one of the most famous ones when was that – 84 or whenever it was. There was a horrific rape up in Inverness that we supported the woman, where they made her re-enact being raped in the back of a car. Cos they claimed it was impossible for two men to rape a woman in the back of a car." [Jan Macleod]

"I remember…being on Radio Clyde…an issue round rape. It was the time of that Miss X …I don't know if it was about that or if it was some other issue…a representative from Rape Crisis was to give their opinion. And I remember being very nervous and hearing myself on it and I was working at Gartnavel at the time at the College of Nursing there and they all heard it and I remember going in the next day and they were really, really proud of me…they got my point…I was just saying…rape is a crime…it's not what women want…what bit of no do folk not understand…all this…bit about women dress to be raped. I think I remember being questioned on that and how that was just all red herrings… I do think though there was a…thing about, you know, feminist weirdos and …people sort of calling you names….I remember that, but I remember you know we kind of took a pride in that…I don't mean by encouraging it, but we didn't mind." [Helen Mackinnon]

"Early on, we did press cuttings – between us, we covered the Scotsman, the Herald, the Record, the Evening News, and anything else we could pick up on the way, some of the Sundays, and we ran a successful lobbying campaign to get the Editor of the Daily Record to stop putting the rape trials on page three. That was one of our successes, was we said you're linking sex and rape and it's not helpful, and he did, in the end, he did." [Lily Greenan]

"We didn't get attacked, we didn't have a negative image in the media, there was never a suggestion from any of the newspapers that we were a bunch of rabid feminists waving our bras around – there was nothing like that. We were seen as, if anything, we were seen as quite serious and maybe a bit humourless." [Lily Greenan]

"I took part in a Radio Tay phone-in along with a police officer and a priest, Father Aldo, who's quite famous. The phone-in was about domestic abuse, rape and sexual assault, and there was a call from a guy who said that his brother had been accused of rape but in fact she was only saying it… to get criminal injuries…So Radio Tay were certainly prepared at that time to have that opened up on a Sunday morning.

Also I spoke on a radio programme…Norma Gamble was the presenter on Radio Tay, and that was about rape and sexual assault, because I could remember her sharp intake of breath when I said 'You have to remember that by law, rape is only where the penis is inserted to the vagina' and there was a very sharp intake of breath at that point [laughs], and I thought 'I better not go on and say what I was gonna say after that' because I was about to explain on air that therefore insertion of the penis to any other orifice of the body is not constituted as rape, but I managed to say it in other ways that perhaps would be more acceptable to the general public!" [Margaret Brown]

In Inverness, the bete noire of Highland Rape Crisis in terms of the media was a woman, Miss Barron:

"Miss Barron didn't like us… She was the matriarch proprietor of the Inverness Courier at the time… completely privately-owned newspaper…Extremely idiosyncratic…And she wrote the editorials, and… they were not favourable." [Sue Owen]

"And if you wrote a letter in, she'd put a little postscript expressing her own view following the letter… You never had the last word with her. She was dreadful…[laughs] Oh, what did she say? Yeah…She saw no reason why there should be a Women's Aid…They were already up and running before we came." [Gale Chrisman]

Sue Owen recalls Highland Rape Crisis input into a radio phone-in:

"We were asked to go onto Radio Highland…and Women's Aid had a representative, we had a representative, and I can't remember if there wasn't a policewoman there or something like that as well, but there were three women and the woman interviewer, and … it was a phone-in about violence against women, not necessarily sexual violence… Well, about the fact that there's no violence at all against women in the Highlands."

A man from Skye phoned into the programme:

"He said, eh, he didn't know what happened on the mainland, but on Skye the men didnae hit the women unless they deserved it…Everybody's…stuffing things in their mouth, and nobody feeling in a fit state to respond, you know?" [Sue Owen]

Sometimes, however, the media could be very helpful in raising issues of sexual violence in the public consciousness:

"There's instances when abuse is highlighted in the media. But it's not really picked up on as being important…before Brookside came off and years ago they did this really interesting thing where, with

165

Woman's Own, August 23rd, 1986

the Grant family, they had Bobby raping Sheila… she'd been raped by a stranger in the park, but then …later on…they had not had sex for ages and she did the whole thing really, really well and she'd be nervous she'd be jumpy she'd be, she'd be doing all the sensible things like, you know well I can't go there because…I don't think people picked up on that unless you were aware of it…and then she was raped by him and what she said I think was really poignant was, 'You know you're all the bloody same'. And then…the Grant family…they got rid of them. But I think people don't pick up on the whole essence of things…we're such …an instant society and it's like we just want things really quickly and you see them and they're gone… which is quite good in terms of like nothing in life is permanent, but the impact of that, it stays with you." [Heather Forrest]

"Since soaps began to portray rape…such as it is… you know, for real…I can't remember which soap it was…but one of them anyway featured a rape… one of the very earlier ones and…we got such a lot of calls after that, so it had to be quite significant… so women felt more able to report it or to speak to us about it…" [Norma Benzie]

The publication of research which confirmed what Rape Crisis workers had been saying for years helped:

"Chambers' and Millars' reports and Lynn Jamieson's report, what they did is they proved what we had been saying all along. There was nothing in there that was against what we had been saying…then that meant it was like oh, the big boys and girls were agreeing with us…maybe what we were saying was true – so in that sense there were changes, and there were changes in people's attitude. You no longer felt so secretive about doing it, or so paranoid." [Aileen Christianson]

166

Professional prejudice and conflict

This acceptance was not universally shared, and in their efforts to support women and gain experience of a type of work that no one had ever attempted before, in areas which had always been hidden and unspoken, sometimes exposed Rape Crisis workers to great suspicion and criticism:

"The history in working…in the area of sexual abuse, is that you can be pilloried and enough professionals have put their head above the parapet and …been shot down and lost jobs, so there's a lot at stake. And I think, for us who did become involved in Aberdeen, it was probably because we were very ignorant. We just didn't know, until it all unfolded and we stuck in there and we pieced things together, and we learnt a lot from the women we were working with. They were the experts, and what they were telling us fitted in with what we were then reading. And the reading, I suppose, informed us and we were able to kind of then have a better understanding of the kind of context." [Sue Hunt]

"Developing experience and developing skills through experience…experiential learning as they call it, I think has a great place to play…it's a good way of learning. It isn't the be all and end all…but you can take that and use it to develop or to support theoretical learning or just as a way of understanding…I think it also allows you to see how people develop as well if you've developed…there's nothing wrong with being professional, but if you're a professional person then you actually have to get skills, get that understanding from somewhere…It's an issue…that we had with social workers who didn't actually understand… how you could work with women and do this without being qualified as a social worker…I mean there's nothing, nothing to do with the social work training that makes you any better or any worse." [Sheila Brodie]

"These days, we have an excellent relationship with most agencies, and Rape Crisis does as well, I'm absolutely certain, but these days we approach it in a more professional way and I think they do as well. I think they've learned about us. I mean, the first time I went with a woman to the police, the woman was hanging on my arm saying 'Please don't leave me, Laurie, please don't leave me!' and I was saying 'I won't leave you, don't worry', and the police officer said…'You, you're from Rape Crisis – you get out and wait there, right?' And I said 'No, I'm staying with this woman' and she said 'No you're not, you're do as you're told.' And I said 'No I won't, I'm staying with her.' Now, that whole thing could have been prevented, right? She could have been saying this to me, 'You'll wait out there' and I could have said 'Can I have a wee quiet word with you a minute, right? I'm not wanting to interfere in an investigation, I promise to stay quiet, but the woman will be able to talk much better if she's got some support. Is that OK with you?'… We're not amateurs because we're volunteers, and the voluntary sector get that anyway, you know? " [Laurie Matthew]

The attitude shown by the GP who advised the first woman Morna Findlay took a call from (and subsequently supported) in her work at Glasgow Rape Crisis to terminate contact with the centre was not atypical:

"I'm sure there was an attitude around – just put it to the back of your mind – don't think about it, you know, it'll be fine …that was the attitude." [Moira Kane]

And sometimes, paradoxically, the worst attacks and criticisms of the new approach taken by Rape Crisis workers came from their own professional colleagues:

"I mean, I was probably the first person in this country to identify someone with multiple personality disorder…It was extremely difficult. I mean, we had the false memory people around, we had someone in the department who was really sceptical…We had psychiatrists who were malevolent about psychology. We had people who were very scathing about any work you did, and we were learning by the seat of our pants but we thought we knew what we were doing. Looking back, I don't think we did at all, and I think I'm only now learning." [Liz Hall]

As a lawyer in the only women-only practice in Dundee, Fiona Raitt quickly discovered that some aspects of her professional work were in direct conflict with her commitment to women and to redressing the injustices that working for Dundee Rape Crisis had exposed her to:

"We were doing a lot of work...with Women's Aid and...with children's hearings...we were also...I sort of started off doing court work where I was the duty solicitor. If you were starting off from scratch with an empty filing cabinet...you do really whatever work comes your way. But I stopped...within a few months, because I discovered that the man I was seeing in the cells that morning had been picked up the night before was the husband of the woman that had seen me the earlier afternoon about abuse.

And I suddenly thought no, no, no...you're gonna have to make a choice here, you can't do what lawyers say they do which is just be on the fence...I'm gonna have to be on one side of the fence or the other so, I decided I would stop doing that kind of work. And...the bad bit about that was it took me out of the criminal courts in a way...I was no longer there to influence anything other than from a, a bit of an outsider's position. But... the good bit was I could then fully commit myself to really acting for women and it wasn't that I'd never acted for men...but if it was men who wanted to fight to the end, then I just would refer them on somewhere.

So...it did definitely affect my long term professional practice, it affected my behaviour with other solicitors...they would talk about me as being very radical and feminist, and the only problem with that is, you can get seen as very biased and then people don't take you seriously... So, over time I think I've found...ways of trying to deal with this, you have to somehow slip into the mainstream at some level so that...you're respected and recognised for a certain level of knowledge and then you put across your viewpoint... to try to acknowledge where other people are coming from and then gradually try to persuade them round, rather than just getting into straight arguments all the time." [Fiona Raitt]

The development of the Scottish Rape Crisis Network

The Scottish Rape Crisis centres campaigned jointly on a range of issues from very early on. In 1981, for example, they produced a joint response to the 1979 MacPhail report, calling for an end to sexual history questioning in rape trials, and in 1988 centres made a joint appeal by letter to the Crown Office complaining about the grossly inappropriate use of the charge 'wasting police time' they knew was being levelled at some women whose cases had been dropped or who had felt unable to endure the prospect of a trial and so withdrawn a complaint.

Strathclyde Rape Crisis drafted a formal response to "Prosecuting Sexual Assault" on behalf of the Joint Rape Crisis Centres so that this could be widely circulated among agencies and individuals across Scotland along with the report itself (which was published at the end of 1986).

The stronger voice, mutual support, opportunities for lobbying and campaigning that the development of a network could offer, were evident, and centres began to develop stronger links with one another, in the same way that other women's organisations had elsewhere:

> "We met as the joint Scottish Rape Crisis Centres from about 1982 onwards…there were centres in different parts of the country, varying levels of funding support and only Glasgow…(they were Strathclyde at the time)…money for a paid worker…the rest of us didn't have paid workers, had limited amounts of money – so we met twice a year, and we rotated it round the country…a different centre hosted it each time, and we used it just as an opportunity to get together, share common experiences, see whether we could come up with new ways to tackle some of the things that we were all struggling with and to get support from the fact that there were other centres in other parts of the country doing this work…
>
> And then, in …1994…we had a letter from one of the English centres saying…centres in England and Wales are going…to become a federation and we want to know whether the Scottish centres would be interested in becoming part of a federation that, perhaps, could have regional sort of focuses and so, we had a meeting that was in Dundee, at which we took the decision that there was little point in us becoming part of an English and Welsh federation, because our legal system was so different and our social services and housing…so much was different in Scotland and we would just be spending money to probably go and attend meetings in England that wouldn't be that relevant to what we were doing. But that maybe it was time for us to be more formal about our relationship with each other in Scotland, and we began the process then. We started by setting up a subgroup to look at a statement of common policy…there were ten points on it, it was very simple. It wasn't really common policy, it was just this is our credo, this is what we believe in…" [Lily Greenan]

> "What I also remember is that it was very active across Europe, they had these meetings 'Women Against Violence Europe', WAVE meetings that we started going to and they were in these places like Sheffield and Birmingham and Leeds and Liverpool and you would go down to England and they'd shout at each other and in particular accuse each other of being racist. And we used to leave, 'Oh thank God we live in Scotland'. I mean they were quite scarily sort of like in your face and challenging and not necessarily aggressive, but there was a lot of sort of political tension that we didn't have here. And that may well be because maybe like they had more black women involved or something like that." [Jan Macleod]

> "I remember us coming out of hibernation, you know, cos we'd managed to get some women in, and I don't know if I was one of the ones that went to one of the first meetings but I was certainly along at some of the meetings…We went to Edinburgh, we went to Glasgow, we had one…in Dundee…And that was quite early on, and it was amazing, because it was that bit about OK, you needed a bit more

169

energy to do that, but once you did it, you realised you weren't alone. That was the thing…and we had no money to go to meetings, you know, so you were taking it out of your pocket. It was hard for me because I had four young children, you know? I was pretty well on my own by then, having left the man and, you know, sort of added difficulties to it, but… but it became worth it." [Laurie Matthew]

"We had sort of group working parties and a lot of that was…around the issues in the law. Aileen Christianson was quite involved with that." [Heather Forrest]

"I remember one meeting in Stanley Road, I don't know whether it was the first or not…I think it was probably… a woman-only house at the time. And women kept coming down from Aberdeen and women from Dundee and Edinburgh women and Glasgow women so it was great – it was an opportunity to meet all these women that you hadn't met before and also to say…what the other collectives were doing and what the issues were and I think I remember the debates about…how would we actually meet, how often we would meet, what would we meet about, how would we fund it, you know and everything was always funded…you brought food or you paid a little bit and somebody had made soup and provided a roll and all that kind of stuff… I remember that happening probably about 1984 or so."
[Margaret McCutcheon]

"All of the Rape Crisis Centres had a meeting once a year…three times, I think, in the years of the Highland Rape Crisis Centre, it was held here and we hosted it. We organised the food and the location and all that…And that was very good. I thought that was very good that we did that. We…had contact, it was official, limited but official, with others." [Gale Chrisman]

"I do remember there being a…network because I remembered I still had friends who were in the Aberdeen group…there were sometimes…weekend meetings, cos I remember going up to Aberdeen… And that was a very strong group, and we had some good kind of meaty discussions I remember…that were about just real issues of …just how do we handle the police and different groups had different experiences, sometimes very good liaison officers, getting a liaison officer was a crucial first step and that took quite a while." [Fiona Raitt]

"I guess people began to see it as a good idea and also that Women's Aid were getting together…I suppose there was a bit of like, 'Oh well there's…Women's Aid stuff in England, there's a Rape Crisis network in England, wouldn't it be good to do the same here.'" [Sheila Brodie]

"We had a network…I think it had just been established…it was kinda new…because I remember we still talked about what…we wanted from the network…what could we get from that that would benefit us all… I don't know when we first attended…but we would…each take a turn…each centre would "hostess" each meeting and…at one point I remember…we thought that we were very well off compared to all the other groups, because we had a grant from our council to employ workers, and everyone else maybe had one and a half posts at best…so we always felt quite favoured, really, that we had all this money to work with. We never had enough, but it was far more than anyone else had…" [Norma Benzie]

The more established centres helped the newer ones get on their feet:

"We did training for them. I mean, I remember doing training in Aberdeen and Dundee, and I think possibly Stirling…we also set up joint Rape Crisis Centre meetings which would rotate round the place… and then Lily moved to Dundee, and she was involved in that centre…So there was a reasonable amount of contact, and it was about support because if anybody was gonna understand what you were doing, it was that Rape Crisis at the other end of the country. And…there were two groups, one in Ayr and one in Kilmarnock and there was a Highland Group for a while and so we did try, but the problem was, the Highland Group, they were the ones who wanted to dump the name Rape Crisis Centre, and so there could be differences about feminism. The newer groups didn't always see feminism as being at the centre and we did…

We had a very good informal contact and we would…go up for a day and go over lots of stuff, often the legal stuff because we had so much knowledge by then…" [Aileen Christianson]

"We used to meet up with Edinburgh…There was a Scottish Rape Crisis meeting I think once or twice a year, and we would try and move that round the different towns… to call it a "centre" was probably a little bit of a…[laughs] an overestimation. But we would usually find a room and, like, I used to be able to get a room at the university or somebody would get a room somewhere else. And then when Dundee was starting up, they came to visit us… and… we'd pass on the knowledge that we had." [Siobhan Canavan]

Later on, as it developed, network members produced a business plan and Network leaflets:

"The real miracle was…going in to all these different collectives, you know, and we actually managed to agree a leaflet and I think that's pretty amazing. I think it's amazing that small handfuls of women and individuals managed throughout that period… with no money, with barely a roof over our head. I mean, Dundee started in a corner of Women's Aid with a box and a phone, you know? That's just amazing…and the very positive stuff…the countless women that would come in…even just for a week or two…to do their bit and then sort of move on, I mean, you cannae beat that, you know?" [Laurie Matthew]

And there was a lot of movement even within the Rape Crisis network: Isabelle Kerr and Morna Findlay both started Rape Crisis work in Glasgow but moved on to Aberdeen and then back – to Glasgow, and Edinburgh respectively.

"People moved around. Moira, when she moved to Edinburgh got involved in Edinburgh Rape Crisis. When I moved down to Glasgow from Aberdeen, I did some work with women, before I got a paid job, I did some work with the Women's Support Project." [Elizabeth Shiach]

The debate around supporting men and the importance of maintaining a women-only service was often aired within the network and was a challenge that centres wrestled with for many years. It was divided opinion on this issue in particular that created the fissure that ultimately separated some centres from those that went on to form Rape Crisis Scotland, which retained the feminist gendered analysis of rape:

"There were some centres who wanted to work…with male survivors and the Rape Crisis movement had been…set up by women, for women and they were saying…these are survivors of rape and abuse… but Rape Crisis isn't necessarily the right place to deal with that and I think that was the kind of main issue. And some women felt…you know they're doing it for men…setting up support for men and why can't men set up that support for themselves." [Sheila Brodie]

"I always felt a bit sorry but…I knew perfectly well why we didn't do it…you know you would get phone calls from men who had been sexually abused as kids and you'd have to say 'Sorry, we don't counsel men, we don't take men on' and you know we just couldn't, there weren't enough of us and there was a deluge of people…

There was nowhere to refer them on and in actual fact…I started a group with a male social worker… but it was for the partners, the male partners of women who'd been sexually abused as children. So it wasn't a group for men. I think a few groups for men did sort of come out of that. Cos they then got together and started organising themselves for themselves." [Brenda Flaherty]

"None of us would have contemplated there being male volunteers in the group, and we had a clear stance on taking calls from women only…our attitude was that if men wanted a support group they could go and set one up just as we had!" [Isla Laing]

"If men are being sexually assaulted – cos it's not rape in the law…then that also has a feminist analysis… And I would, my concern would be…that men's experience would taint women's experience, because we live in a world where we don't have equity as women, …and the male experience is therefore always, always the one that is seen as more valid…and I would be concerned, for those reasons, that what we provide for women… and young women at the moment, could be tainted, it could be taken away down another route, and I don't know how you ensure that that doesn't happen.

That would be my concern…and another point that I would make is that…if I want the world to recognise that female experience is different from male experience, and therefore female experience has got its valid place and needs to be addressed in a certain way, then in fairness, that would be the same for male experience, so perhaps…I would be saying well, perhaps there needs to be organisations that are particularly addressing and supporting men and the issues around their experience of sexual assault…I recently came across a leaflet of a group of men in Taunton in Somerset…and it's an organisation that are providing support for men who experience domestic abuse, and as you read through their aims, their last aim is to remove gender politics from the…debate around domestic abuse. And that shows where that group are coming from, and that's what I'm meaning. I would be concerned that we would end up with actually going complete full-circle and be away back to where we were actually in the fifties." [Margaret Brown]

The wider feminist network, though it broadly shared the same aims and could be very beneficial, did not always take account of or reflect the situation and needs particular to Scotland:

"I remember doing an article for Spare Rib about the differences in the law, and it got published at the back, and it was all about, you know, rape in marriage is a crime in Scotland, and at the front, it had this little bit about how shocking it was that rape in marriage wasn't a crime in Britain [laughing]. So we were kinda playing with two things. There was the Women's Movement in England which was deeply Anglocentric and thought they were talking about Britain and didn't understand we had a different legal system, and there was the male attitudes in Scotland about women [laughing] so…if you were a feminist in Scotland…the main problem was men in Scotland and society and bureaucracy and everything set up in Scotland, but there was also the problem of Anglocentric assumptions in the Women's Movement in London…" [Aileen Christianson]

Lesbian women

The contribution of lesbian women to the development of the Rape Crisis movement in Scotland was enormous:

"The other issue that's not spoken about a huge amount is the amount of lesbian women who've done work…against sexual violence. And I think that is something that has been incredibly important and still is incredibly important… it's something that has been talked very much over the years… should…the Rape Crisis Centre or other women's organisations be more or less upfront about the fact that it is…seen as [the] type of organisation where very often lesbians have been at the front of setting up services for women who have been abused by men…it puzzles people I think as to why that should be the case.

But I mean I think that when people are coming at it from a political feminist thing then it is quite a lot easier… if you're not in a relationship with a man at various stages to challenge rape and the attitudes…I mean it's clearly not impossible, I don't mean that…there's been obviously heterosexual women who've been very involved…and some of them have had really supportive male partners… there's a lot of men that have donated to Rape Crisis and so on, but I mean I think there is something that frees your thinking in a way…especially in the early days…of feminist consciousness-raising groups." [Jan Macleod]

"When I started in Rape Crisis, I would say 75% of the women involved were lesbian and that doesn't happen anymore and I don't know why that is. It's just something I find really quite odd…I think it was an era where there was a lot of political activity and a lot of lesbians were involved in that activity in, you know, women's rights stuff and feminism and what have you, maybe not to the same extent anymore. Maybe people aren't politicised in the same way. Maybe there's more general interest in women's stuff… What's been lost is a kind of…opportunity for a whole lot of women…who have…maybe slightly different viewpoint. Of course, there was all that attitude 'Oh men haters, you know that's why they're involved in Rape Crisis and all these feminists hate men as well blah de blah de blah'. But I think it has made a difference maybe – maybe there were issues about feeling that like Rape Crisis or Women's Aid weren't lesbian-friendly organisations and that they weren't too happy about lesbians being the face of feminism or?… I think there's a little bit of that, and maybe pressure from the outside… I think there's something. Maybe it will change. Who knows?" [Sheila Brodie]

Heterosexual women involved in the centres sometimes had to overcome their own ignorance about lesbian women, as well as challenging assumptions that had emerged from their own sexuality:

"I remember one woman who joined the centre saying that she'd moved into a flat…and the first night she was there a new flatmate had said to her she was a lesbian and…this woman had sat sort of thinking… it's obviously not the done thing to look shocked, but then sat there for the whole of the rest of this night thinking, 'Oh my God am I gonna have to have sex with her?'…Then the woman who was a lesbian just went off to bed and she was sat there thinking, 'Hmm doesn't want to have sex.' Do you know what I mean? But …she was talking about it, about her own ignorance… and lack of awareness coming from a background where she's not been aware of lesbian women at all…I suppose when you think about a lot of the women who write about violence against women like. Andrea Dworkin and Sheila Jeffreys… you know there's quite a big theme there…I think there's a lot of the work on prostitution and sexual exploitation led by lesbian feminists as well." [Jan Macleod]

"One of the main memories I have was…we'd a very difficult discussion around…our own sexuality… in the Rape Crisis group. We were working with real violence, and the majority of us were heterosexual woman, in live-in male relationships, and I can remember one collective, when the whole issue of lesbian politics and working as a lesbian within that collective was raised, it was very, very difficult…

I think because we were being challenged, you know, the heterosexual women in the group were being challenged to look at, well, what have we been doing? What assumptions have we been making? So it challenged us, and obviously for the women…who raised that…they're raising it 'cause they're saying 'Well, we feel that our voices aren't being heard'…Lesbian women…within the collective were saying 'Well, we're feeling not heard' and the heterosexual women are thinking 'Well …we've got to look at this, what have we been doing?'

So I think that was quite tough…I think it made me stop and think… because *[of]* the hidden-ness of our sexuality within the collective…It only emerged at a certain point – I mean, we all knew that there were a mixture of heterosexual and lesbian women within the group, but we never discussed our sexuality…We discussed our own experiences of abuse…but I don't think we discussed how, as a group, what it meant to be a lesbian woman working in this area…We didn't have…that discussion within the Rape Crisis group. I had that discussion with individuals. I can't remember us having that discussion within the Rape Crisis group… So that's one of the things that really… I remember being …quite challenging for people, difficult discussions…all around their sexuality and the hiddenness, particularly of lesbianism within the collective, being something that was hard to raise, for the women who raised it, and hard to hear. But was raised, heard, talked about and out in the open…I think the group was better for that. And…it wasn't before the group had started operating before that happened." [Elizabeth Shiach]

For some lesbian women, involvement in Rape Crisis work was an integral part of their own personal development and somewhere they could be free to acknowledge fully as well as feel comfortable within a lesbian identity:

"I found it really a growing place…it was also part of my growing up period of really exploring my sexuality…at that point in my early 20s I thought 'Oh well it's all right I'll be a lesbian when I'm 40. I can do it then and my mother won't take my daughter from me' and all that kind of stuff and then I realised actually, no it's possible you could actually just define your sexuality and be who you want to be a lot earlier and that'll be a lot better for you so, part of that was also as well was about exploring and meeting…women who actually said 'Yeah…I'm a lesbian.' And that was fantastic for me because it gave me a lot of strength. And being able to come out myself." [Margaret McCutcheon]

"I think lesbian women certainly contributed masses to the feminist movement…In all sorts of different ways in unpaid work…sexuality was always under discussion, I remember, in the sense that when we were talking about violence against women, and we talked about heterosexual relationships… how they defined women and how men were defined within that and about power and patriarchy. Sexuality then came up because…in the late 70s women were talking about women's land and, you know, separatist lifestyles etc so there was a whole kind of like package of things to learn about… how different lesbian women lived their lives and it was important for me just on a personal level to be around really strong women who identified with other lesbian women and…with other women in general." [Margaret McCutcheon]

Black & minority ethnic women

"There remain problems we have not dealt with – we are all English/Scots speaking and almost all white. We recognise that we are not equipped to support Black women who are sexually assaulted whose experience is located within a different cultural context. Language is another barrier; at the moment we can only offer support to women who speak English or Scots. Leaflets translated into other languages and support through interpreters will help us to begin to address the issue. However, we are aware that only with more Black members of our collective will we be able to fully support Black women." [Edinburgh Rape Crisis workers in Grit and Diamonds (Stramullion, 1990)]

There were very few women involved in the first Rape Crisis centres who were black or from ethnic minority backgrounds:

"A lot of the ethnic minority women went to Shakhti, to Women's Aid…which is quite specifically, [why] they set that up…over the years, one or two would come and go, and there was an American lass who was…Japanese I think, in origin, so that would come up…but not as a huge big issue…where our racism we could identify was in terms of Irish and not Irish, so if we had a racism discussion, it often came round to that, 'cause there was always one or two or three Irish women involved over the years. So the racism wasn't such a big thing, largely because there were no black, African origin, or Chinese or whatever, until later in the group." [Aileen Christianson]

"Marcia D'Oliveira. She was the only black woman in the collective…at that time…I think she did the first year of the Women's Support Project, she was Brazilian and then eventually went back to Brazil… she was in…the Communist Party…this black woman who had done her degree in English which was her second language…she did a degree in I think it was Politics and History and she was a tremendously strong public speaker…I remember at rallies in George Square…and different things to do with Greenham or CND, Marcia speaking." [Helen Mackinnon]

"There were…one or two women from black and minority ethnic background. We did try to encourage it but I think culturally it was quite difficult…I mean we advertised, did all the usual things, but…we weren't that successful." [Sheila Brodie]

"Certainly not early on…there was later on…it wasn't for the want of trying… we did, in a lot of our publicity, make it very clear we're looking for women from…a different range of backgrounds and keen to get ethnic minority women on board and we would…put out publicity…to black women's groups, not that in these days there was a huge amount of black women's groups in Aberdeen. They were just starting themselves…about that time, is my recollection. So no, I don't think we…did at the start, although I know that we did later on." [Leslie Brown]

Anecdotes:

Some of the most vivid and revealing impressions to emerge in the course of the oral history project were through anecdotes, in accounts of incidents, conversations and accounts of personal experience, both as lived by Rape Crisis workers themselves, and as recounted by women they knew:

Sexual violence in Stirling

"A friend was followed coming back from an area of campus late one night and got quite a scare. A couple of friends were chased by a gang of guys at a party, like during a party and were, and now, I'm horrified at our lack of response to that, I mean, and amazed at their response to it…They were, it was dismissed as a bit of a lark. It was seen as a 'God that was a close thing', you know? But at one point, one of them was on the ground, and there were six men on top of her, and the other was in a toilet cubicle thinking 'Oh what the fuck am I gonna do here?' And what stopped it was a male acquaintance who had realised something wasn't right, you know, had seen them running and had kinda wondered what was going on – and he was a bit of a nutter, he was known on campus as a bit of a nut-case [laughing] but he appeared suddenly in the toilet, swinging a martial arts weapon, and…he was the kind of scary person that would just frighten, and all the lads scattered…they were young lads from the town and they just took off and it was all then this big, 'Phew'…you know, almost like it was a big adventure. But I remember talking to the woman who'd been in the toilet cubicle about it, and her saying 'I really thought that [I] was gonna be raped.' And, but then we just kinda went 'Wheesh', you know? Just move away from that thought." [Lily Greenan]

"And then a woman…had gone down to the village…to make an international call from a phone box…she was phoning her boyfriend who was in America, and she was standing in a phone box in the middle of a deserted village street, and a man came up to the phone box, and basically stood outside the door and stared at her for half an hour and wouldn't let her out. And she's on the phone to her boyfriend on the other side of the world saying, 'There's this guy', and he's saying 'Hang up and phone the cops', and she couldn't do it. She couldn't phone the police 'cause it would have felt like making a fuss…" [Lily Greenan]

Challenging sexism in Glasgow

"We always went to the pub next door…and Lorraine Warmbath did a shocking thing one time. We went in, and we always had a good relationship with the pub next door which was really spit 'n' sawdust…I don't know if it's under the same management, but it's very rough. It was a real Glasgow man's pub…I think it stopped at ten o'clock, our shift, and it was like ten 'til maybe quarter to eleven, at that time… we went into the pub next door, and it was just choc-a-bloc all the time, and it was very smoky and everything, it was good, it was a good Glasgow pub, and we always had things like half pints of lager or something like that, a half pint of lager and lime, or whatever – and there was this kerfuffle up at the bar, and Lorraine, who was very tall, and she was pointing to someone, and I said to Naomi, 'What is Lorraine doing? What's happening up at the bar?' And there was a lot of aggression, and the man behind the bar was like this, and we went up, and there was a calendar behind the bar…and she said 'This is inciting violence against me…Take it down', and he said 'I'm not f***ing taking anything down, what's wrong with you?' She says 'What is wrong with you that you have – you take that down.' The police were called…And she was taken (laughing) out by the police, because she started shouting. She really started saying 'You're woman-hater, look at that, you're a bloody disgrace.' And she just did things like that. We were like, 'Oh my God' – and of course, that was publicity…

The next day, I said 'Lorraine, my God, what did they say to you?' Oh, and they gave her a really rough time. Wasting police time and all sorts of things, and she gave them as good as she got… 'I just bloody told them.' You know, this, that and the other and she was just full of it, and so we'd such a laugh, but she could do that radical thing, just in the most public places, and not be harassed about it at all, would just take it completely in her stride." [Jane Dorby]

Secret biscuits

"Part of the training *[of Safe Strong & Free]* is you tell kids, 'You know, if anybody asks you to keep something a secret, you know, don't' [laughs]. 'Tell somebody, tell your parents.' And…this kid had been told by a neighbour who gave this kid…a chocolate biscuit, 'Now don't tell your mother that you've got a choc' [gasps]. The kid was so shocked and horrified, so of course she went home and told her mother that she'd been given a chocolate biscuit… [laughs] you know, that kids are gonna apply the instruction, you know, when it's relatively innocent. So yeah, that was great, that was great." [Gale Chrisman]

Paedophile Information Exchange

"We had discussions about incest and it was at that point…what do you call them Paedophile Information Exchange were lobbying Rape Crisis centres to support them being allowed to freedom of speech, talking about having sex with children…they had a huge campaign at that point wrote to all the Rape Crisis centres…they were pushing very much this thing about incest should the laws on incest should be removed, because it was a matter of mutual consent. And I remember that caused a lot of debate." [Jan Macleod]

Feminist consciousness-raising in London

"I remember we went down to London to some feminist thing…I don't remember how that happened, but there were speculums and all sorts of things going! …How we ended up there I do not know, but we went on some kind of awareness training…a couple of us went down…it was real typical 70's women stuff, and it's like 'Oh my goodness, did I really do that?'" [Kathy Litteljohn]

End of a relationship

"It was my last relationship with a man and that would have been in '84 and I remember …I was going to Rape Crisis to do my session, and we happened to be living together actually, but it was only because it was like a shared flat and he kind of moved in sort of thing. I was sharing a flat with another woman, I was a single parent and anyway he ended up moving in. I had this relationship with this guy, and I'm going to do my session and I bumped into him in the street and I said 'Oh, I wasn't expecting to meet you' and he just looked like Mr Guilty and…he had a porn video in a brown bag. I was absolutely incandescently angry and that was it. It was ended, ended. Literally ended it was like 'How the fuck can you have a relationship with me, why am I having a relationship with you?' That was really, it really was powerful, dead powerful." [Margaret McCutcheon]

Liberation

"One of the things that really, really affected me a lot was one of the women I spoke to who had been abused by her father from a very young age, all the way up to being 28 and she started phoning the centre when she was 27…her dad bought her a house that she moved into when she was like 16/17. She never worked because she was agoraphobic. She never went out the house. She did have access to money, but because she'd been so emotionally abused and her dad had set her up in this house so that he could come to the house and continue to rape her and sexually assault her, emotionally abuse her for years and years, you know like from 2 till 28. When she eventually kind of said to me, 'I've phoned a locksmith and changed the locks'…that… knocked me off my seat…I was having to hold back the tears …and that really resonated …that was, incredibly powerful. So that, sort of on a personal level…like a lot of the work we did…with people…they did get their lives back, they were able to move on. But I think that story's particularly powerful because she was a prisoner for all of her life. She didn't know who she was, she was her dad's plaything. So, so those individual stories are really important." [Heather Forrest]

Influences: reading

In addition to the practical experience they gain through working with Rape Crisis, a wide variety of reading informed and shaped the views of the women involved:

"Then I read '**The Women's Room**' – the Marilyn French novel?…And it said on the cover, 'This novel changes lives' and I've always said, I read that book and it did. [laughing]. And it wasn't about my generation, it was about my mother's generation, but something about really seeing what went on for my mother's generation began to move something for me…" [Lily Greenan]

"I remember reading Angela Davis, '**Women, Race and Class**', and I mean if you thought about… my travels in India and Nepal there were the connections there. I thought that was a very strong and powerful book and I did like the feminist analysis that Rape Crisis had…round the…women's position. And the issue about rape, I found that tremendously motivating. And energising. And clear." [Helen Mackinnon]

"I ended up going and buying all sorts of books I'd never read at university because that wasn't the kind of law that I was being taught. But I had to get myself informed quickly so that I could challenge what was the dominant view and, and be sure I had the facts and the figures…there'd be a whole set of books from the 70s and 80s…from London Rape Crisis Group and the sort of standard classic texts…Susan Brownmiller… and there's a whole pile of things which are still very, very important texts, but for me it was like scales falling from my eyes…" [Fiona Raitt]

"I've got one student I know…And he said that he was so affected by what happened in the gender class about rape, that he bought Susan Brownmiller's book for every member of his family…in fact… so much so he said mine got dog-eared, cos they'd been lending it to each other so … he brought me back a new one…that was the time of the Bosnian wars…he went off to join the junior Red Cross and to spend time out there with victims of rape…he was astonishing…he's almost qualified as a doctor and he wants to go off and do this kind of work abroad. So there are, you can reach men as well that's what I say to myself you know if you just, if you only ever speak to one constituency, you won't change people." [Fiona Raitt]

"When anthologies were being published of women writing about their experiences… where there were TV programmes being made, where…you got… issues relating to violence against women and children in soaps, in novels…I would say things like '**The Color Purple**' was really important… it was growing and it was much more in the public domain and public consciousness, I think, and I think women were saying 'Me too.'" [Siobhan Canavan]

"There was a book published by the Women's Press called '**In Our Own Hands**', and it was a groupwork book for working women's groups, different sorts of women's groups and we used to look at that book… just looking for warm-up exercises, just ways to help assist folk express their anger or express their grief or loss, just to find some creative ways of doing things." [Elizabeth Shiach]

At Edinburgh Rape Crisis, workers discovered that they themselves had become the subject matter, when Naomi Wolf's book '**Fire With Fire**' was published:

"Naomi Wolf was a member of our collective, briefly…I liked her. She was, well, she was American, she was very, very pretty and she was very confident – came from an academic background…anyway, Naomi promised…in her case, she got a big screening because we were worried at the fact she was writing a book, and she said 'No, no, no, it's about this and that and the other…I will never write about what's happened in Rape Crisis.'

The book that came out… it's an attack on the Women's Movement, and there's…at least one chapter about Rape Crisis. In that chapter, she says 'Oh it was on the first floor and there was this woman that we all used to talk about behind her back, what a, what a bully she was' and that was me…And one of my colleagues…she went and looked at it in the book shop, and she said 'Aileen don't read it, it's all about you, it's horrible' – so of course, I went and read it, and when Naomi came to promote the next book…I was at the back…and at the end, I went up just to say hello, and she said 'Well it was…they did talk about you behind your back and I said 'Yeah, it doesn't matter if it was behind my back, it didn't affect the work we were doing.'

So have a read of that, get a hold of that book…it's unpleasant, but it's also funny. I mean, I find it quite funny…so if you want a negative view of a collective. And she was terribly upset because we didn't have flowers in the women's centre, it wasn't beautiful – we had no fucking money and we were getting it painted at the time, and she's completely twisted it, so Naomi Wolf, her name is dirt [laughing]…And of course she had to pretend it wasn't us – it was a sort of composite centre, and anyone who'd been involved in it, it was perfectly obvious [laughing]. What a besom eh! …every time she comes over to promote things, it's to the sound of some of us snorting!" [laughing] [Aileen Christianson]

As if she had been witness to this misrepresentation or a similar incident, Germaine Greer had issued a salutary warning:

"Germaine Greer…was interviewed for [an] article, and her closing statement I found very telling… her closing statement was that really what we need to guard against is the misogyny, as women, in our own hearts." [Margaret Brown]

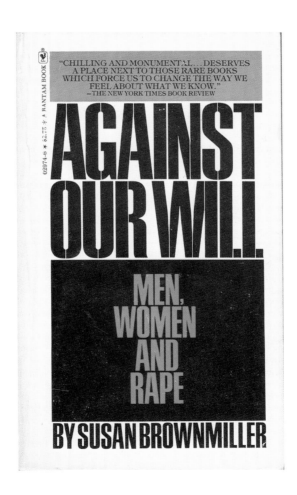

Testimony: the personal impact of Rape Crisis work

Involvement in the Rape Crisis movement and in developing the first services in Scotland figured hugely in the lives of many women and largely shaped many of those lives as much as the new services. The significance of that work and what it meant to women, many of whom continue to work in services dedicated to fighting violence against women, was clear among everyone who took part in this project:

"Well it's sort of taken over my life would just about sum it up but not, or not necessarily Rape Crisis but work on violence against women. I mean I've made a lot of really good friends through the Rape Crisis Centre and through the project and the work that I've done since…whereas you'll definitely never get rich in this work, it does give you a certain freedom…in the Rape Crisis Centre like I've said I learnt an awful lot – an awful lot of skills and it opened an awful lot of doors… And through working at the project, being a small voluntary organisation, you've got that sort of mixed blessing of being able to have a bit of choice about what you're doing in your work and learning new stuff all the time cos otherwise you would definitely go off your head. So you've got this mixture of like carrying an awful lot of responsibility and having to earn your own wages and all that against having that freedom in your life." [Jan Macleod]

"Sometimes it worries me that women in women's organisations don't take the credit for the roots that they've kind of planted. I think, often, that we're so caught up in just providing services that we actually forget how we started, where we came from and what we've actually achieved…we don't give enough credit to a bunch of women who are a bit tired and a bit rough and a bit scared and a bit emotional, getting together, because most of our violence against women services have been set up by those women, you know? So I'm very proud of that. Very, very proud of that." [Frances Monaghan]

"When we're doing all that work, you know, I'm constantly aware of the history that that's steeped in. I don't know if that's just because I'm personally very tapped into my own history and how my history has made me who I am, but I can see that reflected in the services, you know? And we have got a lot to be proud of in this city, and I just wish that, sometimes, we would stop and go 'Look, we know we've got a lot to do, and we're not going to do it all in our lifetime, let's face it.' You know? Because there's new stuff coming up. Internet stuff's coming up, trafficking stuff is there, all these things are going to be getting dealt with. We've got a society that makes it totally easy to exploit us, you know? In fact, it encourages the exploitation of us, but you know, I still want us to remember, if we hadn't have done all that, what would it be like, now?" [Frances Monaghan]

"It was really important…feminism, coming together…and I think what, looking back, and it's only when you do have the time to sit back and think about these things…as a younger woman, it was really important you had that strength…and…a movement behind you – I really took to it like a duck to water, because it was so obviously correct…it still is…the essential core belief of women's powerlessness and issues of power…that still pertains…" [Caroline Armit]

"It's really sort of changed my life and…as I said, there was no turning around…it wasn't an easy ride. But I've always preferred…truth, no matter how unpalatable…so that was just the right environment for me. I think at the time it has raised maybe more questions, for me personally…than it had answered, and…even not having got an answer, I'm sort of much more, much more at peace. What it's given me I think is, is a confidence in, in speaking out…the belief that…you can nurture that confidence in others so that they can speak out as well." [Florence Germain]

"It was completely all consuming and…it absolutely encapsulated everything that I turned out to be really good at …empathising and supporting and all the rest of it…I was also not frightened of standing

"I think that one thing that maybe hasn't come across is that it was fun, the other women were great and I really enjoyed being with them…We had meals and every week there was something so it wasn't all hard work and, I suppose that I kind of miss that really. I mean I've got very good colleagues here that I talk with but I can't imagine discussing feminism with anybody here." [Maureen Porter]

"Very strong friendships formed because I'm still friendly with both Siobhan and Elizabeth. And we've all moved around…It was through Rape Crisis that we made those sort of friendships …I suppose because we had other common interests like hillwalking and stuff. I suppose the bonds grew between each other because you were doing very sensitive and emotional work… it did really create closer friendships because…it touched things in ourselves so we shared things. Not necessarily that we'd all been raped but we'd all had some sort of experience of, well, as most women have. So we shared things that you wouldn't normally share when you were in doing other voluntary work or other kind of work." [Dorothy Degenhardt]

"In those days there were more women's social events …the Tay Hotel that big old hotel as you come opposite the station…it's been standing empty now for about 10 years, but I remember that there was at least one big social event there, women's night or women's party. So Rape Crisis and Women's Aid workers would be there… And …in some other premises I remember. So there were social nights, but it wouldn't just be Rape Crisis. But because Dundee's quite small there was this women's scene in Dundee and so you knew which women were involved in Rape Crisis and Women's Aid. Those were the two main… organisations that were working with women." [Dorothy Degenhardt]

"I think just because of the nature of the way you got to know people, it's a very kind of intense, intimate experience, being in that room, you know…most of the friends that I've got now I've all met through Rape Crisis, so they are friendships that are really intense…so I look back on it as a kind of exhausting at times, quite frustrating experience but mostly I'm really glad that I was part of it for a long time, it was a really empowering experience…there were really strong feminists in there and it was just smashing being around them…" [Linda Reid]

"After we had had our meetings, we would go to the pub, and then because we had only got a short time left in the pub we would say 'Mmm, where's open? [laughs] and we would go to the nearest disco, and such like. Get wrecked…it was nice, and we would go out for Christmas dinners and we would try to do lunches and things when we could, but that…never worked very well…we very quickly got really quite busy as workers, to be doing that kind of stuff." [Norma Benzie]

The need to challenge people in everyday life was a common experience for Rape Crisis workers whose eyes had been opened to the silence around the issues, and the damage myths and misconceptions around rape and sexual violence could cause:

"Social settings, social gatherings, family, you know. I was raising those issues as we all were." [Elizabeth Shiach]

"I had rows with two of the professors here and a boss of mine because they made a joke about me being involved in Rape Crisis at a social event, so I just tore into them." [Aileen Christianson]

"I think that some of us were quite bolshie… we didn't care!…It was more the stamina that you needed, and the resources, and the workload…" [Kathy Litteljohn]

"Attitudes of society…initially when people would say man and mean woman…the sort of political correctness thing right at the beginning was good, you know they wanted people to think about using

185

the word man. I mean I've read books here that say pregnancy and man. You know it's ridiculous so we wanted to wake people up." [Maureen Porter]

"I had a friend who was a young people's psychiatrist…a consultant psychiatrist…and I remember going out for a meal with him and his partner and one or two folk, and…leaving that restaurant in tears, because we'd had a terrible row. I remember him sort of attacking me and saying 'I can't believe that somebody of your sort of solidity would buy into all this'. And I remember just being in floods of tears over it and just being very upset by it. Partly annoyed with my own self for not having the words to debate it." [Helen Mackinnon]

"I was interviewed to be a trainee social worker, and I can remember the guy's name, I won't say, and he said 'I've read your paperwork…very interesting…this Rape Crisis, what is this?' …and he said 'Well you know, I've seen a pretty girl get on a bus' …I remember it vividly 'And she goes …up the stairs on the bus with a short skirt on' says he, and I said 'Look, just, gonnae no talk like that', I really was just quite assertive…and he did shut up after that and kinda try and kid on he was being flippant, and I just said 'Well, it's not at all funny'…but I did get on the course!" [Caroline Armit]

"I was challenging somebody at a party…just last week…I was saying, on the assumption that this woman would share my point of view, which is…a mistake I make often, that she would be as horrified as I at the news that 5 percent is all that men who actually get to the point of being in a court room, which is minute… and I was saying 'You know, this is absolutely appalling after how many years?'… and she said 'Well, em…' and she began on this… 'Well, you know, sometimes women don't tell the truth about these things.'…Oh God! I could tear my hair out, I could have torn her hair out, really. After, what, 25 years later, this woman is saying, she's not a stupid woman, she's intelligent and knowledgeable. Why… why is she saying that? I mean, does she honestly think… unless they're very disturbed women, that they want to go through the humiliation and activity…of being in a courtroom and having to, you know? Mostly it is of course the opposite – women don't come forward, not that women come forward with false allegations. What is she thinking of? And I was so depressed about that." [Gale Chrisman]

"I was a bit of a firebrand in those days…sort of go in and shout at men that I was working with and [laughs] the boys that I was teaching and, you know, my partner and things like this…But I quite enjoyed that…and it wasn't very nice, really – the sort of classic, I think because of my involvement in party politics, it was just very much point scoring and putting people down and being really aggressive. It wasn't really doing it in the appropriate way. I wouldn't have done that with women – I would have tempered my approach with women. But yeah, yeah – I did it all the wrong way. It was just the usually confrontational stuff, you know?" [Rona Clarke]

"To be honest, in the early days, I was more prone to challenge jokes, bad jokes and idiotic remarks, which you do hear in pubs and things like that, but now that I no longer pub crawl, I'm a bit reluctant to get into the kind of arguments that I used to do when I was younger. I used to feel quite angry if people said insensitive things but now I'll say what I think I need to say, and then, 'I'm not fighting with you – I'll sow the seeds, and I'll leave it with you.'…

I don't know if that's enough or not, but no I don't think that it's gotten very much better, and it's still a conversation stopper. People say 'Where d'you work?' And it's quite a drawback, because sometimes, if I've been working late and I get a taxi home – you know taxi drivers…and they'll say 'Where d'you work?' and I'll say 'Tescos' or something like that (laughs) 'Oh my wife works there!' – that happened once. I was like 'No, I don't actually know her'…

Sometimes when I have said I counsel women who've been raped or sexually abused as children, there's a silence. And then, once or twice, I've had disclosures…from the taxi driver, and then…sometimes

186

they're like 'That must be a difficult job hen', and then they're quite happy to leave it – they don't want to talk about it…I did put that taxi driver down as a session…" [Norma Benzie]

"It was demanding…I mean it took its emotional toll, I would say. It certainly took its emotional toll on me…I think you could, because what you hear is about the particular issue you're working with in this one, you know, sort of sexual violence, and male/female relationships, that is, it starts to warp your view of male/female relationships, and even though I'm in a heterosexual relationship…I think all of those things… affected me, affected my relationship with my partner…it's changed my view of the world." [Elizabeth Shiach]

A combination of attitudes that were prevalent at the time, and ignorance around many of the areas within which Rape Crisis workers were operating, meant that many paid a high personal price for their involvement:

"I think it's very mixed. I think it was extremely exciting…and it's nice to think that… I was quite touched when you said that other people had commented on my contribution, cos I didn't think it was very significant. I've been hurt by the experience as well. It's taught me a hell of a lot. I'm still working with people…nearly 30 years on, still working with people who've been abused … so it's been hugely influential…It's been my life…but it's also been part of the fabric of my sadness and probably my illness … so it's very mixed, very, very mixed. When I left Aberdeen I was probably depressed, I was certainly burnt out." [Liz Hall]

Several of the women involved in developing Rape Crisis centres spoke of the impact that the work they did with Rape Crisis had on their daughters:

"It influenced her in becoming a much stronger woman, I'm sure…I mean, I remember her as a seven-year old, you know, ringing up the City Library and ticking them off cos they hadn't got the book she wanted and I'm thinking 'My God, this is my daughter!' and somebody said 'Well, you know, kind of like… like mother, like daughter.' And she's so… well, she's quite prone to telling me off as well…but she also saw the downside of me getting exhausted and tired and not always being there for them, so… and she's much more sensitive than my son would have been." [Liz Hall]

"I feel as if I've made an impact on…what my daughter is like you know, I mean I just listen to her talking sometimes and I think I done that to you, you know…She has a partner, and she's got three children and she's at home. Well she's probably at the gym right now. But she's at home…looking after the children and I'm no saying she's not working cos she works bloody hard. But, she doesn't get caught up in, you know, 'I'm the only person responsible for this, I need to look after this family'…she does not have these, these expectations…What she does, she does by choice and knows that that is a choice that she has, she's got the right to make and if she chose to do something else, she would have no qualms whatsoever about going doing it. Her choice at the moment is that she likes to be there, looking after her children – that's…where she really sees her kind of role at the moment. And values it…but she certainly doesn't see that happening for the rest of her life…she's making plans about her future…and I just think in the way that she treats her partner as well in that you know she doesn't buy into that whole, you know 'I'm the breadwinner therefore…' she doesn't buy into that at all…and my granddaughter as well…She's 9 and…we affectionately call her the Princess of Darkness and she is a very strong-willed assertive young woman…she really is…And long may it last." [Isabelle Kerr]

"My daughter in particular absorbed a lot of what I was doing and the way I was with people, and although she hasn't had any formal involvement with anything like that, she's actually really good with women and she has a really good awareness and understanding of that kind of thing…she's the sort of person people tell things to, so quite a lot of her friends will have told her that over the years they've been raped or sexually abused or something like that and she comes to me and says 'Well I said this and I said that, and is that all right?'…so I'm quite, I'm quite proud of the way she's responded to that." [Brenda Flaherty]

"I think it had quite a significant impact…my children…I can get quite tearful about this because I think they quite suffered, when I look back. And although I was never as extreme as some of the members of the group, I think the work I got involved with, and there were two women particularly, who I became very heavily involved in, who were very, very, very dependant and demanding of time, and certainly to the neglect of my middle daughter, who started having some problems and you know, I have to sort of accept that, at times, I wasn't as much there as I should have been." [Sue Hunt]

"I've got a daughter who's 15 and I have had some regrets that I haven't had more political involvement while she's been growing up because I'm not sure how much of it has rubbed off on her. I think she's at the moment part of that generation that – it's not just that she thinks the battles have all been won, I don't think she thinks there's anything to fight about. And I will sometimes make remarks that I think are quite Gothic in terms of, you know, how conservative we are, you know, about silly things…My wee boy – I'd kept some of the clothes that Rosie had, and I'd give Jim one of these t-shirts – and I'm not talking about a pink flowery t-shirt – he felt the fact that it had been owned by a girl meant he shouldn't wear it. He thought it was somehow demeaning to his dignity or something! How did I have a daughter who thinks like this? It's because…she doesn't hear these discussions and I regret that a wee bit." [Morna Findlay]

And inevitably, the heightened awareness workers had of the possibility of abuse, could strike very close to home:

"The worst thing, from a personal point of view, was there was a minister in Aberdeen … who was convicted of sexual offences, and he was the minister of the church my daughter went to Brownies in, and I remember having to ask her whether he'd done anything to her. That was horrible." [Liz Hall]

"There was a church minister, who lived at the end of my road, then, and what this woman said was that he had said to her, she said he'd been part of the abuse… And she said that he had said to her, 'You know that little girl that lives at such and such a number,' who was my daughter, who was seven, 'She goes to Brownies, doesn't she?' So it came over as an implicit threat, and I think that shook me as well. He was, soon after that, he was arrested. Nothing came out about ritual abuse, but he was sentenced to prison." [Sue Hunt]

Having experienced the movement in its hand-to-mouth resource-free infancy, some of the women who were involved in the earliest Rape Crisis centres shared their perceptions of Rape Crisis today and the changes intervening years have brought:

"I think there's been a huge step forward structurally since the Scottish Parliament, since the network were successful in getting a national office, that has definitely increased the profile and the influence that Rape Crisis movement's got. Through the Rape Crisis Specific Fund we've got the new centres, I don't think it's been easy." [Jan Macleod]

"I think that the issue of violence against women has gone up the agenda in terms of the Scottish Parliament and that has brought *some* funding. I don't know much about exactly how much money is coming into the Rape Crisis network in Scotland in terms of how adequate it is, but I do know in respect of other organisations, for example SAY Women that it is a continual struggle to secure funding, but at least in terms of…Rape Crisis there are now some paid posts which was never the case in the past, I mean in Aberdeen most of the volunteers were coming from having spent a full day either working in paid employment or looking after children…to spend a few hours covering the line…" [Isla Laing]

"I just have a wee feeling of, we're on the edge of something that could be really, really good and I'm looking forward to that. In terms of Rape Crisis, I'm glad that you've been able to negotiate the change in the relationship between the national office and the network, to get…the independent sort of articles to do that process. I think that will help, certainly, for Rape Crisis Scotland." [Lily Greenan]

"The trouble with all voluntary organisations is that they depend on the women who are the volunteers… and there's never enough money to pay lots of people, and people get really tired because it is so draining, and I think that's the bit that gets forgotten, is that you get really into the heady days of challenging the world and, you know, 'We can do this', to being defeated and exhausted because the world actually keeps basically telling you to go, or to fuck off, really. And so it's a very tough battle. As I say, we keep turning the wheel, we keep on having to fight the battle again." [Liz Hall]

"I think one of the things has been it's always been a very secret, it's a very secret thing… and, you know, it's not associated with men, so half the population has nothing to do with it and it's almost seen as anti-male, and I think that's a great pity, cos it isn't. I think that's a real pity.

I think one of the lessons I learned, strongly, from involvement in Women's Aid and Rape Crisis has been a thing about have a reaction which is we shouldn't be hiding – we should be very public…Very public, very vocal. We should not be saying to survivors of abuse 'You need to sneak into this secret address', you know? What there should be is a big placard saying 'Rape Crisis Centre', 'Women's Aid', and anybody going in there should be holding their head up with pride, you know, because it's not our shame, and I know the reason it was made very secretive in the beginning…

Where that originally came from in Dundee was supporting the workers, because when we went to see women we didn't have a place we saw them initially, so we went in twos. So it was for safety…

And I like what I've seen the network doing. I'd like to see, you know, Scottish Rape Crisis being much higher profile, out there, in people's faces…And I think all the local Rape Crisis should be doing exactly the same and not hiding. I mean, the days of that are over. The days of being shut away in a pathetic building where you're stepping over drunks, because that's how much we cared about women, not us, but that's how much the needs of women were catered for." [Laurie Matthew]

"It's been really good to see how Rape Crisis has evolved and changed and developed, I also think that it's really good to be in a position now where…we're asked to be involved…we are consulted about things, whereas often in the past, I mean many, many years ago…the scenario was…'You lassies mean well'. You know? 'But all these lassies tell lies really.' So…I don't see that, that disnae happen now. People might still be thinking it but they don't actually say it to us. I think the recognition that the Scottish Executive has had for women's organisations and the funding and how that's taken very seriously I think has just been a fantastic achievement. But that hasnae happened in a vacuum. I mean that's because women's organisations…have been there biting at their ankles for 30 years…and I think that has to be recognised as well." [Isabelle Kerr]

"I was hugely impressed…I was really interested in how…things have…become a bit more structured and how there's a lot more…appreciation of…the whole community of women…more inclusive… and targeted, and stated approach to looking at the issue, and …not being just focused on an act which happens to a woman, but…experiences that people have had that are sometimes hard to pigeonhole…" [Kathy Litteljohn]

"I just think even when people talk about the Cross-Party Reference Group…I just think 'Wow!', you know? From our little cave up in Aberdeen and everybody else's little cave …in the other towns, look what it has come to. The world has turned and it will never, no matter what happens…go back in the box again. Never, ever, ever. And I think that's a phenomenal social achievement…and women have done it and children have done it. Not men." [Siobhan Canavan]

"I think, through the Scottish Executive, there's been a fair amount of interest in…women's issues… the very fact the Crown Office has been looking at…cases of rape, what's happening through the Prosecution Service, in what ways the Prosecution Service isn't, you know, geared up to dealing with it, is…a very positive sign that it's being taken seriously…and Women's Aid have been quite fortunate in getting additional funding and …we've been seeing some new offices and refuges emerging and I think that's because the Scottish Executive has been quite sympathetic to seeing change…they were quite keen to develop sort of consultancy mechanisms as well…involving quite a lot of women. So if that is sustained, then…it gives you the base from which to start dealing with that, and getting it taken seriously." [Sheila Gilmore]

"I think that women's expectation of getting support…has probably shifted as well. We have an expectation now of, as a consumer…as being provided, you know, as service providers or somebody who's using a service, what the quality of that is gonna be about. So I think that's significantly different…I think it applies to Rape Crisis." [Margaret McCutcheon]

"I think as feminists and in organisations we have to really be constantly thinking…re-theorising – we need to be the ones who are shaping the theories really. And I think that for me there's possibly a sense that we've lost a little bit of not writing down and sharing that kind of written work amongst ourselves to then say ok this is our position on it…the internal debate in feminist organisations…I think as well when you're holding very large budgets…there is something for me about our job of work is about saying 'Well ok, what does feminist management look like? What does feminist leadership look like? What is it, what is that about?' Because I think…there was such a fear that if you weren't operating as a collective you'd lost a bit of your feminism. And I don't believe that." [Margaret McCutcheon]

"I think that people may have felt that over the years that…maybe the battles hadn't been won, but some of the arguments had been won and had become mainstream…I think that people know now that children are abused by family members…friends – everybody knows that. Although there may be a perception that there are paedophiles lurking about, I think that people realise this goes on and have accepted that. I think it's interesting the way some of the debates have changed in the press over women's culpability in rape – in the past it would be…'You shouldn't be out at night, you shouldn't be wearing a short skirt'; now it's like, 'You shouldn't be pissed.'" [Morna Findlay]

"It has been very significant for us as individuals and hopefully in creating services for other women and for all women to get involved…not just as survivors…And I think that whole thing about empowerment and partnership working and all the stuff we now use in social work and so on has come about because of all that, the Rape Crisis work and the whole notion of…survivorship. Cause I think…incest survivors was probably the first time the word was used …it's really had an influence. It's certainly had an influence in mental health work which I've …worked in professionally and taught …I think that whole notion of survivorship and involving service users in working with others and so on, it's had a fundamental effect on that. But I don't think it's always recognised as such." [Dorothy Degenhardt]

Looking forward

How much have things changed? What still needs to happen and what might the future look like for today's young Scottish women? Pioneering women of the Rape Crisis movement give their views:

"I don't know where young women, nowadays, ever get to that stage because they don't have the advantage that women of my generation have of coming up through that development of their own personal politics and…to name yourself as a feminist… nowadays is still, what would you call it, people would say it was an insult, you know? They think as, as a term of abuse. Whereas, I mean, I would wear it as a badge of pride, rather than a term of abuse." [Elizabeth Shiach]

"In the eighties when I was going about the job of trying to bring women together, I certainly had a sense of a sisterhood…now, that's not to say that everything was hunky-dory in that sisterhood, you know? I think I'm not looking through rose-coloured spectacles when I say this, but…there was a sense of women coming together… with their anger and frustration…towards a common goal, and to channel it so that it was taken into action that was positive. And what I find now is that when I speak to… particularly, well, I'm in my fifties now – women who are younger than me, they are experiencing the same anger, the same frustration, but they don't know what to do with it." [Margaret Brown]

"If I were to put my energy anywhere in something in this area ever again, it would be… with children and young people, about all the stuff Gale's said about Safe, Strong, Free, and young people…if anyone ever wants to have a vigilante group going round with a Stanley knife slashing all that sexualised clothing for the under-eights, I'm with them." [Sue Owen]

"I'm kind of finding that a lot of the old attitudes are still there and people are not getting the support to kind of say, 'Well it wasn't my fault, there's nothing I could have done'. So there's no one there that's able to say to them…'Look it's not your fault…you didn't do anything to cause the abuse'…that's actually probably what is missing in terms of the messages out there…We need a lot more of people to kind of to be non-judgemental and to recognise that lots of things happen when you're raped or sexually assaulted or abused as a child…if you're a child, the chances are you've got no power at all physically or emotionally. If you're a young woman or you're probably still in the same positions as being a child, but if you're sort of like 18, 19, 20, you still don't have a lot of power either. And to have somebody that you can turn to in your social group, they can say 'You know it really wasn't your fault' and 'Don't blame yourself for what happened because the man was stronger than you'…that's not out there now and I kind of think, gosh 2006 and I was working in 1980 as a volunteer and what has changed, you know how come that message has, where has it gone?" [Heather Forrest]

"Being involved in primary education is so important and I really think…when people become parents it should be a prerequisite that they actually go on to a parenting class where they learn about basic things – you know, as a child your son should be encouraged to do X, Y, Z. Your daughter should be encouraged to do X, Y, Z. If your child is, you know, dreamy and kind of like vulnerable in their own wee world, this is the kind of thing that might help you to know that they're confident. So whether it's a boy or a girl…encourage them to do…self confidence classes, so when they're out, be aware of the world and get them to kind of think, you know 'Ok so who's around, do I know them? Who's my safe adult, who'll look after me?' Teach them basic self defence and get them to use their voice so they're not afraid to scream, to shout, to make a noise, to hit a car that's gonna set off an alarm or whatever… and make it fun…but I think it has to be at a very early age." [Heather Forrest]

"My daughter is 18, nearly 19. She just sort of says she's a feminist but doesn't really think about it and doesn't realise what we went through. She just takes it all for granted. I think now, I'm sort of proud to call myself a feminist, although when you read some of the stuff, you realise that there's a lot of different types of feminist and I'm probably what's called a liberal feminist. But I suppose on the other hand, it's sad that's there's still so many things to be put right. When my daughter's generation think it's all done and nothing to worry about." [Maureen Porter]

"I think younger women when I speak to them…They wouldn't call themselves necessarily feminists but I think you know if you scratch the surface and point out what we did in the 70's and 80's they'll you know, you realise that depends a lot of it… they take a lot for granted now that we really fought for them… So I think it's still there, it's called something different, I think it has had a big fundamental influence on women, but unfortunately it still isn't really accepted, I think people are still battling against the word, they're battling against a notion of feminists… Equality for women and support for women all that sort of thing there's still a long way to go, a long, long way to go." [Dorothy Degenhardt]

"The whole thing about the sexualisation of girls and young women…very often in precocious ways, and giving them all sorts of messages about their sexuality and no messages at all about safety and ownership and the right to say no…and the right to say no to being sexualised as well… If I hear something in the news that says, you know, my 13-year old daughter's weekly magazine that's aimed at pubescent girls is talking about how to give good oral sex, I think 'I don't believe this.' And I go out and get them off the shelf, and it's true…

And also, although things have moved on drastically amongst law enforcers…the canteen culture still exists…and I do think there's still lots and lots of work to be done with police…You know, not at the top of the hierarchy. I think they've got the message. But I don't think the message is on the street, and that's where the women, if they're going to report it…that's going to be their interface, you know? OK, they've probably got their most sensitive officers in Family Protection Units, but it has to be more than that. It has to go further than that." [Sue Owen]

"One of the objectives was to give women confidence to come forward and…I think [it] still probably comparatively is true that there's more reporting than there was before all that activity, but…in practice…the attrition rate on the cases is so high…that for all that apparent sort of success that we were having in changing things, it just seems to have stalled somewhere and not moved on." [Sheila Gilmore]

"I think it's still difficult. I think the burden is still taken up, largely, by women – often by choice, because they want to do that. I mean…is there any point in having kids if you're never going to see them?…I think women are very conscious of that. It's not that they're necessarily shoved aside – they make choices which are probably the right ones, to me. It's how you definitely get society to accept that…and if you have taken time out, or if you do reduce your working hours…there is still quite a sort of macho culture…I think a lot of law firms are still…you know, this sort of notion that if you're not there from the crack of dawn…I mean, whether they're actually doing anything or they've just got a jacket on the back of their chair, looking busy…it is certainly a bit of a question. But no, I think we have made a difference… we haven't got there, we've just made huge advances, and I think given opportunities to ourselves… that would have been unimaginable…to our mothers and grandmothers who had much more restricted opportunities. And that's good." [Sheila Gilmore]

"I think there's still a long way to go…in the workplace. In childcare issues I see it all the time – young women out working part time and they get left behind because of that…cos they're not there five days a week…I mean where I'm on secondment just now, the Chief Executive is a woman, but all the directors are men for instance, and, at the council where I work normally…they just have recently appointed two youngish women as directors out of six so that's two out of six, which isn't bad, but I mean…the law is riddled with discrimination." [Brenda Flaherty]

"It's how much violence against women is still used as entertainment…I'm looking forward to a Saturday night serial killer series where it's …not a succession of young women because I just don't see that changing at all – that sort of enjoyment of, you know, women in peril…to me it doesn't matter if the

192

forensic psychologist is a woman or if the detective who solves it all is a woman, it's still showing the women as victims more entertaining." [Morna Findlay]

"I think women's liberation's very far from here, you know, when you look around at statistics, at what's happening, one of the things that keeps striking me these days, I sometimes watch these comedy programmes on television, and it's like a boy's club…they're all men…occasionally Jo what's her name gets invited along…Even the fashions I have to say…back to these blooming awful high heels that people can't walk in…really…that's the sort of thing we were trying to get away from before…girly girly girly. …Now it's girly girly girly plus!" [Moira Kane]

"The more it's out in the open, the more women speak out, the more men …are challenged I think that the better it will get. But not to be sort of deluded that it will disappear from the face of the earth because it won't. It's also the strength of the friendships it has given…birth to. The…value of collective working, how a small group of dedicated women could make such a phenomenal change…I have great pride in that. And I would just encourage more women…to take the work on." [Florence Germain]

"I've had some contact with the Dundee Rape Crisis and Sexual Abuse Centre because I've had student placements there so I've been back to chat to them. And now the Perth one setting up…the woman that runs that…is an ex social work student of mine at Northern College…a couple of weeks ago when she was showing me round her new premises…isn't it funny how all these things come full circle?" [Dorothy Degenhardt]

"I still think we've got a long, long way to go and…when I look back, it's been such slow – I wouldn't even call it progress, it's just been such a slow struggle, and I don't know whether it's this area or whatever it is. However, it's very heartening that the local schools are starting to take an interest because that kind of takes a shortcut as far as I'm concerned, cos it's giving those children information that they can use to prevent something happening or to stop what's happening to them. I think that …that's more proactive – that feels good." [Norma Benzie]

"Women [are] being blamed for their behaviour, and one sadly wonders how much it has changed…I think there are movements in the right direction, but…I don't think it's changed anything like enough – you just need to look at some of the media coverage that's around just now…" [Isla Laing]

"I don't think you can just stop the move, stop the…kind of energy that has been sort of unleashed, but at the same time one should not underestimate the danger of either diluting or diverting women's energy into areas which are …not worth it because we need to transform…the power relationship." [Florence Germain]

"You move in a glacial pace to make small progress and you can easily take a big step back. But at least once the ground's been broken, I think you can pass through it again a bit more quickly. And you mustn't give up hope, I think is the key thing." [Fiona Raitt]

"I think it's marvellous, where we've got to…there are threats which have always been there on the horizon…What I've learned over this long time is that any gain, any ground that we gain, we need to hold onto, because the minute that we relax, it is actually whipped away from under our feet. So it's being sure that we're all moving in the same direction and only by, I think, coming together, can we ensure that we'll be able to…sustain it indefinitely and wear the threats and see them off." [Margaret Brown]

"I think what we need to be doing is to be getting rape and sexual assault…to the stage where we're at the moment…with domestic abuse…there are no questions about it. Rape's wrong. Don't do it. And to be getting away from…the sort of the advice on well this is 20 things you can do to stop rape…I think there's only one thing we can do stop rape. Guys, stop raping." [Isabelle Kerr]

Rape Crisis Scotland's network of centres has gone through a period of expansion in recent years with four new centres established since 2005 in Western Isles, Lanarkshire, Argyll & Bute and Perth & Kinross.

Other affiliated centres from which RCS evolved are based in Aberdeen, Dundee, Edinburgh, Glasgow and Kilmarnock.

There are a number of other Rape Crisis centres in Scotland outwith Rape Crisis Scotland's network. These are in Dumfries, Fife and Stirling.

Reading & References

Bain, Ouaine & Sanders, Maureen – **Out in the open: a guide for young people who have been sexually abused.** London: Virago Press, 1990

Bass, Ellen & Davis, Laura – **The Courage to Heal**. New York: Harper & Row, 1988

Breitenbach, Esther & Mackay, Fiona (editors) – **Women & contemporary Scottish politics**. Edinburgh: Polygon, 2001

Brownmiller, Susan – **Against Our Will: Men, Women and Rape**. New York: Simon & Schuster, 1975

Chambers, Gerry and Millar, Ann – **Investigating sexual assault.** London: HMSO, 1983

Chambers, Gerry and Millar, Ann – **Prosecuting sexual assault.** London: HMSO, 1986

Davis, Angela – **Women, Race and Class.** London: The Women's Press, 1982

Driver, Emily & Droisen, Audrey – **Child sexual abuse: feminist perspectives**. Basingstoke: Palgrave Macmillan, 1989

Ernst, Sheila & Goodison, Lucy – **In our own hands: book of self-help therapy**. London: The Women's Press, 1981.

F.A.S.T – **Feminists Against Sexual Terrorism Newsletter** No. 2, April 1979

Graef, Roger (Producer) & Stewart, Charles (Director) – **Fly on the Wall: Police, Episode 3: A Complaint of Rape**. BBC Bristol, 1982

Greenan, Lily – **Violence against Women: A literature review commissioned by the National Group to Address Violence Against Women**. Edinburgh: The Scottish Government, 2005

Hall, Liz & Lloyd, Siobhan – **Surviving child sexual abuse**. London: The Falmer Press, 1989

Harper, Ross & McWhinnie, Arnot – **The Glasgow Rape Case**. London: Hutchinson, 1983

Henderson, Shirley & Mackay, Alison (editors) – **Grit & Diamonds**. Edinburgh: Stramullion, 1990

MsPrint – Issue 1 – Published by the MsPrint Collective, August 1978

Nelson, Sarah – **Incest: Fact and Myth**. Edinburgh: Stramullion, 1982

Spring, Jacqueline – **Cry hard and swim – the story of an incest survivor**. London: Virago Press Ltd., 1990

Toner, Barbara – **The Facts of Rape**. London: Hutchinson, 1977

Walker, Alice – **The Color Purple**. London: The Women's Press, 1983

Wolf, Naomi – **Fire with Fire: New Female Power and How It Will Change the 21st Century**. London: Chatto & Windus, 1993